Barriers and Bounds to Rationality

PRINCETON STUDIES IN COMPLEXITY

EDITORS

Philip W. Anderson (Princeton University)
Joshua M. Epstein (The Brookings Institution)
Duncan K. Foley (Barnard College)
Simon A. Levin (Princeton University)
Gottfried Mayer-Kress (University of Illinois)

TITLES IN THE SERIES

Lars-Erik Cederman, *Emergent Actors in World Politics: How States and Nations Develop and Dissolve*

Robert Axelrod, *The Complexity of Cooperation: Agent-Based Models of Competition and Collaboration*

Peter S. Albin, *Barriers and Bounds to Rationality: Essays on Economic Complexity and Dynamics in Interactive Systems*. Edited and with an Introduction by Duncan K. Foley

FORTHCOMING TITLES

Scott Camazine, Jean-Louis Deneubourg, Nigel Franks, and Thomas Seeley, *Building Biological Superstructures: Models of Self-Organization*

James P. Crutchfield and James E. Hanson, *Computational Mechanics of Cellular Processes*

Ralph W. Wittenberg, *Models of Self-Organization in Biological Development*

Barriers and Bounds to Rationality

ESSAYS ON ECONOMIC COMPLEXITY AND
DYNAMICS IN INTERACTIVE SYSTEMS

Peter S. Albin

EDITED AND WITH AN INTRODUCTION
BY DUNCAN K. FOLEY

PRINCETON UNIVERSITY PRESS
PRINCETON, NEW JERSEY

Copyright © 1998 by Princeton University Press
Published by Princeton University Press, 41 William Street,
Princeton, New Jersey 08540
In the United Kingdom: Princeton University Press, Chichester, West Sussex

All Rights Reserved

Library of Congress Cataloging-in-Publication Data
Albin, Peter S.
Barriers and bounds to rationality : essays on economic complexity and dynamics in interactive systems / Peter S. Albin ; edited with an introduction by Duncan K. Foley.
p. cm. — (Princeton studies in complexity)
Includes bibliographical references and index.
ISBN 0-691-02676-9 (cloth : alk. paper)
1. Economics, Mathematical. 2. Statics and dynamics (Social sciences).
3. Computational complexity. I. Foley, Duncan K. II. Title. III. Series.
HB135.A555 1998
330'.01'185—dc21 97-33634

The publisher would like to acknowledge the authors and editor of this volume for providing the camera-ready copy from which this book was printed

Princeton University Press books are printed on acid-free paper and meet the guidelines for permanence and durability of the Committee on Production Guidelines for Book Longevity of the Council on Library Resources

http://pup.princeton.edu

Printed in the United States of America

1 3 5 7 9 10 8 6 4 2

To Pat with love and appreciation

IN MEMORIAM
Minna and Joseph Albin
Lillian and Louis Grudin

Contents

Preface   xiii

Acknowledgments   xxxiii

1 Introduction   3
    1.1 Dynamical systems 3
        1.1.1 Linear dynamical systems 4
        1.1.2 Nonlinear dynamical systems 7
        1.1.3 Cellular automata as models of nonlinear dynamical systems 15
    1.2 Dynamical systems in social and physical science 17
        1.2.1 Local and global interaction 18
        1.2.2 Topology and geometry in physical and social models 18
        1.2.3 Time and causality 20
        1.2.4 Identity and diversity 21
    1.3 Economic models of fully rational behavior 23
        1.3.1 The rational choice program 23
        1.3.2 Individual decision models—intertemporal optimization 25
        1.3.3 The finite-horizon Ramsey problem 25
        1.3.4 Market models 28
        1.3.5 Game theory models 33
    1.4 Definitions and measures of complexity 40
        1.4.1 Computational complexity 41
        1.4.2 Linguistic complexity 42

	1.4.3	Machine complexity	44
	1.4.4	Decidability, computational complexity, and rationality	46
	1.4.5	Dynamical systems and computational complexity	47
1.5	Complexity in cellular automata		48
	1.5.1	Complexity types	50
	1.5.2	Computability, predictability, and complexity in cellular automata	52
1.6	Modeling complex social and economic interactions		53
	1.6.1	Self-referencing individual agents	53
	1.6.2	Organizations	55
	1.6.3	Industries and economies	56
	1.6.4	Markets	58
	1.6.5	The local interaction multiperson Prisoners' Dilemma	61
1.7	Complexity, rationality, and social interaction		64
	1.7.1	How complex are social systems?	65
	1.7.2	How smart do agents need to be?	67
1.8	Toward a robust theory of action and society		68

2 The Metalogic of Economic Predictions, Calculations, and Propositions — 73

2.1	Introduction		73
2.2	Preliminaries: Automata and structural formations		76
	2.2.1	Finite automata	76
	2.2.2	Finite formations	77
	2.2.3	Generalized formations and finite surrogates	79
	2.2.4	General computation and computability	80
2.3	Undecidability in generalized formations		83
	2.3.1	An economy with finite automaton components	84
	2.3.2	Structural properties of a finite economy	85
	2.3.3	Archival expansion: An economy with Turing machine components	85

CONTENTS ix

    2.3.4 Conditional forecasting: Economies with universal machine components 86
    2.3.5 Undecidability propositions 87
    2.3.6 General comments 88
2.4 Social welfare evaluations 91
    2.4.1 The decision setting 91
    2.4.2 The political process 94
    2.4.3 The computability of a political program 95
    2.4.4 Predictability of restricted programs 97
2.5 Conclusions 98
Appendix: Proof of Theorem 2.5 103

3 Microeconomic Foundations of Cyclical Irregularities or "Chaos"   105

3.1 Introduction 105
3.2 The research problem 106
    3.2.1 The meaning of "chaos" in dynamic systems 107
    3.2.2 Nonlinearities and underlying microeconomic interactions 110
3.3 A model of microeconomic interaction 114
    3.3.1 Specification of interaction neighborhoods 114
    3.3.2 Specification of interaction conventions 116
    3.3.3 Simulation of firm behavior 117
    3.3.4 Classification of simulated time series 118
    3.3.5 Preliminary indications 125
3.4 Interpretations 127
    3.4.1 The background model 127
    3.4.2 The computation irreducibility hypothesis 131
    3.4.3 Reexamination of economic implications 131
3.5 Extensions and applications 135

4 Qualitative Effects of Monetary Policy in "Rich" Dynamic Systems   137

4.1 Introduction 137
4.2 The experimental setting 138
4.3 Complexity classification of dynamic behaviors 140

		4.3.1	Qualitative types of dynamic behavior	140
		4.3.2	Projective properties	147
		4.3.3	Modeling considerations	148
		4.3.4	Dynamics and expectations	148
		4.3.5	Industry structure	149
	4.4	Policy interventions		149
		4.4.1	Simulating monetary interventions	151
		4.4.2	Properties of the system and experimental protocols	155
	4.5	Results and preliminary interpretations		155
		4.5.1	Incomplete stabilization	156
		4.5.2	Economic implications	156

5 Decentralized, Dispersed Exchange without an Auctioneer: A Simulation Study — 157

	5.1	Introduction		157
	5.2	A model of dispersed exchange		158
		5.2.1	Endowments and utilities	159
		5.2.2	Advertising neighborhoods, information costs, and trade protocol: The rules of the game	159
	5.3	Strategies of agents		161
		5.3.1	Boundedly rational agents of fully rational players	161
		5.3.2	Truthful disclosure	162
		5.3.3	The agent's computational capacity	162
		5.3.4	The candidate algorithm	163
		5.3.5	The expected gain from signaling	163
		5.3.6	Estimating the likelihood of neighbor actions	164
		5.3.7	Simulation procedures	165
		5.3.8	The coefficient of resource utilization	166
	5.4	Simulation results		166
		5.4.1	Reporting format	166
		5.4.2	Illustrative results	167
		5.4.3	Trader accounts	168
		5.4.4	Comment	169
		5.4.5	A second illustrative example	169
	5.5	Information cost and efficiency		169
		5.5.1	Interactions of advertising cost and neighborhood size	170
		5.5.2	Interpretations	171
	5.6	Concluding comments		174

6 Approximations of Cooperative Equilibria in Multiperson Prisoners' Dilemma Played by Cellular Automata 181

- 6.1 Introduction 181
- 6.2 The model 183
  - 6.2.1 Subgame and sub-subgame structure of MPD 183
  - 6.2.2 Threshold conditions for equilibria in repeated play . 188
- 6.3 Strategic equivalence and the complexity of cellular automaton rules 190
  - 6.3.1 Digression: Study of cellular automaton complexity properties 190
- 6.4 The complexity of bounded-rationality forms 192
  - 6.4.1 Classes of strategic equivalence in multiperson games 193
- 6.5 A theorem on "Nash-like" equilibria in MPD 197
- 6.6 A "Nash-like" solution to MPD 198
- 6.7 Conclusions 204
- Appendix 205

7 The Complexity of Social Groups and Social Systems Described by Graph Structures 210

- 7.1 Introduction 210
- 7.2 Directed graphs and their representation: An overview . . . 213
  - 7.2.1 Arbitrary system functions: "Structure generators" 216
  - 7.2.2 Analysis of the undirected graph 218
  - 7.2.3 Parameters of the undirected graph 218
  - 7.2.4 The function "rumor transmission with recorded path" 218
  - 7.2.5 Complexity of the rumor propagating machine . . . 222
- 7.3 The directed graph 231
  - 7.3.1 The graph that is less than total 231
  - 7.3.2 Complexity measurement for the directed graph . . 235
  - 7.3.3 Case example: Complexity of organizational structures 236
- 7.4 Conclusion 241

Works Cited 243

Index 251

Preface

Peter S. Albin

In the social sciences, generally, and in the literature of economics, particularly, "structure" and "complexity" are poorly defined concepts which are invested with weight, depth, and magical significance and presumed to be well understood by the reader. Skimming texts and journals, one sees "complexity" connoting singly or in a melange: "ramified specialization," "intractability," "strategic interaction," "uncontrollability" (or "controllability through intricate maneuver"), "cognitive depth," "cognitive breadth," "nonprobabilistic uncertainty," the "obstructions of detail and organization," (or the "challenge" of same). Equal ambiguity surrounds the term "structure." Yet, "complexity" can have precise meaning. It does within the cognitive and informational sciences disciplines—most notably, within automata theory, the study of models of computer architectures, computation, and formal languages. The disciplined application of this meaning is transferable and therein is the subject of this book: rigorous analysis of an advanced economy's connective and supportive structures and the informational, evolutionary, and adaptive processes that occur within them. In setting out an automata-theoretic design for the study of complex economic structures, I will play several roles beyond that of a researcher compiling findings from a program of study. The role of text expositor is necessary, since automata-theoretic methods—although now coming into vogue—have not previously been systematized for the economist reader. The need for codification is especially great when it comes to complexity assessment. Here, I act as advocate as well as pedagogue. There are actually a number of candidate technical approaches to complexity measurement and each has distinctive advantages in particular problem areas. I believe, however, that one schema best suits the requirements of economic analysis and I will press strongly for it. This approach, Noam Chomsky's original complexity hierarchy for formal languages as extended to dynamic systems by Stephen Wolfram and elaborated in some details by me, encompasses automata as the building blocks of system architecture, data structures, levels of decision-making competence, and dynamics. It disentangles the various connotations of "complexity" alluded to in the previous paragraph and avoids one dangerous intellectual trap. "Complexity" is not so simple a notion that it can be captured by a single index labeled "randomness," "entropy," "size of a computer program," "dimension," "computer time," or any of a number of parameters of a graph. To be sure, the Chomsky-Wolfram synthesis can subsume certain of these indices in certain appropriate contexts. Its value lies, however, in its power to codify the full range of informational properties intrinsic to advanced economies and their dynamics.[1] This position is strenuously maintained throughout the book.

My advocacy of automata-theoretic resolutions to economic complexity puzzles is of long standing and the reader may wish to know the history of this commitment. It originated when I first encountered "The Game of Life," John Conway's recreational version of John von Neumann's system of self-reproducing automata. "Life" went on then for the most part within the emerging raffish subculture of academic computer hackers. For me, "Life" revealed a way to gain hands-on experience with a model system that could literally build for itself the capacity to communicate and calculate while accomplishing astonishing organizational transformations. The configurations built autonomously by "Life" demanded to be seen as structural institutions formed with hidden, but seemingly inevitable logic, from the simplest of building blocks. They expressed in the purest sense attributes of complexity but they were too featureless to model an actual economy. I played for a while and then went back to the source.

Von Neumann's creation (1966), a constructive proof posthumously completed by his associate Arthur Burks, demonstrated the assembly of simple parts within a preexisting framework of interaction paths to form

---

[1]The Chomsky-Wolfram schema defines the *qualitative hierarchy* of a system as its position within a four-step hierarchy. In formal computational terms, the steps correspond to (1) computers without memory, (2) computers with memory of fixed size, (3) "fixed program" computers with memories that can expand with time and the demands of a problem, (4) "universal" computers which can replicate the behavior of any fixed-program computer. In the original Chomsky formulation the four complexity levels pertain to the symbol-processing capacities of an artificial or natural language and to the language-recognition capacity of an artificial intelligence. These capacities translate directly into decision-making capacities of economic agents—modeled, for example, as game-playing automata. In terms of dynamics the first three levels correspond to discrete deterministic systems with capacities to generate trajectories equivalent, respectively, to those with limit-point, limit-cycle, and strange attractors in continuous dynamic systems. The fourth level corresponds to irregular "structure-changing" dynamics with no strict analogue in continuous dynamic systems but many associations in developmental and adaptive economic systems.

a coherent whole that possessed essentially unlimited powers of fabrication and computation. The notion of "complexity threshold" was critical in von Neumann's reasoning. In overall size and number of differentiated parts the composite had to exceed scale bounds. If it did not, the system would fail to accomplish one or more stipulated functions: building parts and scaffolding; putting together the replica according to blueprints and instructions; checking (computing) the accuracy of the construction, and equipping the clone with a copy of the construction instructions and blue prints before sending it on its independent (self-reproductive) way. As I saw it, the von Neumann system literally represented factory organization, supporting communications, degrees of hierarchy in control, and roundaboutness in dynamics.[2] The highest von Neumann complexity threshold, that for self-reproduction, seemed to suggest the attainment of a critical frontier in technical development, the capacity to spawn new viable technologies. Subsidiary thresholds formed a declining sequence of subsidiary stages of economic development: systems capable of importing techniques and adapting them to local conditions; systems capable of running imported "turnkey" facilities but without adaptation; and systems unable to support industry.

In our view this line of study constituted a fresh approach to one of the oldest problems in the discipline, the division of labor and its effect on productive efficiency. We opened up the black boxes of control technology and job design at least some of the way to uncover largely unsuspected trade-offs between productivity growth and short-term labor costs. The terms of these trade-offs relate to organizational features which can be represented by complexity attributes of computer architectures representing different principles of job design. Our subject was today's automated work floor, but the terms of the problem were defined in the *Wealth of Nations*.

As Adam Smith argued in his famous comparison of the pin factory with the craftsman pinmaker, systematic organization can facilitate enormous productivity gains. Clearly the organization of work in hierarchic or roundabout ways permits maximum power, energy, mechanical advantage and specialized learning to be applied to simple separable operations. The skills of Smith's craftsman represented a type of generalized complexity embodied in the experience and knowledge of an isolated individual. However, physiology and neural capacity place natural limits on what one

---

[2]My initial view was that von Neumann must have had economic applications in mind when he was originating his cellular automaton model—the connections did seem that striking. However, von Neumann's co-workers during the 1940s and 1950s insisted that his thinking followed quite different lines and that he saw his computational forms as pure mathematical objects with some biological referents (personal and telephone conversations with Morgenstern, Burks, Goldstyne, and Whitman, among others). Absent a metaphysics of subconscious influence, von Neumann's understandings of economic theory did not enter this, his last creation.

worker can do at one time, and the balance of capacities within a representative individual does not necessarily match the mix of capacities required for efficient production. The factory solution is, in some sense, the substitution of organizational "complexity external to the individual" for natural "complexity within the individual" to obtain the balancing advantages of specialization and rationalization.

It happened that at the time of my immersion in the von Neumann world of self-replicating abstract automata I was also trying to find a way around the many discrepancies between what one observes happening on the factory floor and what is representable by the parameters of a production function.[3] It came to me that with suitable modification of von Neumann's system it would be entirely practical to model production from the bottom up, using as data literal engineering specifications of individual pieces of hardware and playing the decision requirement of the technique against the skills and capacities of the work force. With a computer (itself part of the schema) reproducing decisions of managers at the margins of adjustment, the system could calculate detailed microeconomic reactions to changing local factor availabilities and skill levels, while adjusting to external factor and product prices. Finding another way to write a production function is hardly news. The point of the exercise was in its implications for dynamic projection. The model would have the same intrinsic scale and informational complexities as its real-world referent. The attributes played a determining role in the choice of appropriate production techniques and in developmental structural change that depended for its productivity effects upon encounters with system complexity thresholds.

In sum, my associates and I came to view the automata-theoretic methodology as providing a constructive and practically insightful way to capture the informational dimension in economic analysis, that is, the processes, institutions, infrastructure, and logical structure that characterize decision making and control the knowledge-based subsystems which are the distinguishing characteristics of the contemporary economy.

Fritz Machlup (1962) has suggested that "information and knowledge services" and "information and knowledge machines" be classified as distinct sectors of economic activity. Since 1962 the value-added and employment weights of these activities have increased many times over. These can be no doubt that this development is of great quantitative importance; however, interesting divisions exist on whether the change is of historical qualitative significance and on the distinctiveness—if not, uniqueness—of its embodiment, the computer, as an economic good. On the one hand, battalions of technologists and social commentators assert that economic

---

[3]This work resulted in a series of papers on complexity and job design, which the interested reader may consult: among them, Albin (1978b, 1982b, 1984, 1985); Albin and Weinberg (1983); and Albin, Hormozi, Mourgios, and Weinberg (1984).

PREFACE   xvii

life and productive activity have changed dramatically in recent years and that linked revolutions in information use, information-oriented occupations, and information-handling technologies are central in ongoing transformations.[4] Economists, however, have been prepared, by and large, to see continuity, incremental adjustment, and smoothed processes in their observations of technological change. The computer has put on weight within sectoral, national, and trade accounts;[5] but this growth does not necessarily mean that the computer has played a distinctive causal role—let alone, a revolutionary one. Vision within the discipline of economics sees the similarities with past adoptions of technique rather than a transforming change in regime. The computer can enter the conventional analysis as a faster widget-maker.

There exists, simultaneously, within the policy domain, substantial practitioner disenchantment with the relevance and effectiveness of the standard solutions of applied economics which once appeared to have such power and range. Evocations of policy impasse abound:[6] two are germane here. The first is specific to labor markets. Outside the discipline, computerization is often viewed as a prime cause of stagnating general employment growth and deteriorating job quality. Although the factual basis for the claim is controversial and the causal reasoning of the critics is frequently muddied, the perception of computerization as an economic problem untouched by economists remains. That perception is reinforced in the debates over macroeconomic policy that are closest to determining action. In this economists' domain, technological unemployment and labor-displacing automation are seen most often variously as: (1) transient phenomena, (2) invisible as symptoms, or (3) dismissed as untreatable with the prescriptions at hand.[7] The second domain of policy concern is more conjectural. It involves a hypothesis that transformations of production, finance, and consumption—largely around new computation and communications technologies—have promoted new patterns of international de-

---

[4]The sociologist James Beniger (1986) provides the definitive citations list on the perspective of revolutionary change—a classification and tabulation of diagnoses of information-related structural change in major postwar works describing social, technological, and economic transformations.

[5]Economists working in a Schumpeterian tradition (e.g., Freeman, Clark, and Soete, 1982; Dosi, 1981; Nelson and Winter, 1982; Best, 1990) know to exempt themselves from this criticism. I will argue subsequently that the modern information technologies have distinctive features even from the perspective of Schumpeterian dynamics.

[6]I will not attempt to sort out the roles and possible influences of energy shocks, deregulation, disasters, multinational competition, monetarist or supply-sider zeal, financial innovation, debt crises, and many other factors said to change the rules of the stabilization game.

[7]Economists who engage these and related matters must do so at one remove from the prevailing "nonselective" perspective on policy. Structuralist perspectives appear in works of Leontief and Duchin (1985), Bluestone and Harrison (1982), Freeman (1986), and Piore (1984) among others.

pendence and have altered the dynamic response of the domestic economy in ways that invalidate old rules for guidance, stabilization, and control. It may be possible to explain many of these changes, retrospectively[8]—even to capture them as parameter variations in standard formulations. But repeated failures and omissions in prospective analysis suggest a disjunction between the economic system and the economists' system on matters that count.

I happen to be an economist who believes that transformations in informational technology and information use have affected the functioning of the economy in determining ways. I also share in a view that many of the analytical tools used by economists are poorly adapted to the study of informational phenomena and that some are intellectual blinders. The criticism applies directly to descriptive formulations but extends to the theoretical core of the discipline itself. A fundamental flaw of the dominant scholarly paradigm is its mechanistic treatment of information-handling, signaling, decision making, and knowledge institutions.[9] One is equipped with tools to measure resources committed to information and cognitive activities but not their systemic effects. One can footnote a market study with the observation that increased interdependency and shortened lags have increased the complexity of the decision tasks faced by agents but can say little more of substance since consensus on a rigorous definition of "complexity" is lacking.

However, I believe that better tools are available. In effect, economics, the analytical discipline of decision and choice has remained peculiarly untouched by advances that have transformed the pragmatic arts of decision making and information management. This book is about ways in which the economist can draw techniques from the cognitive and computational sciences to advance the analysis of informational phenomena that impact on the functioning of actual economic systems and their theoretical counterparts. Its range is the *informational dimension*: the Machlup activities, their special efficiency and cost properties, their systemic and dynamic implications, and analytical and mathematical forms that can represent them within economic theory.

---

[8] Although the whole must be inferred, elements of the hypothesis can be formalized. For example, if the production of informational machines and their use increases the number of sectors subject to increasing returns, the stability properties of the (general-equilibrium) system are dramatically worsened, exacerbating tendencies toward stagflation (Heal, 1986). The "financial-fragility" restrictions on the scope of monetary policy (Minsky, 1986) are particularly severe within a Eurocurrency environment and hardly eased where financial trading is automated. (The preceding sentences were written prior to Oct. 17, 1987.)

[9] This theme is prominent in works drawing on Kornai (1971).

PREFACE   xix

Exploring the information dimension

The core of my argument is a claim that informational technologies and processes have critical properties which are imperfectly captured by models in the mechanistic analytical tradition but which are well defined when building blocks of the economy are represented as abstract automata. (Real economies contain agents who have adapted to these information technologies, while economists on the whole have not.) Abstract automata, mathematical models of computing devices and informational processes, have obvious referents in literal hardware installations. Additionally, automaton modeling of economic structures can be highly informative when the identified parts and links of an economic unit studied correspond to conduits for information flow, barriers to information flow, decision making entities, stores of data or knowledge, and technologies devoted to decision making, computation, and control. The real power of automaton-based methods as a foundation for economic methodology, however, lies in their formal attributes. These include as elements: resource-dimensioned measures of computational requirements; a hierarchy of rigorously defined complexity levels, which serves to classify the information content of economic activities; rich dynamics which cover within a single family of models the widest possible variety of "stylized facts" pertaining to system growth, fluctuation, and historic development; and natural representation of system building from component parts. The essays reprinted here explore these attributes both in the abstract and as they associate with properties of real and model economies.

Model or metaphor

Some delicate questions of exposition and style should be aired at this point. Reasoning which associates a referent system with an image system can range from scientific model building, through heuristic exploration of a detailed analogy, to intuitive play with loose metaphor. Associative reasoning of any type may contribute to analysis; however, an appeal to an association can only communicate understandings where there is a fund of shared experience with and appreciation of the image system. Certainly we, as economists, understand one another when we speak among ourselves of "equilibrating market processes" even if there is no physical market place, when the goods involved are amorphously defined, and while fluctuations abound in the empirical referent. Common sense, common mathematical training, and a shared background in working with exemplar cases help to bind what others might see as a loose metaphor into a working model appropriate to the context. With their rich connections to pure science, the cognitive disciplines, and mathematics, automaton formulations also invite associative translations of all types. Unfortunately, few economists have developed the easy familiarity with the computer—as an object of study, as opposed to an object of use—that would make a demonstration of association or correspondence between economic forms and automata instantly interesting, and meaningful. My tasks, then, are to demonstrate the necessity of pursuing the association at the level of rigorous model building, to provide easy access to the more powerful tools and to develop exemplar analyses.

Formal models of informational activities

In a nutshell, many informational and decision making processes of economic importance require computation or equivalent data handling and organization. Accordingly, it is a natural step to tie an informational process or function to a reference computing device which has the capacity to handle the process or solve the function. The referencing is bidirectional: given a process, it is appropriate to ask for a measure of the computational resources required to accommodate it: "How elaborate a personal computer (PC) is needed to solve this production-control algorithm in real time?" Or, given computational resources, one can inquire into their capacities: "How large a regression program can be fitted on this PC?"

A microcomputer with restricted memory, however, represents only one level in a hierarchy pertaining to computational capacities or the implied requirements of informational functions. These levels, which are frequently called "indices of system complexity," register threshold combinations of scale, differentiation, and interconnection of computational resources. Although in some instances it is possible to trade off one aspect of complexity for another within a qualitative level, the levels themselves are absolute. The microcomputer has capabilities beyond 12 or 1,200 or N calculators wired together. And, as one already suspects, there are qualitative levels beyond a memory-restricted microprocessor with a fixed budget for diskettes.

Complexity

The matter of qualitative complexity level is critical because at the heart of many informational processes of economic interest are transformations and functions—virtual or implied—which encounter complexity thresholds in significant ways. For example, firms in the United States and Japan install the same microprocessors to control the same production equipment but assign decision responsibilities to workers according to different principles. In a formal translation of the observation, abstract automata are used to model the actual combinations of human and machine resources committed to decision making and control in the two locations. Study of the derived forms indicates that one approach to work organization leads to a combination of decision resources that crosses a critical complexity threshold, whereas the other does not. In context, the threshold implies the capacity to perform the "knowledge functions" required for continuous upgrading and reconfiguration of the production system. Thus, an objectively determined complexity threshold registers as a precondition for "learning-by-doing," and "adaptiveness." On this interpretation, the analysis permits strong inferences as to rates of productivity change in the two nations. Astute commentators have drawn similar conclusions from other indicators but only via ad hoc means.

In other explorations of the informational dimension, we examine standard expectational and decision making assumptions by translating the assumptions into implied calculations on the data. The computing procedures implied by the theory associate with formal automata. In some cases complexity thresholds are inescapable: seemingly plausible anticipational assumptions require for their fulfillment volumes of computational resources that are beyond the mass of the physical universe. For example, "rational expectation" assumptions entail each actor in a system having a model of the decision making apparatus of every other actor. It may also be the case that problems which are seemingly well specified are at intrinsic complexity levels that permit no rigorous inferences as to solvability.

The power of complexity classification as a tool of theoretical analysis comes out most dramatically in the study of highly interactive systems modeled as N-person nonnegotiated games. In the many-person repeated prisoners' dilemma analyzed in Chapter 6, for example, there are a multitude of possible behavioral strategies. Yet the search for a solution is relatively painless. First, one can readily demonstrate that a cooperative solution can not be sustained in any dynamic system formed from player strategies if the overall complexity of the system falls below that of the highest of four complexity classes. This complexity threshold wipes out most candidates including those analogous to "tit-for-tat" and other popular ones that fare well in two-person tournaments. Of the remainder in the sparse highest class an effective cultivator of cooperative behavior turns out to be—gratifyingly so, I may add—the "Game of Life."

"Life" can be implemented by the most simple-minded of bounded-rationality agents to yield payoffs close to those of uniform cooperation and offers self-enforced security against wiseguy defectors. In effect, "Life" players rely on the built-in complexity of a network of social interactions. The robustness of the solution can be demonstrated, but only through simulation. The complexity theory that guides one to an effective strategy bars definitive proof of its optimality.

In these cases and in several others, patterns of organization, interconnection, and differentiation matter as much as does "scale," defined as an absolute measure of hardware and time resources devoted to computation. This means that we can not treat an expansion of informational resources uncritically as "investment" or as a "substitution" for ordinary labor or capital, even though the installation may be viewed as such by the decision makers involved and may have many investment-like or substitution-like qualities. Informational functions carry within themselves the potential for profound change in complexity level—qualitative variation or structural change, as it were—with no apparent variation in economic measures of conventional inputs. To get the analysis right it is necessary to open up the black boxes of technical, institutional, and organizational givens.

Inside some black boxes

As economists we are accustomed to working on one side of a line that separates us from the technologist, the programmer, the engineer, and the production manager. Ordinarily we would be quite comfortable with a study that took as givens the terms of a trade-off between instantaneous labor cost and longer-term productivity change (the main *economic* variables in the work-organization application) and used these data to calculate production, cost and employment impacts, changes in comparative advantage, alterations in dynamic properties, and the like. Unfortunately, the necessary trade-off data are not available in ready-to-use form nor have we suitable qualitative information on function properties. Furthermore, the actors who design computers, program them for production control, alter job assignments, and build communications systems are generally aware of only the most narrow economic implications of their work; so it would be blind faith to expect far-reaching optimal adjustment. In short, if we are to pursue the major implications of the ongoing revolutions in computing technology and work organization, it is necessary by default to model and evaluate these production systems at the level of fine technical detail—at least until we can get a fix on parameters and critical indicators.

I have taken it as an obligation to do more than just identify a gap in our knowledge. The essays reprinted here provide tools with which an economist can take apart an informational system—whether a control facility within an actual firm or micro-organization or a formalism implied by pure theory—and determine its capabilities and effectiveness in performing the economic functions ascribed to it. In most instances sample analyses using the tools are carried to definitive conclusions or to a point where the terms of the problem are sufficiently well defined for conventional analytical tools to be applied.

PREFACE   xxiii

   Comparisons over time between older control systems that required mechanical controls and current systems based on digital electronics lead one to distinguish the earlier era as one in which a clockwork control technique drives a clockwork basic machine and delivers productivity improvements at the same rate as the driven facility. The difference in productivity growth rates between the clockwork and digital control techniques suggests the usefulness of applying unbalanced growth analysis (as in my 1978a book and Baumol, 1967) to the setting to identify the associated trends in product and service costs and the related income distribution.

   The most important of the technical black boxes is the one enclosing the logic and architecture of computational devices. At a minimum, it has become necessary for economists to have an intuitive understanding of the complexity properties of informational systems equivalent to the physical intuitions which they bring to analyses using models deriving from the study of mechanical systems and equilibrium processes. The closer look at the theory of computational devices will certainly disclose that representation of the informational dimension of economic processes is an important scientific step. Treating the dimension in terms of ordinary investment or substitution can cloud understanding—an assertion which will come to life as we expose the cost barriers and scale properties of actual information technologies.

Informational perspectives on economic analysis

From the foregoing, the reader can anticipate that some economists will have problems in reconciling the approach here with established perspectives within the discipline. Fortunately, there are a few important predecessor works in the literature which can frame the formal analyses and the message of this book.

Antiequilibrium

Janos Kornai's *Anti-equilibrium* (1971) stands out in this regard. Kornai's now-classic work develops a broad critique of analyses which rely on the presumption of general equilibrium. In doing so, it provides foundations for a general information-based approach to institutional functioning, the formalization of which leads to significant classification concepts such as the "pressure" and "suction" categories of macroeconomies. The concepts have proven to be operational as in Kornai's many studies of microbehaviors in suction economies (e.g., 1982) and to be eminently transferable, as in Weitzman's investigations of alternative incentive structures (1984). It has passed almost unnoticed that Kornai's main arguments are based explicitly on formal properties of automata as models of information systems (1971, 51). Kornai had been working within a community of active computer-science theoreticians, so it is not at all surprising that his work took the line it did. It is a measure of his skill as an expositor that his analyses were accepted largely on grounds of theoretical elegance and institutional realism rather than on arguably stronger[10] grounds of automata-theoretic reasoning from informational foundations.

Kornai's critique defines an essential point for epistemological inquiry. If informational properties are foundational and distinctive in the ways he indicates, then the presumptive basis of general equilibrium is impaired and the associated welfare conclusions become ephemera at best. However, if informational properties are not both foundational and distinguishable, then market forces can be relied on to dominate the system—distinctive structural forms become ephemera (or local imperfections). In the antiequilibrium domain of inquiry, "positive" economic analysis is directed toward uncovering persistent institutional regularities; whereas in the "equilibrium-school" domain positive economics is directed toward identifying parameters of processes conditioned on and supporting general equilibrium—as in Reder's description of the "tight priors" of the Chicago school (1982, 11–19).[11] It seems impossible to straddle the fence on this matter; a study of special informational properties is hardly meaningful outside the antiequilibrium framework and such is the position taken here.[12]

---

[10] Kornai opposed the institutional fact that enterprises rely on highly differentiated information to the presumption of the "general-equilibrium school" that price-type data suffice for the guidance of economic activity. It might seem that one could accept the Kornai critique for "real" economies and at the same type accept the informational presumptions of the general-equilibrium school as appropriate for a meaningful abstract economy. The argument based on formal properties of automata whittles down the domain of "meaningfulness" to a few trivial cases. Kornai alluded to the complexity properties of automaton representations on several occasions, either directly or through references, and gave an intuitive sketch of the full formal critique. Since the formal argument was not presented mathematically it may have been regarded as a heuristic (or metaphor!) and escaped wider attention.

[11] It is interesting to note that studies of informational processes taken within the antiequilibrium framework can yield results that might either confirm or invalidate its priors. In the latter case one might reject the approach and fall back to general equilibrium as a limiting case. Within the stacked deck of the general-equilibrium framework, however, results consistent with the existence of distinct information structures are epiphenomena that can be resisted as "imperfections." The analyses presented in later chapters do not shake any of Kornai's basic arguments for his theoretical critique. In fact, the "positive" results add significant supplementary and confirmatory detail. The automaton approach provides rigorous demonstrations of informational properties which are only alluded to in Kornai's work and the applications extend the scheme to new sets of institutional phenomena.

[12] Given the neat fit with the anti-equilibrium frame, I see no reason to write another version of the standard dissident's introduction. Consider as read the invocation of Kuhn and Lakatos and the recital on the impasses and irrelevancies to which standard theory

Bounded rationality

The information-oriented institutional perspective, of course, has its genesis in Herbert Simon's work and "bounds on rationality" will appear here as a recurrent theme—recall, for example, the construction in which available decision resources are counterpoised against decision requirements imposed by theory. Simon, however, is a protean figure in all of the senses of the allusion; and to grapple with Simon, the economist, it is necessary to be prepared to grasp him as a computer scientist and cognitive theorist. In terms of another image, he has kept the black boxes of computer technology, software design, and artificial intelligence closed in his economic writing, although full understanding of his research program relies on knowledge of their contents as explicated in his work within the cognitive disciplines. Simon has certainly left the keys in plain sight on his citation pages; but except for a few prominent economists—in particular, Kornai again, Montias (1976), Williamson (1975), Nelson and Winter (1982)—they have not been picked up outside the original Carnegie-Mellon community.

Simon's own "architectural" approach to complexity (Newell and Simon, 1972) finds a common cognitive hierarchy in the ways chessmasters identify pattern in board positions, successful organizations assign coping responsibilities, and insightful decision makers filter information. A guiding model for such hierarchical procedures is the methodology for computational decomposition of large otherwise-intractable systems. Simon is most persuasive when the information presented by the economy for interpretation is inadequate for global analysis but is prestructured so that there is a breakdown into fast processes working within nearly integral subsystems and slow processes working between subsystems. The more fully these conditions are met, the better a hierarchical approach that separately analyzes subsystems and their linkages can work. Hierarchy also seems to be a natural way for human intelligence and institutions formed by human intelligence to organize their cognitive processes. Even if the technical conditions of near decomposability are not met, the model is still appropriate for a behavioral analysis of actual institutions in realistic frustrating environments such as some bureaucracies. The schema is flexible enough to accommodate the variety of forms studied by Simon, the behaviorist and organization theorist, and yet is tight enough to serve as a foundation for Simon the methodological critic in his dismissal of global optimization and unbounded individual rationality as foundations for pure theory.

There is a surface similarity between Simon's approach and that here: an explicit model for the organization of computations is proposed as a model for social and economic organization. Yet the theme of qualitative

---

leads. Kornai's critique is sufficiently filled out and extended by those of Nelson and Winter (1982), Simon (1978, 1984), and Elster (1989a, 1989b).

complexity levels, so prominent here, is absent in Simon's work. This omission can hardly be an error or an oversight and is best seen as reflecting Simon's judgment that behavioral regularities—for example, the hierarchical organization of natural cognitive processes—are primary as compared to technical properties of the data. There are epistemological pitfalls along the path I take; but I argue, nevertheless, that the technical properties matter a great deal—particularly in analyses that deal with changing computational technologies. I treat rationality bounds as conditional and variable—endogenously determined, as it were—and employ different informational architectures at several distinct qualitative complexity levels[13] as templates for the construction of economic models.[14]

Is this economics?

In short, the Simon-Kornai perspective: (1) reduces the system property of actual or potential equilibrium from a prior condition to one of several testable hypotheses that depend upon technical and institutional givens; (2) shifts attention toward organizational behaviors and information usage; (3) calls for explicit specification of information processes and functions; and (4) calls implicitly for consideration of informational resources.[15]

---

[13] It is perhaps premature to bring out the fine points before actually getting into the technical questions. However, any work that proposes a bridge between computer science and the social sciences needs to be positioned vis-à-vis Simon. I see my approach as complementary to his with respect to positive analysis of institutions and reinforcing with respect to his critique of rationality assumptions.

[14] As is well known, the Simon-Kornai perspective is referenced and partially incorporated in many works which are primarily critical including writings by "post-Keynesians" (Eichner, 1991), "institutionalists" (Solo, 1991; Tool, 1986), "behaviorists" (Cyert and March, 1963), "evolutionary Schumpeterians" (Nelson and Winter, 1982), and "rationalists" (Hollis and Nell, 1975). Results deriving from automaton modeling will provide these schools with additional ammunition. However, since my main concern is with applications, I have confined critical comments to this chapter and to side notes scattered in the text.

One additional point should be brought up in this context however. A common focus of many critiques of neoclassical and "equilibrium school" analysis is reliance on mathematical methods which are intrinsically time-reversible and ahistorical. Development, evolution, technical revolution, knowledge accumulation, and qualitative progress are thus extrinsic categories for analysis within the standard paradigms. Computational forms including automata models are intrinsically time-irreversible (time-reversible abstract automata exist, but as special cases) and inherently accommodate such processes as knowledge accumulation. The crossing of qualitative complexity thresholds as can occur in a dynamic sequence may be interpreted as "development" or "structural change" but this is metaphorical usage and subject to the qualifications noted earlier. My own view is that dynamic automata models are rich enough to illuminate aspects of historical processes but are no substitute for historical and institutional analysis. They provide only partial relief with respect to the critical charge of ahistoricity in pure theory.

[15] Of course there are significant exceptions. Economists who have specified automata as economic units without necessarily endorsing a broader informational perspective

Is a study in this perspective "economics"? Obviously not, if the Chicago "tight priors" are taken as definitive. Yet it is economics, in the trivial sense that it represents the "doing of economists" in problem areas that are recognizably economic. I advance narrower and stronger grounds for an affirmative response. Economics is the study of rational choice and the consequences of choice under restrictions imposed by productive technique, a legacy of institutions, and finite resources. By and large the technology of rationality has remained unexamined. This book represents a reconstruction of economic analysis where rationality is subject to the rules and restrictions of informational technology.

My first attempts at simulating structure change in systems with high intrinsic complexity were combined with theoretical studies of such changes and the information properties of finely detailed complex systems. These studies formed the principal subjects of my 1975 book, *The Analysis of Complex Socioeconomic Systems*. The book stressed the potential power of the methodology for structural representation and the generality and scope of the von Neumann forms when suitably translated. In effect it advocated a constructive approach to economic modeling and it sketched in broad outline a research program which is largely realized in these pages. The specifics of this program involved: (1) working out the practical details of a method of structural description that would reveal critical complexity thresholds; (2) developing a theory of "structural formations," entities which possess capacities for computation and information exchange but are not optimally designed in any architectural or economic sense; (3) developing an associated theory of decentralized, parallel, quasi-autonomous entities; (4) identifying the practical limits on economic decision making that stem from intrinsic data complexities; and (5) completing a taxonomy of economic agents and institutions organized according to the intrinsic complexity levels of the functions they perform.

The theoretical side of the research was augmented and shaped by parallel case analyses, participant-observer studies, and technology reconstructions, all aimed at testing the applicability, practicality, and scope of the approach. A critical test ground was the work floor where I sought to model and reproduce the decision-complexity content of an entire installation, covering the full range of choices from the most primitive routine tasks, through intricate operational decisions to the deepest optimizations. I recruited a team with credentials in industrial psychology, industrial so-

---

include: Ames (1983) on information exchange and signaling; Gottinger (1983) on bounded-rationality organizational design; Chenault and Flueckiger (1983) on adaptation; and Rubinstein (1986) on game-playing surrogates; Gottinger (1978a) and Piccoli (1973) on decision requirements. While Binmore and Dasgupta (1987) examine unrestricted rationality. Warsh (1984) provides an intuitive description of a "complexity perspective" as an emerging tendency in the discipline.

ciology, industrial engineering, computer science, and job design. Together and separately we ran lathes, prowled construction sites, and coded the content of jobs as we attempted them, as they were performed by experts, and as they were coordinated (or not) by managers.

Subsequent structured interviews and informal discussions told us to what extent, how, and in what ways the formal complexity properties we identified entered the considerations of workers and managers. The feedback provided gratifying confirmation that the automata representations we used captured essential features of the choices presented by the technology and the thought processes and heuristics employed to resolve them. These were actually thrilling moments. Unprompted, a shovel operator at a New York City excavation site described the hierarchy of decisions involved in doing his job so as to maintain an efficient flow of work for his satellite loaders, dump trucks, and drilling crews. The formalisms and complexity orderings we had identified came to life. A lathe operator, asked an innocuous question about what made for a satisfying day's work, replied with a categorization of significant job "complexities," routine "complications," and how what we have come to call "learning-by-doing" rested on his resolution of the former. In short, complexity thresholds mattered a great deal.

The empirical work and the research program, as I had initially conceptualized it, were essentially completed several years ago. However, an important expository element seemed absent. I lacked a persuasive demonstration of the distinctiveness of high-complexity systems—a firsthand means to communicate to the reader the kind of insight I had gained during many hours spent with "Life" and had reinforced in the recapitulations of job content. I feared that unless that insight were cultivated the reader would not see complexity assessment as a central new development but rather as a side aspect or metaphorical adjunct to yet another technical means of modeling bounded-rationality systems. Short of bundling "Life" software with the book, it appeared that I would have to proselytize with secondhand evocations of privileged visions—a sufficient apostolic basis for founding a religion but not for influencing my colleagues.

Coincidentally, at about that time, I was invited to present a paper at a conference on *Dynamical Systems and Cellular Automata* held in Lumigny, outside Marseilles. There, physicists Norman Packard and Stephen Wolfram showed crude early versions of their now-celebrated slides of the evolution of one-dimensional cellular automata. My first impression was that they had simply found effective pictorial means to display results that were implicit in the work of Alvy Smith and others in the immediate post-von Neumann generation of automata theorists. But on reflection, I came to understand how much more they had accomplished. The pictures were the final evidence that tied the complexity hierarchy to an equivalent hierarchy

PREFACE

for dynamic systems. The supporting calculations and documentation gave definitive support to their conjectures but the pictures told the story.

At this point I developed the "snapshots of complex systems" which both decorate the present text and form the basis of the substantive chapters on complexity measurement and dynamics. The pictures will, I am sure, cultivate the reader's intuitive understanding of the complexity hierarchy, particularly as it applies to economic data structures. But one does, of course, still have to read the captions. The new work illuminated many aspects of the original program, especially those that dealt with decentralized systems and the essentially parallel architectures which characterize the fields of interaction of many economic processes. The results could even be dramatic as, for example, in a pictorial record of the misfiring of policy attempts to fine-tune an expectations-driven economy.

This brings us almost up to date. I had planned to complete the compilation of these essays into a polished manuscript during a sabbatical stay at Nuffield College. Yet one loose end of exposition remained. I still lacked a compelling—direct, as opposed to inferential—example of an important economic problem whose resolution required the attainment of the highest complexity threshold. I reshelved my manuscript in my tower room and went downstairs to the computer room to pursue a hunch. I had long felt that complexity properties were the key to what Martin Shubik calls the N-person game with "many" players. My focus was on an iterated version of Thomas Schelling's "multiperson prisoners' dilemma" where "many" equated to the many thousands who could be portrayed through parallel computation. It turned out to be simple enough to prove by standard game-theoretical reasoning that no system in the lower levels of the complexity hierarchy could support an equilibrium other than universal defection or an all-or-nothing trigger strategy of the sorts proposed by Roy Radner and James Friedman. But did a self-enforcing cooperative equilibrium exist at the highest level of system capacity? It took some billions of simulated games to demonstrate a close and robust approximation of cooperative equilibrium by a strategy suitable for a bounded rationality player. The strategy is unique and to my astonished delight it turned out to be the "Game of Life." I am sorry to be the one to turn "Life" from an object of intellectual dalliance to an instrument serving a utilitarian purpose, but such is frequently the obligation of the economist.

With the story of this work told, I can at last pass to the most pleasant part of presenting it—the recollection and compilation of the many courtesies received, the guidance and criticism that helped so much to shape the work.

I owe thanks for many valuable criticisms of this work. Eileen Appelbaum has reviewed most of these pages. Others implicated, if only for side comments that made a difference, include: Ed Ames, Luca Anderlini, Brian Arthur, Michael Bacharach, Christopher Bliss, Stephen Brams, Ivan Christin, Richard Day, Robin Cowan, Christophe Deissenberg, Gerald Flueckiger, Duncan Foley, Frank Hahn, Geoff Heal, Oskar Itzinger, Janos Kornai, Robert Kuenne, Cigdem Kurdas, Bill Lunt, John Miller, James Ramsey, Ariel Rubenstein, Andrew Schotter, Willi Semmler, Avner Shaked, Tom Vietorisz, and Chuck Wilson. My coauthors Roger Alcaly, Eileen Appelbaum, Charles Bahn, Duncan Foley, Hans Gottinger, Farokh Hormozi, Ross Koppel, Stergios Mourgos, and Art Weinberg will surely recognize their influence and perhaps their thoughts. Al Eichner, James Meade, Hy Minsky, Bruno Stein and Aaron Wildavsky, regrettably, cannot acknowledge my thanks for their encouragement and unshaking support for the entire project. On the technical side I have gained much from discussions of automata forms with Per Bak, Norman Margolus, Norman Packard, Thomas Toffoli, and Stephen Wolfram. I should like to thank for their particular assistance Bob Tater of Automatrix Inc., the intelligence behind CAM-PC, and our contact at Thinking Machines Corporation, David Ray. Cam-6, a Toffoli and Margolus production, and "cell-systems," written by Charles Platt, were used for many of the graphics displays. Hang Kim is owed special thanks for the support given to automata-based structural methodology in the pages of *Mathematical Social Sciences.* To David Warsh, thanks in general. I would like to acknowledge helpful comments from participants in seminars at the Universities of Oxford and Cambridge, the University of California at Irvine, the State University of New York at Albany, Vassar College, the Jerome Levy Economics Institute, and New York University. In addition I should like to mention the contributions of Ariel Rubenstein, my Seminar Group at CUNY Graduate Center, and the artists who helped with this work.

My debts to institutions are also great. I received financial support from the National Science Foundation; the OECD; the U.S. Congressional Office of Technology Assessment; the State of New Jersey, the PSC-CUNY Faculty Research Fund, the John Jay College graduate program, and the Jerome Levy Economic Institute. Workers, managers, and researchers at IBM (Amsterdam), Phillips Electric (Einthoven), Mitsubishi Heavy Industries (Kobe), Brown and Williamson (Louisville), and Reynault (Boulogne) are owed much gratitude. Special thanks are due President Monty Gettler, lathe operators, and forge teams at Nepco along with site managers and heavy-equipment operators at several Tishman excavation locations. I can only regret that research-design considerations forced anonymity on so many who contributed to this study. As is so often the case, ideas flow in new surroundings; leaves spent at the Institute for Advanced Studies in Vienna, the Medis Institute in Munich, the University of Paris (Pantheon), Nuffield College, the Santa Fe Institute, and the University of Bonn proved this to my satisfaction.

Very particular thanks are due to Pat Albin, without whose practical and emotional support this book could not have been completed, Joanna Koldynska–Pekala, who gave me irreplaceable personal assistance, and Ted Yanow, who provided invaluable help in the preparation of the manuscript.

New York, 1991; revised December 1996.

Acknowledgments

We would like to thank Elsevier Science-NL, Sara Burgerhartstraat 25, 1055 KV Amsterdam, The Netherlands, for its kind permission to reprint:

Chapter 2 from *Mathematical Social Sciences* 3, Peter S. Albin, The metalogic of economic predictions, calculations, and propositions, 329–358, 1982;

Chapter 3 from *Mathematical Social Sciences* 13, Peter S. Albin, Microeconomic foundations of cyclical irregularities or "chaos," 185–214, 1987;

Chapter 5 from *Journal of Economic Behavior and Organization* 18, Peter Albin and Duncan K. Foley, Decentralized, dispersed exchange without an auctioneer: A simulation study, 27–51, 1992;

Chapter 6 from *Mathematical Social Sciences* 24, Peter S. Albin, Approximations of cooperative equilibria in multi-person Prisoners' dilemma played by cellular automata, 293–319, 1992;

Chapter 7 from *Mathematical Social Sciences* 1, Peter S. Albin, The complexity of social groups and social systems described by graph structures, 101–129, 1980.

We would like to thank M. E. Sharpe, Inc., 80 Business Park Drive, Armonk, New York 10504, USA, for its kind permission to reprint the material in Chapter 4 from Willi Semmler, ed., *Financial Dynamics and Business Cycles: New Perspectives*, Peter S. Albin, Qualitative effects of monetary policy in "rich" dynamic systems, 168–187, 1989.

Small changes have been made in these texts to correct typographical errors and to adapt them to the format of the present book.

The camera-ready copy for this book was prepared in LaTeX using the Textures typesetting system of Blue Sky Research, Inc.

Barriers and Bounds to Rationality

Chapter 1

Introduction

Duncan K. Foley

1.1 Dynamical systems

One of the most fruitful conceptions in scientific investigation has been the idea of representing the state of a system of interest (whether the system is physical, biological, or social) at a given time as a vector, $\mathbf{x}_t$ in a space X, the *state space* of the system. Interesting systems are those that change through time. Thus we are led to consider the idea that the evolution of a system is governed by certain laws that define a dynamical process. In a large class of situations it turns out that the state of the system in the current time period is the only information available about the influences on its state in the next time period. Thus whatever lawful regularities the system possesses can be summarized by the relation:

$$\mathbf{x}_{t+1} = F_{\mathbf{a}}(\mathbf{x}_t) \qquad (1.1)$$

In this expression $F_{\mathbf{a}}$ is an operator on the state space and the vector $\mathbf{a}$ represents potentially changeable parameters of the system.

The operator $F_{\mathbf{a}}(.)$ may represent a deterministic or stochastic process. In the deterministic case the lawful regularities determine $\mathbf{x}_{t+1}$ uniquely given $\mathbf{a}$ and $\mathbf{x}_t$, while in the stochastic case some margin of uncertainty may remain about the exact value of $\mathbf{x}_{t+1}$. The systems studied in this book are deterministic. Since deterministic systems can be regarded as degenerate stochastic systems, the conclusions we draw about deterministic systems apply to at least some stochastic systems. Negative results and counterexamples established for the deterministic case must apply a fortiori to stochastic systems as well.

The method of dynamical system analysis has been successfully applied to a huge range of phenomena in the physical and biological sciences, as well as to a wide range of social and economic problems. Thus a great deal of mathematical effort has gone into studying the behavior of dynamical systems like (1.1).

1.1.1 Linear dynamical systems

The possible range of behaviors of one class of dynamical systems, linear systems, is completely understood. In a linear dynamical system the operator F_a is a matrix, A, so that the system can be written:

$$\mathbf{x}_{t+1} = A\mathbf{x}_t \tag{1.2}$$

The trajectories of this system can be decomposed into independent motions of three types (see Hirsch and Smale, 1974, for a complete exposition of this theory). One type of motion is geometric expansion or contraction along a particular ray. This motion is associated with a real, positive eigenvalue of the matrix A; the ray is the corresponding eigenvector. A second type is geometric expansion or contraction in which the system jumps from one side of the origin to the other on a particular line in alternate periods. This motion is associated with a real, negative eigenvalue of A; the associated eigenvector again determines the line to which the motion is confined. The third type is inward or outward spiraling in a particular plane. This motion is associated with a pair of complex eigenvalues of the matrix A; the corresponding real and imaginary components of the associated eigenvector define the plane in which it takes place. (The use here of the word "complex" to describe numbers having a real and an imaginary part is, of course, quite different from the use we will make of "complex" to describe properties of whole systems in what follows.)

The magnitude of the eigenvalues determines the stability of the corresponding motion. If an eigenvalue (or pair of complex eigenvalues) has a magnitude smaller than 1 the corresponding component of the motion will be stable, moving toward the origin. If an eigenvalue (or pair of complex eigenvalues) has a magnitude greater than 1, the corresponding component of the motion will be unstable, moving away from the origin indefinitely. Eigenvalues with magnitude just equal to 1 are neutral, neither stable nor unstable. The corresponding component of the motion is neutral as well: if the eigenvalue is $+1$, the system will remain indefinitely at any point on the line corresponding to its eigenvector; if the eigenvalue is -1, the system

1.1. DYNAMICAL SYSTEMS

will indefinitely oscillate in reflections around the origin; if a pair of complex eigenvalues has magnitude 1 (thus lying on the unit circle in complex coordinate space), the system, started at any point in the plane defined by the corresponding eigenvectors, will rotate indefinitely on a circle around the origin through the starting point.

The actual motion of a linear system starting from any initial point $\mathbf{x}_0$ can appear quite complex, but can always be decomposed into a combination of these simple independent motions.

1.1.1.1 Example: The linear oscillator

Consider the linear system defined by the equations of motion:

$$\begin{aligned} x_{t+1} &= \lambda \cos\omega x_t - \lambda \sin\omega y_t \\ y_{t+1} &= \lambda \sin\omega x_t + \lambda \cos\omega y_t \end{aligned} \quad (1.3)$$

Here $\lambda > 0$ and $\omega \neq 0$ are parameters that govern the equations of motion of the system. The matrix A in this case is

$$\begin{bmatrix} \lambda \cos\omega & \lambda \sin\omega \\ \lambda \sin\omega & \lambda \cos\omega \end{bmatrix}$$

The eigenvalues of this matrix are $\lambda(\cos\omega \pm i\sin\omega)$, which are stable if $\lambda < 1$, and unstable if $\lambda > 1$. The trajectories of this system from any arbitrary starting point except the origin are inward spirals if it is stable, outward spirals if it is unstable, and circles in the borderline case $\lambda = 1$. The sign of the parameter ω determines the direction of spiraling, and the magnitude of ω its speed.

1.1.1.2 Linearity and predictability

The possibility of decomposing the trajectories of linear dynamical systems into simple independent motions suggests that it might be possible to predict the motion of linear systems by observing their past trajectories. A clever predictor might use the past trajectories of this system to infer the values of the matrix A, and then could use standard mathematical techniques to extrapolate the future trajectory of the system. Sophisticated and robust techniques for estimating the structure of linear systems, even when the observations of the trajectories are contaminated by errors of observation, have been developed by econometricians, epidemiologists, physicists, and engineers who deal with time series.

Linear systems have the convenient property that their behavior in all regions of the state space is proportional to their behavior in a small neighborhood of the origin. Thus observation of a linear system in a small part of the state space is potentially sufficient to understand its behavior everywhere. This behavior contrasts sharply with those of systems that evolve in different ways at different scales.

Linear systems also have the convenient property that smooth changes in the parameters **a**, which in the case of linearity define the elements in the matrix A, lead to smooth changes in the behavior of the trajectories. The speed of expansion or contraction of a solution along a ray, and the location of the ray itself, may vary with the elements of A, but in a smooth and gradual way. Two real eigenvalues may coalesce into a pair of complex eigenvalues, their eigenvectors becoming the real and imaginary components of the complex eigenvectors, but this takes place so smoothly that the corresponding trajectories are close to each other for small changes in the parameters.

Linear systems may have many dimensions, and their trajectories may seem to be quite complicated, but in fact they are simple, because with enough information, even local information in one region of the state space, about the past trajectory of the system, it is possible to infer the future trajectory to any desired degree of accuracy.

1.1.1.3 Example: The linear oscillator continued

The linear oscillator we have studied exhibits the smooth dependence of linear systems on changes in parameters. It is convenient to rewrite this system in polar coordinates, (r, θ), where $r(x,y) = \sqrt{x^2 + y^2}$, and $\theta = \arctan(\frac{y}{x})$. In these coordinates the laws of motion become:

$$\begin{aligned} r_{t+1} &= \lambda r_t \\ \theta_{t+1} &= \theta_t + \omega \end{aligned} \qquad (1.4)$$

In polar coordinates it is clear that the expansion or contraction of the system depends on the parameter λ, while its speed of rotation depends on the parameter ω. If we hold ω constant and increase λ from a value smaller than 1 through 1 to a value larger than 1, the trajectories change smoothly from inward spirals to circles to outward spirals as in Fig. 1.1. If we hold λ constant and vary ω, say from a negative value through 0 to a positive value, we see the spiraling on the trajectory slow down, stop, and then reverse direction, as in Fig. 1.2. When $\omega = 0$, the eigenvalues of the system are no longer a complex conjugate pair, but two real numbers, both equal to λ. In this situation the system decomposes into pure motions in

1.1. DYNAMICAL SYSTEMS

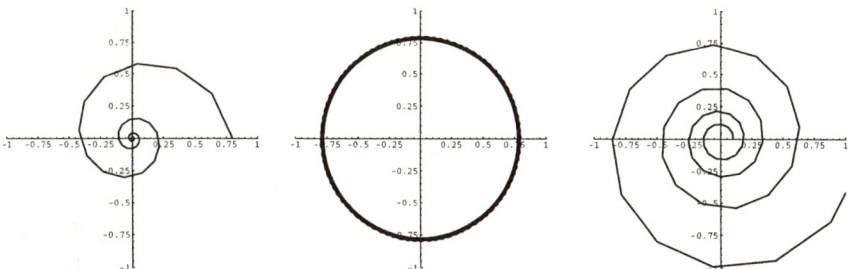

Figure 1.1: As λ moves from stable to unstable values, the trajectories of the linear oscillator change smoothly from inward spirals through a circle to outward spirals.

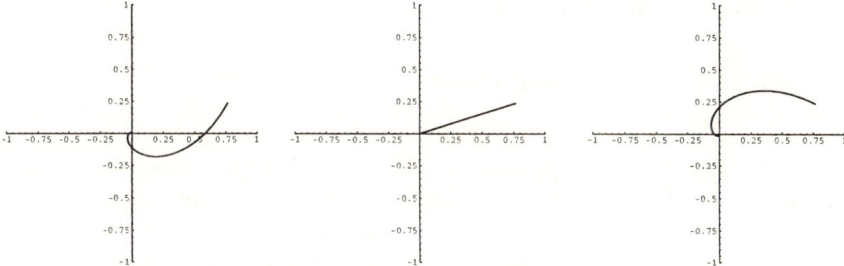

Figure 1.2: As ω moves from positive to negative values, the spiral trajectories of the linear oscillator slow down, and reverse direction. When $\omega = 0$, the system moves along a straight line toward or away from the origin.

the x- and y-directions, which are both unstable or stable, depending on the value of λ.

1.1.2 Nonlinear dynamical systems

The situation where the operator $F_\mathbf{a}(.)$ is not linear is quite different. Suppose, for convenience, that the origin of the state space is an equilibrium of the system, in the sense that the laws of motion require that if the system starts at the origin it will stay there:

$$0 = F_\mathbf{a}(0)$$

For points close to the origin the laws of motion can be approximated by expanding the operator $F_\mathbf{a}(.)$ as a Taylor's series:

$$\begin{aligned}x_{t+1} &= F_{\mathbf{ax}}(0)\mathbf{x}_t + \frac{1}{2}\mathbf{x}_t^T F_{\mathbf{axx}}(0)\mathbf{x}_t + \ldots + \\ &= (F_{\mathbf{ax}}(0) + \frac{1}{2}\mathbf{x}_t^T F_{\mathbf{axx}}(0))\mathbf{x}_t + \ldots +\end{aligned} \quad (1.5)$$

Here $F_{\mathbf{ax}}(0)$ represents the vector of first derivatives of $F_{\mathbf{a}}$ evaluated at the origin, and similarly for $F_{\mathbf{axx}}(0)$. This approximation suggests that we regard nonlinear systems as perturbations of linear systems, where the perturbing effects appear in the quadratic, cubic, and higher order terms of the power series. The second form emphasizes one important aspect of the nonlinearity of the system; the laws of motion of the system change as the system moves in the state space. In a nonlinear system it is no longer generally possible to make inferences about the global behavior of the system from local information.

1.1.2.1 Bifurcations and chaos

Nonlinear dynamical systems display a much greater range of behavior than linear systems. For example, if we gradually vary the parameters in a linear system with a pair of complex eigenvalues so that the eigenvalues move from being stable to being unstable, the corresponding motion changes from a stable spiral toward the origin, through neutral circling of the origin, to an unstable spiral away from the origin. In particular, the motion can remain bounded and cyclical only in the knife-edge case where the eigenvalues have magnitude exactly equal to 1.

In a nonlinear dynamical system matters are quite different. As a pair of complex eigenvalues moves across the unit circle (the *Hopf bifurcation*) the system becomes locally unstable, since the linear forces tend to push it in ever widening spirals. But as the system moves away from the origin, the nonlinear forces become more important. It is possible that the nonlinear forces will be stabilizing, so that the system will develop a stable limit cycle, generating bounded oscillations indefinitely for a range of parameter values and a range of initial conditions. This behavior is qualitatively different from the possible behavior of linear systems, which can produce indefinite bounded oscillations only in the fragile case where the parameters lead to a pair of neutral complex eigenvalues; even in this special case the cycle that results changes with each change of initial conditions.

The interplay of destabilizing linear forces and stabilizing nonlinear forces in a nonlinear system can produce even more complicated trajectories. The nonlinearities may couple the independent motions of the linear system. In this situation the system may be unable to achieve a limit cycle, because its motion disturbs a third variable, which in turn changes the

1.1. DYNAMICAL SYSTEMS

local laws of motion. The system may wander indefinitely in a confined part of the state space, so that it is globally stable, never exactly repeating its previous trajectory. The resulting patterns of motion are called *chaotic*, a terminology that does not do complete justice to the combination of organization and unpredictability that results.

Chaotic systems are organized in that their asymptotic trajectories (or attractors) occupy only a part of the available state space, so that knowledge of the underlying dynamics of the system allows an observer to predict that they cannot assume certain configurations. (This type of knowledge would be of great practical value, for example, in speculating on the motions of financial asset prices. Even though an observer might not be able to predict the exact trajectory of prices very well, knowledge that certain related movements are impossible would allow for profitable informed speculation.) Furthermore, chaotic systems are locally predictable, because the laws of motion change only gradually over the state space. If the system returns to a position in state space close to an earlier trajectory, its trajectory will for a while follow the previous trajectory closely. Furthermore, chaotic systems produce statistically regular outcomes; every trajectory tends to spend the same proportion of time in different portions of the state space. Knowledge of these statistical properties is also of great practical value, since certain risks can be excluded from consideration.

1.1.2.2 Example: The perturbed linear oscillator

We can introduce a stabilizing nonlinear force into the linear oscillator easily by adding a quadratic term that tends to push the system back toward the origin when it gets far away from it. This is particularly transparent in polar coordinates:

$$\begin{aligned} r_{t+1} &= \lambda r_t - \lambda r_t^2 = \lambda r_t(1 - r_t) \\ \theta_{t+1} &= \theta_t + \omega \end{aligned} \quad (1.6)$$

This modified oscillator continues to behave like the linear oscillator when the linear part is stable, that is, when $\lambda < 1$, as Fig. 1.3 shows. The system continues to spiral inward to the origin. The reason for this is that in this case both the linear forces and the nonlinear forces are stabilizing: as the system approaches the origin the nonlinear forces, which are proportional to the square of the distance of the system from the origin, become negligible in comparison to the linear forces.

When we destabilize the linear system by increasing λ above 1, however, we see a dramatic difference between the behaviors of the linear and nonlinear systems. The linear system with $\lambda > 1$ always spirals indefinitely

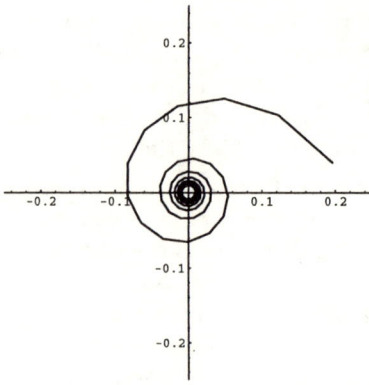

Figure 1.3: The perturbed linear oscillator behaves like its linear counterpart when $\lambda < 1$, spiraling inward toward the origin from any starting point.

outward from the origin, but the nonlinear system establishes a limited, stable oscillation at a particular distance from the origin that depends on λ, when λ is not too much larger than 1, as Fig. 1.4 shows. In this situation the nonlinear stabilizing forces are in conflict with the linear destabilizing forces on the system. When the system is close to the origin, the nonlinear forces are very weak compared with the linear forces, so the nonlinear system behaves like the linear system and spirals outward. But as the system moves farther from the origin, the stabilizing nonlinear forces become stronger, and eventually balance the destabilizing linear force, creating the observed limit cycle through a Hopf bifurcation.

If we continue to increase λ, the stable limit cycle itself begins to break up into more and more cycles as in Fig. 1.5, until finally the nonlinear oscillator reaches the chaotic state illustrated in Fig. 1.6. Trajectories of this system that start at very nearby points will diverge exponentially over time: small errors of measurement of initial conditions will lead to larger and larger errors of prediction.

Figure 1.7 illustrates a further nonlinearization of the oscillator. Whenever this system enters the small window of states, the value of λ is reduced to .5, the value of ω becomes 0, and the system moves on a straight line to the origin. We might think of the window as representing the solution to some difficult problem: the system casts around almost randomly seeking it, but once it has found it, finds its way to the ultimate equilibrium. The trajectories of this system diverge initially, but sooner or later all of them will converge on the origin. As we will see, this type of regime shift, in which the diversity of behavior of the system first expands and then contracts, is characteristic of highly complex systems.

1.1. DYNAMICAL SYSTEMS

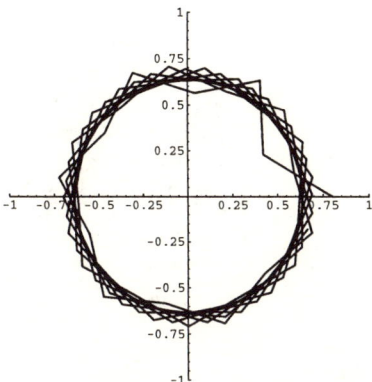

Figure 1.4: When λ is increased moderately above 1, the perturbed, nonlinear oscillator establishes a stable limit cycle at a distance from the origin depending on λ.

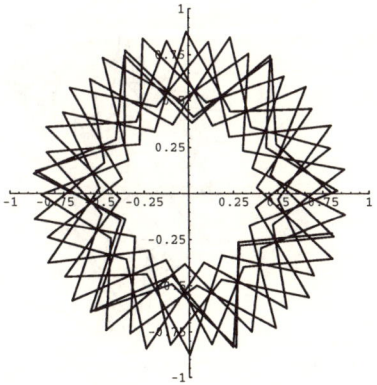

Figure 1.5: As λ increases above 1, the limit cycles of the perturbed oscillator break up into multiple cycles.

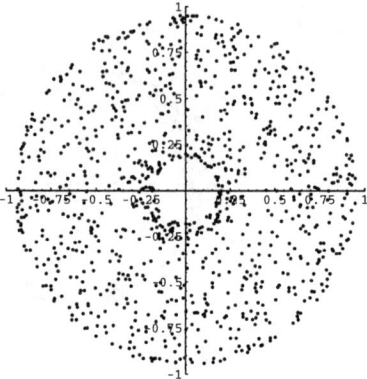

Figure 1.6: As λ approaches 4, the trajectories of the perturbed oscillator become chaotic. Here only the points of the trajectory are plotted.

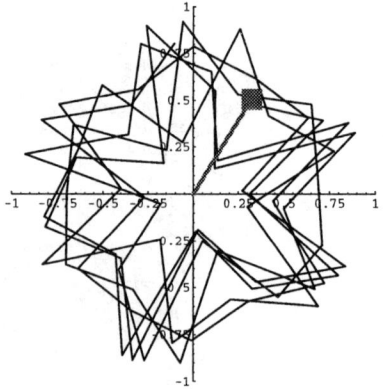

Figure 1.7: When the system enters the window (the gray square), its dynamics change and it moves on a straight line to the origin.

1.1. DYNAMICAL SYSTEMS

1.1.2.3 Dynamical systems from an informational viewpoint

A fruitful way to think of a stable dynamical system is as a signal processor. The input to the system is its initial condition, and its output is the attractor set representing the asymptotic trajectories. A dynamical system, for example, that maps each initial condition onto a finite number of point attractors can be seen as a pattern recognition device: the initial condition represents the data the system confronts, and the particular equilibrium to which it tends from the initial condition can be interpreted as the underlying pattern it associates with these data.

Chaotic systems, on the other hand, are unpredictable. It is relatively easy to predict the trajectories of a stable dynamical system with a simple attractor such as a point or a stable limit cycle. Wherever the system starts, its trajectory will approach the stable attractor, which itself has a relatively simple structure. Furthermore, trajectories that start from nearby initial conditions will actually become closer together as the system evolves. Thus small errors in measuring the initial condition of the system will become negligible factors in disturbing the accuracy of the predicted trajectory. Chaotic systems also tend to attractors, but the attractor is a geometrically complicated structure. One trajectory, starting from one set of initial conditions, may be very different in detail from the trajectory starting from a very slightly different set of initial conditions. In fact, in chaotic systems trajectories starting from slightly different initial conditions diverge progressively as the system evolves. Thus small errors in measuring initial conditions of a chaotic system are magnified over time, and lead to increasingly inaccurate predictions.

Chaotic systems are familiar aspects of human life, the weather being a paradigmatic case. Modern research suggests that chaos is the rule in real nonlinear dynamical systems, and that systems with simple attractors like points and limit cycles are relatively rare results of highly controlled interactions. Furthermore, the widespread existence of chaos suggests that many systems often viewed as being purely stochastic—that is, varying without any discernible order at all—may have the type of structure associated with chaotic dynamics.

1.1.2.4 Complexity and self-organization

Human experience also embraces the phenomena we associate with living organisms, which are, in principle, dynamical systems, moving on a trajectory through some large state space. Living organisms display behavior that is qualitatively different from chaotic systems like geological or meteorological interactions. First of all, living organisms are highly structured, and have powerful homeostatic mechanisms that stabilize important aspects of their behavior. On the other hand, some living organisms, certainly human beings, produce state space trajectories that appear not to be even partially statistically predictable like chaotic systems. Human beings, for example, seek solutions to problems, which may involve an exploration of the relevant state space which does not have the repetitive features of chaotic motions. In solving a problem, a human being may pursue one approach, exhibiting one type of behavior, for a while, and then determine that this approach is a dead end, and suddenly (from the point of view of an external observer) shift to a qualitatively different type of behavior embodying an alternative approach to the problem. Furthermore, if the human is lucky enough to solve the problem, the problem-solving trajectory may come to an end. The terminal state is a kind of stable attractor for the problem-solving system, but is clearly not very well modeled by stable linear or nonlinear systems with simple attractors, because the trajectories leading to it may diverge before they eventually converge on the solution.

Thus there exist at least some nonlinear dynamical systems that are self-organizing and exhibit dynamic behavior qualitatively different both from simple stability and chaos. Although it is not easy to characterize these systems in general mathematical terms, they are called *complex, adaptive systems*. Their basis has to be nonlinear dynamics, since the motions of linear dynamics are not rich enough to support complex behavior. In complex systems the nonlinear dynamics can sustain self-organized and self-reproducing structures, and these structures in turn are capable of interactions that mimic the behavior of living organisms.

Complex adaptive systems are of great interest to human beings, since they include ourselves and other life forms, and in particular our processes of conscious thought. This book addresses the question of the degree to which the social interactions of human beings, especially their economic relationships, also constitute complex adaptive processes.

Human beings are very intelligent compared to systems with simple point attractors, though even these systems sometimes pose subtle problems to human understanding. We are intimately familiar with the behavior of massive objects falling to rest in the field of gravity, for example, though it is not so easy for us to throw a spear with force and accuracy at a distant target. Oscillatory systems pose a more complicated, but still conceptually soluble problem to human intelligence. The oscillatory system falls into a repetitive pattern that we can with long observation and attention recognize and learn to predict. But this process is not easy, either: many generations of human observation and thought were required to unravel the oscillatory motion of the planets, for example.

Chaotic systems pose an even higher barrier to human understanding, because their regularities are subtler, and require more observation and more careful analysis to discover. Our learning and knowledge of chaotic

1.1. DYNAMICAL SYSTEMS

systems take a structural, statistical form, in contrast to the precise predictions we can make about point-stable and oscillatory systems. We often regard chaotic systems as simply stochastic, through missing the subtle structures that determines their attractors. The deepest understanding we can reach of a chaotic system is a knowledge of its underlying laws of motion, even though this knowledge does not practically allow us to predict the evolution of the chaotic system in detail.

Complex adaptive systems pose novel problems for theories of human knowledge and learning that go beyond the realm of the chaotic. The problem is that these systems are inherently at the same (or perhaps a higher) level of complexity as our own consciousness, which provides the tools with which we learn and know the world. There does not seem to be any economical way to predict the problem-solving efforts of another human being, for example. We can try to solve the problem ourselves, thus reenacting the dynamical process which we are studying, but this effort may not (in many cases will probably not) replicate the problem solving of another person very closely. Even if we can solve the problem, that does not allow us to say very much about whether another person will solve it, or arrive at the same solution.

As we will see, the choice to regard human and social interactions as the aspects of complex systems poses deep questions for received models of human behavior, especially for the models of maximizing rationality that are the foundation of much existing social and economic theory.

1.1.3 Cellular automata as models of nonlinear dynamical systems

There is a bewildering variety of nonlinear dynamical systems, and it is unlikely that any very general laws apply to all of them. Our current understanding of these systems is largely the result of two research strategies. The first looks at the consequences of the simplest and most manageable nonlinearities and attempts to understand the resulting systems through rigorous mathematical analysis. The second seeks to identify very particular systems that are capable of a wide range of complex behavior and to study these examples through computer simulation to get clues as to the possible range of behavior of nonlinear systems in general.

The second strategy underlies much of the work reported in this book. One conceptually simple, but exceedingly rich model of nonlinear systems, the *cellular automaton*, serves as a laboratory for the exploration of the difficult general questions raised by nonlinearity and complexity. The cellular automaton is an array of cells with a particular geometry (arranged on a line segment, a circle, a segment of the 2-dimensional plane, or a torus, for example). In each period of a simulation each cell is characterized by a certain *state*, chosen from a finite set of possibilities. This concept is motivated in part by quantum mechanical ideas, since in quantum theory the states of physical systems are confined to a finite or countable range of possibilities, and in part by certain common nonquantum physical systems, such as oscillators, that can be excited only at a certain range of frequencies, and saturating systems that move to a finite range of stable limiting configurations. The restriction of the states of the cells to a finite set is already a reflection of the underlying nonlinearity of the system being modeled.

The cellular automaton advances through time with the cells synchronized to a common periodic clock external to the system. The state of each cell in the next period depends on the current state of the cells in the system as a whole. In most of the cellular automata that have been studied in detail, the evolution of any single cell depends only on the past states of the cells in a neighborhood containing it. Because of the physical motivation for much of the research in cellular automata, where the system being modeled consists of a large number of identical particles or subsystems, it is frequently assumed that all the cells obey exactly the same rule of evolution.

The simplest cellular automaton, for example, might consist of n cells arranged on a circle, each of which can be in one of two states (*on* or *off*). The neighborhood of each cell might consist of the k (perhaps 1) cells on either side of it. There are eight possible configurations of the three cells in a neighborhood, so the law of evolution of a two-state, radius-1 neighborhood circular cellular automaton can be described by a list of eight bits (0 or 1), interpreted as the next state of the cell when the current configuration of neighboring cells is described by each of the eight possibilities (000, 001, 010,...,111).

Figure 1.8 illustrates the evolution of a one-dimensional two-state cellular automaton in a format frequently used in this book. The cells are displayed horizontally, with the state of each cell in one period indicated by its shading (in a two-state cellular automaton typically white and black). The state of the system after a clock tick is plotted directly beneath the original state, so that the time evolution of the state of any cell can be traced vertically.

Cellular automata are obviously very simplified models, but they are capable of a remarkably wide and interesting range of behaviors. They can mimic, for example, all four of the types of nonlinear dynamic behavior we have discussed: stability toward a single state, stability toward a pattern of regular oscillation, nonrepetitive chaotic motions (within the limits imposed by the large, but finite number of states a finite cellular automaton can occupy), and complex evolutions with sharply changing regimes and

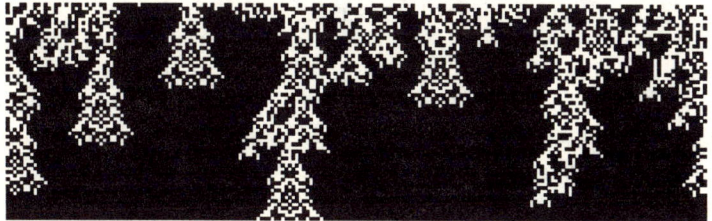

Figure 1.8: The evolution of a one-dimensional cellular automaton.

unpredictable stopping points.

Cellular automata have great research advantages, since they are easy and cheap to emulate on a computer, and exhibit such a wide range of possible nonlinear behavior. Certain cellular automata can emulate general-purpose computers (Turing machines), and are thus capable of producing output at the highest complexity level of formal language theory. They also have limitations as models of human social and economic interaction, which will be explored in some depth in this introduction and in the later chapters of the book. As a result of these limitations the logic of this research is largely that of the counterexample: if certain hypotheses about human behavior can be shown to be impossible or implausible in the environment of cellular automata, they will a fortiori be impossible or implausible in more general (and perhaps even more complex) nonlinear environments. But a demonstration that a certain strategy or behavior is plausible or functional in a particular cellular automaton may not generalize to other automata or to other nonlinear systems.

1.2 Dynamical systems in social and physical science

Social scientists have been tempted to apply the powerful methods of dynamical system analysis to social systems. In carrying out this project, however, one immediately runs into the fact that social systems comprise the interactions of conscious human beings, unlike physical systems in which the behavior of the elements arises purely from their physical properties. The later chapters of this book raise these issues sharply and concretely in a variety of research contexts, but it is worth reviewing them briefly here.

1.2.1 Local and global interaction

In most physical systems the forces carrying the interactions of particles or molecules decay rapidly with distance. It is natural in this circumstance to model the system as evolving through local interactions. Cellular automata reflect this presupposition by making the next state of any cell depend only on the current states of cells in it neighborhood.

Many models of human social interaction, on the other hand, assume that the agents in the society have at least some kind of global information that influences their behavior. In one standard economic model of markets, for example, every agent in the market is supposed to determine her net demand for the commodity in the next period on the basis of a market price established in the current period. But this market price in turn depends on the net demands of all the agents in the market, not just a limited subset that might be regarded as the informational neighbors of the agent.

The essay "Qualitative Effects of Monetary Policy in 'Rich' Dynamic Systems," chapter 4 in this volume, offers another instance of the same issue. Policy signals such as the short-term interest rates largely controlled by central bank intervention in markets are common information to all the firms in the economy. In deciding its investment policy the firm takes into account this global signal in addition to local information consisting of the current investment decisions of its neighbors. In addition to the local interactions modeled by classic cellular automata, there are at least weak global interactions mediated by markets and policy makers that have to be taken into account in economic models.

Systemwide interactions in cellular automata raise novel issues concerning the dynamics and evolution of complex systems. Economists believe, for example, that the relatively limited information contained in market prices is sufficient to stabilize and organize potentially chaotic market transactions. Classical studies of cellular automata give us a good sense of the complexity and instability inherent in even relatively simple patterns of local interaction in nonlinear dynamical systems, but we have very little feel for the impact of weak global interactions in these contexts.

1.2.2 Topology and geometry in physical and social models

Physical systems consist of particles located in a highly structured geometrical space (typically Euclidean space). In this situation there is no ambiguity about the distance between particles or the identity of the particles closest to a given particle at a given moment of time. This geometry carries over into cellular automata, though it is simplified in important

1.2. SOCIAL AND PHYSICAL SCIENCE 19

ways. Rather than considering a full three-dimensional space, it is computationally much easier to study the evolution of cellular automata in one- or two-dimensional spaces. The geometry of the spaces is further simplified by considering only a finite or countable set of lattice points as sites for cells. Rather than coping with the complexity of smoothly decaying interactions (like gravity or electrical fields), the cellular automata are assumed to respond only to the states of immediate neighbors within an arbitrarily chosen radius.

Notions of closeness have played a powerful and fertile role in social and economic theories as well, but are inherently much more ambiguous and rich. The simplest cases are those where the economic agents are deployed in a real physical space, for example, locational models in economics. The notion of closeness and neighborhood relevant to a spatial economic model is almost the same as in a physical model, since, for example, transportation costs are often proportional to geographical distance between agents.

But even this very favorable example of transportation costs as determining economic distance signals additional levels of mathematical difficulty. Transportation costs depend not only on geographical distance, but also on topographical features (mountains, rivers, and the like) and on transportation facilities (railroads, highways, canals, and so forth). In a city built on a grid plan the economically relevant distance between two points is not ordinary Euclidean distance, because travel on diagonals across the grid plan is not feasible. Furthermore, the relevant economic distance measured by the time or cost of movement of people or goods between two points may vary depending on traffic congestion and street capacity. The economic distance between a customer and supplier is really the cost of moving goods from one to another, which may also vary according to the good being shipped. Bulk sea freight may bring cities half the world away from each other economically closer for certain commodities than these cities are to their geographically much closer suburbs.

But spatial models are only one context in which the concept of social or economic distance plays a key role. In models of the business cycle demand is often assumed to diffuse through the economy from customer to supplier. The injection of a given amount of government spending in one sector of the economy creates a cascade of further spending as the immediate producers hire workers and buy supplies to meet the demand, creating demands for other sectors. In this context the relevant economic neighbors of an agent are determined not geographically but functionally in terms of their technological positions in the hierarchy of production. This example also indicates mathematical difficulties. To say that firm A is a neighbor of firm B because orders to firm A will create demand for firm B does not necessarily imply that firm B is reciprocally a neighbor of firm A. Demand for B may have no, or very weak, effects on the demand seen by A. In Euclidean space the distance metric is symmetric, so that the distance from point A to B is the same as the distance from point B to A, but this may not be true for many relevant conceptions of economic distance. Economic distance is also evidently not necessarily additive: the distance from A to C is not necessarily the sum of the distances from A to B and from B to C, because A and C may have economic relations that are independent of B altogether.

The same considerations apply to models of the diffusion of technical change through economies. Technical change in one sector of the economy (say, the introduction of a new metallurgical process yielding a higher strength alloy) tend to ripple through the customers of that sector (the building industry can build higher buildings with fewer structural components). Bottlenecks in one sector are important incentives for technological changes in supplier sectors (power looms require stronger thread to reduce the costs of thread breakage). Cellular automata are natural simplified models of diffusion, but in the social context the problematic character of the geometry of the space in which the cells are located has always to be kept in mind.

1.2.3 Time and causality

Physical theories have progressed in part because of their decision to regard time and causality as flowing in only one direction. The past is allowed to influence the future but not vice versa. This presupposition is reflected in the cellular automata developed to model physical systems in the assumption that the state of the system in the next period depends only on its state in the current period. Human beings, on the other hand, act with an eye to the future consequences of their actions. Thus the future, at least through actors' conceptions of the future, plays a different role in social and physical interactions.

This difference in point of view in the physical and social sciences lies at the heart of some of the most vexing and controversial problems about modeling human action. One resolution is to distinguish between the actual future and agents' conceptions or expectations of the future. If we take agents' expectations as part of their current state, then we can rigorously regard their actions as determined only by the present and past, not by the future itself, even though their conceptions of the future are acknowledged as part of their motivation and calculation. This point of view has its own set of conceptual problems and tangles. Expectations, for example, are not directly observable, and as a result must be inferred from agents' actions, which the expectations are supposed to explain. It is tempting for economists to suppose that agents can use the same processes of rational calculation to form expectations that they are assumed to use in

1.2. SOCIAL AND PHYSICAL SCIENCE

allocating budgets and other resources, leading to the economic theory of *rational expectations*. One of the central questions addressed in this book is the plausibility of the assumption of fully rational expectations in environments evolving according to complex nonlinear dynamics. For example, is it reasonable to assume that agents can costlessly solve mathematical problems of any degree of complexity, or make measurements of the current state of their environment to any degree of accuracy? As we shall see, these issues take on a sharp clarity and poignancy in the models considered here.

1.2.4 Identity and diversity

Physical systems often consist of one or a small number of types of interacting particles. Many interesting phenomena can conveniently be analyzed in systems with only one type of particle, since the interactions of interest (exchange of momenta, resonance, and the like) can take place among identical particles. As a consequence the widely studied cellular automata models of complex system interaction assume that all cells are subject to identical laws of motion.

The situation in models of society and the economy is different, because diversity of interest is often central to social interactions. Take for example the simple standard textbook model of a market. A number of agents (which might be thought of as cells of a cellular automaton) respond to a publicly announced market price with a particular net (or, in economic terms, excess) demand for the commodity being exchanged in the market. A positive excess demand indicates that the agent wants to buy that amount of good at the announced price, while a negative excess demand indicates that the agent wants to sell. The problem to be solved by the market is to find a price at which the sum of the excess demands is zero, so that the market clears.

We could model this system as a cellular automaton in which the state of each cell represents the excess demand for the commodity. (It is traditional in economics to regard excess demands as continuous variables, but it would not do much violence to the conception to restrict the levels of excess demand to a finite, but perhaps large, set of possible values.) As we have already noted, the dependence of each agent's excess demand on an announced market price that reflects, say, the total excess demand in the previous period departs from the usual cellular automaton assumption that each cell's state depends only on the state of the neighboring cells in the previous period. But the traditional image of market clearing involves the division of the agents into buyers and sellers at the announced market price. If all the agents are identical, as in the cellular automaton model, they will all assume exactly the same state once a market price is announced. It may still be possible to clear the market by finding a price at which every agent's excess demand is zero, but this is a somewhat restricted image of the activity of real-world markets, since if every agent's excess demand is zero there would be no actual transactions in the market.

Chapter 5 in this volume, "Decentralized, dispersed exchange without an auctioneer," deals with these modeling problems in some detail. In this essay the agents are identical in tastes (though not in endowments, and thus not in excess demand functions), but the assumption of a single market price announced to all of them is relaxed. Instead we assume that the agents trade with their neighbors, so that effectively each agent sees only a small part of the whole market. Because the agents are arrayed in a circle, the various submarkets corresponding to different neighborhoods are indirectly linked. Simulations show how such an indirect linkage can lead to some of the same results as the textbook model of a single market price, though not all.

The issue of diversity does not arise in all economic models. In fact, contemporary macroeconomic theory tends, for the sake of computability and conceptual simplicity, to make the assumption of a *representative agent*, that is, that the economic behavior arising from the interactions of many agents in the economy can be modeled as if it were the behavior of a single agent. One way this might happen is if all the agents were in fact identical (and there were no externalities, that is, nonmarket-mediated interactions between them). Here the cellular automaton assumption that all the cells are governed by the same law of motion would be consistent with the traditional economic model. These considerations, however, reveal the fact that the traditional economic models have built-in assumptions that simplify their trajectories. Take the textbook market model with identical agents as an example. Suppose that the agents start in a random configuration of excess demands. In the next period a price will be announced, and all of them will pass into the same state, responding to this market price. Then the market price will be adjusted to eliminate excess demand or supply, and all of the agents will move together from one state to another until they reach the equilibrium. This type of behavior clearly has low inherent complexity: there is no local interaction of the agents. In fact, the evolution of the system as a whole after the first period is simply an n-fold copy of the evolution of any individual agent.

To retain the possibilities of complex evolution in economic models we must either relax the economic assumption that all the agents respond to the same systemwide signals (such as market price) or relax the cellular automaton assumption that all the agents are identical.

1.3 Economic models of fully rational behavior

The essays in this volume critically examine some of the most fundamental assumptions in widely accepted economic models. For the sake of clarity in terminology, and as a service to readers who are not familiar with economic modeling practice, in this section we review the general form of economic models of rational behavior and consider the details of a representative sample of such models.

The central issues revealed by this survey concern the information-processing and computing capacities implicitly attributed to rational economic agents in various contexts. These issues become particularly acute, as we shall see, when the modeling context involves decisions over a large number of time periods and when the agent is uncertain about key aspects of the future environment.

1.3.1 The rational choice program

The cornerstone of received economic theory is the idea that human agents behave rationally. Rationality is supposed to underly the predictability of human behavior, and thus to establish it as a candidate for systematic scientific investigation.

The concept of rationality itself has no content without further elaboration and specification. For the economist rationality has come to mean behavior that can be viewed as maximizing some consistent mathematical function of behavioral and environmental variables. The rational agent can be seen as pursuing a definite and unambiguous goal, and her actions are predictable in this light. The most general form of the rational model, then, is that the agent's actions $\mathbf{x}$ maximize her objective function $u_\mathbf{a}(\mathbf{x})$, where $\mathbf{a}$ represents parameters describing the environment. Thus we predict that the agent's behavior can be described by a lawful relation $\mathbf{x}(\mathbf{a}) = \arg\max_\mathbf{x} u_\mathbf{a}(\mathbf{x})$. That is, the agent chooses the action $\mathbf{x}$ that maximizes her objective function $u_\mathbf{a}(\mathbf{x})$ given the environment $\mathbf{a}$. In particular, the economist will try to infer the objective function u from the agent's observed behavior, and then predict that her actions in the face of a change in the environment will follow the law $\mathbf{x}(\mathbf{a})$.

There are some well-known problems with this program of explanation and prediction. In the first place, as suggested earlier, the hypothesis of rationality puts no observational restrictions on an agent's actions. We can always rationalize behavior by positing an appropriate objective function. For example, one might think it irrational for an agent to bet simultaneously for and against a certain event at odds that guarantee her a loss. But if her social position, for example, requires her participation in betting, she may in this way be regarded as rationally meeting social norms at the lowest cost. Second, if we allow the agent to change her mind over time, that is, for the objective function u to change from one time to another, no practical observations can disconfirm the hypothesis of rationality. What appears to be irrational or inconsistent behavior may simply reflect a change in the function being maximized between observations. Third, the program of rationality seems to run afoul of Occam's Razor, in that the utility function that is assumed to mediate between the environment and behavior is inherently unobservable, so that it is not clear what explanatory advantage its presence in the theory confers.

Furthermore, it is not obvious that rational behavior is more predictable than irrational behavior. If we take self-destructive mental illness, for example, as a paradigm of irrational behavior, it may be possible to establish highly confirmable and replicable patterns of behavior associated with particular diseases. On the other hand, the behavior of a presumably rational stock speculator, making complex calculations based on a constant flow of new and subtle information, may be very difficult to predict lawfully.

Economists have long been aware of these problems with the concept of rationality. Economic theory proceeds on a series of more or less tacit assumptions that address them. For example, when economists speak of objective functions, or utility functions, or preferences, there is an implicit assumption that they remain invariant over the relevant period of analysis. Despite the difficulty of actually observing utility functions, economic models typically assume that they are known fully to the economist, or take a particular functional form that makes them amenable to mathematical manipulation. Economic models implicitly assume that the legitimate arguments of the utility function are confined to a certain range of relevant factors, such as the physical consumption of the individual, or her money income, and in most (though not all) cases rule out social status, ritual perfection, aesthetic taste, and the like as arguments in the utility function.

Much of existing economic and social theory consists of the application of this rational choice paradigm to the explanation of human behavior and social interaction. This effort constitutes a rational choice research program, which seeks explanations for all social and economic phenomena through identifying the preferences of the agents involved and uncovering the rationality inherent in their actions.

The essays in this book, however, pursue another fundamental set of questions raised in the work of Herbert Simon (1978, 1984) which challenge the rational choice program. In assuming that the individual behaves so as to maximize a utility function in a given environment, the economist also assumes that the agent can costlessly process the information describing the

1.3. ECONOMIC MODELS

environment and costlessly compute the optimal policy for coping with it. In the past fifty years, however, the emergence of computers has, paradoxically, both drastically lowered the costs of computation and information processing and made us acutely aware of these costs and of the limitations of computability. The investigations reported in this book suggest that it is impossible to formulate the hypothesis of rationality consistently so as to take systematic account of the costs of computation.

It is tempting to think that the problem of computation and information processing costs could be resolved by moving the rational decision to a higher level, constructing a new rational choice problem in which computation is one strategy. This idea, in other words, tries to formulate a metaproblem, in which one component of the agent's behavior is the decision to undertake computation to improve her estimates of the consequences of various fundamental actions. This approach, however, cannot solve the problem, as Sidney Winter (1975) and John Conlisk (1988) have pointed out, because the resulting metachoice problem is just as difficult to solve computationally as the original problem. As we will see in more detail later, one characteristic of computationally complex problems is that there is in principle no way to predict the cost of solving them short of undertaking a computation that does in effect solve the problem. Computation costs might lead an agent to be content with an approximately maximizing, thus only approximately rational solution to her maximization problem: Herbert Simon has emphasized this type of behavior as *bounded rationality*. Computational complexity, on the other hand, raises issues not of costs but of logical feasibility, and thus appears to constitute a *barrier to rationality*.

1.3.2 Individual decision models—intertemporal optimization

The best way to understand how expectation formation in economic models leads inevitably to the consideration of nonlinear dynamic systems and the related problems of complexity is to look at some typical models in detail.

The simplest type of rational decision model considers a single agent acting in effective isolation. Traditional economic theory views this situation as a paradigmatic case of modeling and explanation. The traditional economics research program seeks to generalize the features of this type of model to more complex social interactions that involve several agents.

1.3.3 The finite-horizon Ramsey problem

Consider the situation of an agent with a lifetime of T periods, who has no interest in leaving a bequest, and who begins life with a fund of wealth

W_0, which can be invested at a constant real interest rate r, and faces the choice in each period of how much of her wealth to consume. Thus $W_1 = (1+r)(W_0 - C_0)$, and similarly for later periods, $W_{t+1} = (1+r)(W_t - C_t)$. For mathematical convenience, let us assume that the agent's objective function is the sum of the natural logarithms of her consumption over her lifetime, each period's utility being discounted at the constant factor $\beta < 1$. This objective function has a natural interpretation. In each period the agent experiences a utility proportional to $\log(C_t)$. The shape of the logarithm function reflects a declining marginal utility of consumption, that is, the agent puts lower values on additional units of consumption the higher her consumption already is in each period. Utility in the future counts less for the agent than utility in the present, and this temporal discounting is represented mathematically by multiplying the utility of consumption in period t by β^t, where, since $\beta < 1$, the discount factor declines geometrically with time.

This model can be summarized as a mathematical programming problem:

$$\begin{aligned} \text{choose} \quad & (C_0, C_1, \ldots, C_T) \quad \text{so as to} \\ \text{maximize} \quad & \log(C_0) + \beta \log(C_1) + \ldots + \beta^T \log(C_T) \\ \text{subject to} \quad & W_{t+1} = (1+r)(W_t - C_t) \quad \text{for} \quad t = 0, 1, \ldots, T \\ & W_{T+1} \geq 0 \\ & W_0 \quad \text{given} \end{aligned} \quad (1.7)$$

The constraint $W_{T+1} \geq 0$ is required to make the problem well determined: otherwise the agent could always increase her utility by consuming more and going deeper into debt. Since the logarithm function has the limit $-\infty$ as $C \to 0$, it is clear that the agent will be better off consuming some finite amount in each period than choosing not to consume at all. Furthermore, the agent has no reason to choose a policy with $W_{T+1} > 0$ under the assumption that she has a finite known lifetime. She will be better off consuming her whole wealth in period T, so that $W_{T+1} = 0$ on the optimally chosen path.

There are a variety of equivalent mathematical approaches to the solution of this problem. One approach effectively transforms the problem of finding the optimal consumption policy into the problem of finding the trajectory of a particular dynamical system, thus revealing the close links between the problem of rational optimization and dynamical systems.

To see how this link is established, let us use the *Lagrangian method* to solve the programming problem. We introduce a series of Lagrange

1.3. ECONOMIC MODELS

multipliers, which economists often call *shadow prices*, $\beta^t P_t, t = 0, 1, \ldots, T$, corresponding to the $T+1$ constraints. The Lagrangian function is then:

$$\mathcal{L}(\{C_t, W_{t+1}, P_t\}_{t=0}^T) = \sum_{t=0}^{T} \beta^t (\log(C_t) - P_t(W_{t+1} - (1+r)(W_t - C_t)))$$

The solution to the programming problem corresponds to a saddle point of the Lagrangian function: at the optimum choice it must not be possible to reduce the value of Lagrangian by changing the $\{P_t\}$, nor to increase it by changing $\{C_t, W_{t+1}\}$. The first condition ensures that the constraints are met, since if $W_{t+1} > (1+r)(W_t - C_t)$, the coefficient of P_t would be positive, and it would be possible to reduce the value of the Lagrangian by increasing P_t. The second condition ensures that the objective function is maximized.

The first-order conditions for the problem, which ensure local optimality on the path by testing whether shifting consumption from one period to the next will increase the value of the Lagrangian are:

$$\beta^{-t} \frac{\partial \mathcal{L}}{\partial C_t} = \frac{1}{C_t} - (1+r)P_t = 0$$

$$\beta^{-t} \frac{\partial \mathcal{L}}{\partial W_{t+1}} = -P_t + \beta(1+r)P_{t+1} = 0$$

$$\beta^{-t} \frac{\partial \mathcal{L}}{\partial P_t} = -W_{t+1} + (1+r)(W_t - C_t) = 0$$

The first equation tells us that $(1+r)P_t$ is the marginal utility of consumption in period t, and allows us to eliminate $C_t = 1/((1+r)P_t)$. Then we are left with a dynamical system in the variables (W, P):

$$P_t = \beta(1+r)P_{t+1}$$
$$W_{t+1} = (1+r)(W_t - \frac{1}{(1+r)P_t})$$

The optimal policy must be one of the trajectories of this dynamical system. We have two boundary conditions, W_0 given, and $W_{T+1} = 0$, which choose out a particular trajectory which is optimal. To look at this in a slightly different way, we could consider an arbitrary choice for P_T, which would, from the first dynamic equation, determine the whole path of P_t. Plugging this solution into the second dynamical equation, we would determine the path of W_t. If we start with a very high P_T, the whole path of P_t will be high, consumption will be low, and $W_{T+1} > 0$, which is not optimal. If we choose a very low P_T, consumption will be high and $W_{T+1} < 0$, which is infeasible. The optimal path corresponds to the choice of P_T which just makes $W_{T+1} = 0$.

This relatively simple problem reveals the basic structure of intertemporal optimization. Local optimality considerations establish a dynamical system, whose trajectories are the candidates for the rationally optimizing decision. Some of these trajectories are infeasible because they violate economically important constraints. There are typically many feasible trajectories, each of which leads to a different level of the objective function over the whole time path; the agent must then choose the one that yields the highest value for the objective function, by choosing a trajectory that respects the boundary conditions on the problem.

The problems of complexity and computation costs arise in rational intertemporal decision making when the dynamic systems that result become chaotic or complex. In these cases the rational agent faces the formidable problem of working out the full trajectory corresponding to a whole range of initial choices; only when she has accomplished this task can she determine which one is in fact optimal.

1.3.4 Market models

Many economic models represent the economy as a group of agents independently optimizing, with market prices acting so as to coordinate their potentially inconsistent decisions. The very influential Walrasian model of market equilibrium, for example, posits an auctioneer who cries out a system of market prices. Each agent then maximizes her utility subject to her budget constraint at these prices, and announces her excess demands to the auctioneer. In general the agents' plans will not be consistent: their excess demands will not sum to zero. In the Walrasian model, the auctioneer then adjusts the market price vector so as to try to eliminate the market excess demand. Equilibrium results when the auctioneer has succeeded in finding a vector of prices at which the sum of the agents' excess demands is zero.

Walrasian models in their full generality are quite difficult to solve, because the excess demands as functions of the announced market price vector can be arbitrary nonlinear functions. In order to get some insight into the structure of Walrasian equilibrium, economists often look at simplified economies in which it is easier to analyze the excess demand vectors mathematically. One popular simplification is to assume that all the agents in the economy are exactly alike in that they have the same preferences, technology, and endowment. This assumption might be viewed as a first approximation to an economy in which the agents differ only to a small degree. It has the virtue of greatly simplifying the analysis of equilibrium, but

1.3. ECONOMIC MODELS

the disadvantage that in the resulting equilibrium no trading takes place. Since all the agents are identical, they will always report the same excess demand vector in response to the same market prices, so that the only way to achieve equilibrium is to announce prices at which each individual agent's excess demand vector is zero.

One way to compute the equilibrium price vector in identical-agent models is to maximize a representative agent's utility over the technology and endowment constraints, using the technique of Lagrange multipliers. The resulting production and consumption plans will be the equilibrium production and consumption plans, and the vector of Lagrange multipliers is equal to the equilibrium relative price vector.

Because identical-agent models are simpler than the general Walrasian model, any degree of complexity that can arise in identical-agent equilibrium models must a fortiori be possible in the general Walrasian model. The converse conclusion, of course, does not hold: it may be possible to demonstrate simple structure in identical-agent models that does not hold in general. An example is the observation that equilibrium in identical-agent economies always implies no actual trading among the agents, a conclusion which does not hold in general.

1.3.4.1 The corn-steel model and the stable manifold

To get a concrete sense of the logic of intertemporal equilibrium in market models, consider an economy (see Burgstaller, 1994) with two goods, corn, K, and steel, S, each of which is the sole input into the production of the other. Thus to produce 1 unit of corn in the next period requires a_{SK} units of steel this period; to produce 1 unit of steel next period requires a_{KS} units of corn this period (perhaps to feed workers who produce the steel). The stocks of both corn and steel depreciate at the same constant rate δ each period. The typical agent of the economy consumes only corn in each period, C_t, but has no way to produce it except by producing steel first, so that she has a motive for producing both goods. The typical agent starts with an initial endowment of corn, K_0, and steel, S_0. She has to decide how much of the corn to consume and how much to devote to the production of steel for the next period. We assume as in the previous example that the agent's utility in each period is equal to the logarithm of the amount of corn produced, and that she discounts utility with a factor $\beta < 1$. Thus the typical agent's utility maximization problem can be written:

$$\text{choose} \quad \{C_t, S_{t+1}, K_{t+1}\}_{t=0}^{\infty} \geq 0$$

$$\text{so as to maximize} \quad \sum_{t=0}^{\infty} \beta^t \log(C_t)$$

subject to $\quad a_{SK}(K_{t+1} - (1-\delta)K_t) \leq S_t \quad t = 0, 1, \ldots$

$$a_{KS}(S_{t+1} - (1-\delta)S_t) \leq (K_t - C_t) \quad t = 0, 1, \ldots$$

$$K_0, S_0 \quad \text{given} \tag{1.8}$$

A convenient and economically insightful way to solve this problem is to use the Lagrangian method. Let $\beta^t P_{St}$ and $\beta^t P_{Kt}$, $t = 0, 1, \ldots$, be the Lagrange multipliers (shadow prices) associated with each of the two constraints in each period. Then the Lagrangian function is:

$$\mathcal{L}(\{C_t, S_{t+1}, K_{t+1}, P_{St}, P_{Kt}\}_{t=0}^{\infty}) =$$

$$\sum_{t=0}^{\infty} \beta^t \log(C_t)$$

$$- \sum_{t=0}^{\infty} \beta^t P_{St}(a_{SK}(K_{t+1} - (1-\delta)K_t) - S_t)$$

$$- \sum_{t=0}^{\infty} \beta^t P_{Kt}(a_{KS}(S_{t+1} - (1-\delta)S_t) - (K_t - C_t))$$

The optimal policy again corresponds to a saddle point of the Lagrangian, a sequence $\{C_t, S_{t+1}, K_{t+1}, P_{St}, P_{Kt}\}_{t=0}^{\infty}$ at which no marginal change in $\{C_t, S_{t+1}, K_{t+1}\}_{t=0}^{\infty}$ can raise the value of the Lagrangian, and no marginal change in $\{P_{St}, P_{Kt}\}_{t=0}^{\infty}$ can lower the value of the Lagrangian. The second condition assures us that the constraints must be satisfied, and the first that the utility function is at a maximum, since if it were not, it would be possible to increase the value of Lagrangian by adjusting the consumption and production plans.

These first-order conditions can be written:

$$\beta^{-t} \frac{\partial \mathcal{L}}{\partial C_t} = \frac{1}{C_t} - P_{Kt} = 0, \quad t = 0, 1, \ldots$$

$$\beta^{-t} \frac{\partial \mathcal{L}}{\partial K_{t+1}} = \beta P_{Kt+1} + a_{SK}(1-\delta)\beta P_{St+1} - a_{SK} P_{St} = 0, \quad t = 0, 1, \ldots$$

$$\beta^{-t} \frac{\partial \mathcal{L}}{\partial S_{t+1}} = \beta P_{St+1} + a_{KS}(1-\delta)\beta P_{Kt+1} - a_{KS} P_{Kt} = 0, \quad t = 0, 1, \ldots$$

$$\beta^{-t} \frac{\partial \mathcal{L}}{\partial P_{St}} = a_{SK}(K_{t+1} - (1-\delta)K_t) - S_t = 0, \quad t = 0, 1, \ldots$$

$$\beta^{-t} \frac{\partial \mathcal{L}}{\partial P_{Kt}} = a_{KS}(S_{t+1} - (1-\delta)S_t) - (K_t - C_t) = 0, \quad t = 0, 1, \ldots$$

1.3. ECONOMIC MODELS

From the first set of equations, we see that P_{Kt} measures the marginal utility of consumption of corn in period t, which must always be a strictly positive magnitude, given the assumption of logarithmic utility. If we substitute $\frac{1}{P_{Kt}}$ for C_t in the last equation, we can eliminate C_t altogether, and we get a nonlinear dynamical system in the variables $\{P_K, P_S, K, S\}$:

$$P_{Kt} = \beta((1-\delta)P_{Kt+1} + \frac{1}{a_{KS}}P_{St+1})$$

$$P_{St} = \beta(\frac{1}{a_{SK}}P_{Kt+1} + (1-\delta)P_{St+1})$$

$$K_{t+1} = (1-\delta)K_t + \frac{1}{a_{SK}}S_t$$

$$S_{t+1} = (1-\delta)S_t + \frac{1}{a_{KS}}(K_t - \frac{1}{P_{Kt}})$$

$$K_0, S_0 \quad \text{given}$$

As in the simpler optimal consumption model with a single asset, the optimal consumption/production path for the agent must be one of the trajectories of this dynamical system. But the system has four variables, $\{P_K, P_S, K, S\}$, and the terms of the problem impose only two initial conditions, K_0 and S_0. Any arbitrary choice of P_{K0} and P_{S0} will lead to a trajectory that satisfies the local conditions for optimality. The agent, in order to solve the problem, must then evaluate her utility on each of these candidate trajectories in order to find the optimal one.

In this example the problem is somewhat simplified because the dynamical subsystem involving the shadow prices is independent of the quantities, and is also linear. Analysis of the eigenvalues and eigenvectors of this subsystem reveals that the eigenvector corresponding to the smaller of its two roots in magnitude is positive, while the eigenvector corresponding to the larger of its two roots in magnitude has prices of opposite sign. Any solution that activates the larger root will eventually lead to one of the prices becoming negative, which signals a trajectory that cannot be economically optimal. Thus the only trajectories that are candidates for the optimal policy are those that set the prices of steel and corn on the eigenvector corresponding to the smaller of the two roots, that is, those on the *stable manifold* of the dynamical system. This requirement adds one boundary condition to the problem.

This still leaves the question of the absolute magnitude of the shadow price of corn. As in the optimal consumption model, if we choose the initial shadow price of corn very low, consumption will be high, and the stock of corn will eventually become negative, which is economically infeasible. If we choose the initial shadow price of corn very high, consumption will rise so slowly that the agent will accumulate stocks of corn and steel that will never provide her with increased consumption because of their enormous depreciation costs. The optimal policy corresponds to a choice of the initial level of P_{K0} that maintains feasibility and avoids overaccumulation of the stocks. Once again, the choice of the optimal policy requires the agent to look at the complete trajectories of a dynamical system in order to weed out infeasible or suboptimal policies.

Once we have the optimal solution, with its shadow prices, we also have the market equilibrium for this model. If the market prices are announced proportional to the shadow prices of the optimal policy, the utility maximizing agent will be led to the optimal policy, which will also clear the market since it is feasible. The important mathematical point to be gleaned from this example is that the establishment of a Walrasian equilibrium requires (or is equivalent to) the determination of the trajectories of a dynamical system. In the cases we have looked at, the dynamical systems that arise are fairly simple and exhibit only a small range of the possible spectrum of dynamical repertoire of nonlinear systems. In these cases it is possible to convince oneself that the discovery of the market equilibrium is computationally feasible for highly motivated and clever agents, who might use methods of trial-and-error extrapolation to determine the consistent current prices of assets.

1.3.4.2 The potential complexity of equilibrium paths in investment models

The preceding examples show the close connection between rational choice in an intertemporal framework and the behavior of dynamical systems. From a mathematical point of view the determination of an optimal intertemporal consumption/production policy is equivalent to the solution of a boundary value problem for a dynamical system. The solution of these problems is relatively easy in the examples we have studied, because the trajectories of the dynamical system are relatively simple.

But even highly simplified intertemporal choice models can give rise to complex trajectories. M. Boldrin and L. Montrucchio (1986), for example, have shown that an arbitrary dynamical system can be interpreted as arising from an intertemporal model of optimal consumption with several capital goods (or equivalently, the identical-agent market equilibrium for the same situation) without violating any of the common assumptions of economic models, such as diminishing returns. In particular this means that the trajectories rational agents have to compute may have any degree of complexity that dynamical systems can exhibit: they may be chaotic, have sensitive dependence on initial conditions, and so forth.

1.3. ECONOMIC MODELS

Jess Benhabib and Richard Day (1981), and a substantial literature their work has spawned, have shown that chaotic behavior can arise in a wide range of economically relevant intertemporal models. These mathematical facts raise serious questions for the methodological plausibility of the Walrasian equilibrium concept that underlies these models. If Walrasian equilibrium can be established only through the interaction of agents who must carry out computations we know to be impossible or impractical, what warrant do we have for regarding Walrasian equilibrium as a relevant model of real market interactions?

1.3.5 Game theory models

Competitive market equilibrium theory manages to approach the problem of analyzing the interactions of many rational agents through the assumption that the number of agents is very large, so large, in fact, that each agent can ignore the effects of her actions on any other particular agent. Under these circumstances each agent can be viewed as maximizing against a market price system on which her behavior has a negligible impact. The potential complexity of interagent interactions is finessed by the assumption that all these interactions are mediated by market prices. We have seen that taking computational costs into account calls into question the viability of long-accepted formal solutions to the problem of competitive interaction.

But there are many important spheres of social and economic life where the assumption of perfect competition is a violent distortion. In the first place, perfect competition itself is an ideal approximation to the complex behavior of economic systems with large but finite numbers of agents. In order to achieve a completely satisfactory theory of competitive equilibrium it would be necessary to demonstrate exactly how this approximation works, that is, how the behavior of a large system of interacting agents actually converges to the perfectly competitive limit as the number of agents increases without bound. In order to carry out this program, we need to have a theory of what actually happens when competition is less than perfect.

In fact, it is a common observation of life in market-directed societies that competition always breaks down at least locally. When one comes to make a transaction, no matter how competitive the market, one has to deal with one or a small number of other agents, and there is always some latitude in price, quality, or other dimensions of the transaction for bargaining. These noncompetitive spheres may be negligible from the point of view of the whole economy, or market, and the economic theorist may reasonably choose to abstract from them for the sake of a simple and tractable theory. But a complete theory should at least embrace and account for these pervasive features of economic reality.

Finally, there are many extremely important economic interactions that simply do not involve a large number of competitive agents. Many important markets are oligopolies, in which a few very large sellers interact with an acute awareness of the impact of their behavior on each other. In many cases these interactions are of critical importance for economic development. A large investment in the construction of a transportation facility may be justified if complementary large directly productive investments will be forthcoming to generate a sufficient level of traffic. The investment in direct production, in turn, may be profitable only if the transportation facilities are available to bring the product to market. In this situation the productive investor and the transportation investor are inherently involved in a strategic interaction, in which each has a strong incentive to outguess the other, or, at least, to anticipate the other's behavior.

The formal analysis of situations of strategic interaction leads to the general theory of games. A game is formalized by specifying the number of players, their strategic options, the information conditions that link their actions, and the payoffs or utilities that characterize their evaluation of the outcomes of any combination of strategic choices. The research program of game theory hopes to find general characterizations of the behavior of rational agents interacting strategically. This program is a kind of generalization of the theory of rational agents interacting on competitive markets to the analysis of strategic interactions.

Here again the chapters in this volume show the critical importance of the issues of complexity and computational costs. As we will explain, even games of relatively simple structure rapidly give rise to computational problems of extremely high complexity, in which the assumptions of rationality are impossible to maintain. Once again, the logical structure of the argument is that of counterexample. If serious computational issues arise in relatively simple contexts, they must, a fortiori, be present in more complicated contexts.

1.3.5.1 Cournot-Nash equilibrium

There is a vast literature on various general solution concepts for abstract games (see, for example, Binmore and Dasgupta, 1986). The most popular starting point for most analysis of noncooperative games is John Nash's proposed equilibrium, generalizing an idea of Auguste Cournot. The Cournot-Nash equilibrium singles out strategy choices for the players of a game that have the property that no player can improve upon her outcome unilaterally, by changing her strategy, assuming that the strategies of the other players will remain unchanged.

1.3. ECONOMIC MODELS

This idea has considerable intuitive appeal, since at least in a repetition of the same game it is hard to see why players would be content to continue with strategies when alternatives offering a higher payoff are available. But it also has serious methodological difficulties. To begin with, in general the set of Cournot-Nash equilibria of a game is large, and in many cases includes outcomes that are uninteresting or implausible. Thus the Cournot-Nash equilibrium appears to be incomplete as a theory: we require further considerations to reduce the multiplicity of equilibria. But even when the problem of multiplicity of equilibrium has somehow been dealt with, there is some question as to why we should expect agents to choose Cournot-Nash equilibrium strategies. It is plausible that if an agent knew for sure that her fellow players would play their equilibrium strategies she will play hers, since it is by definition the best response she can make. But why should she have any confidence that her fellow players will behave in the way predicted by the equilibrium? The motivation for the Cournot-Nash concept of equilibrium lies in considerations of symmetry that have more potency as a mathematical postulate than credibility as a theory of human behavior. Once we acknowledge the possibility that an agent might doubt that her opponents will follow the predicted strategies, we must also admit the possibility that the opponents might doubt her commitment to it as well, and the whole structure of the equilibrium concept unravels.

But, as the chapters in this volume show, there are serious computational issues raised by the Cournot-Nash concept of equilibrium as well. Even if players have implicit faith that some version of the Cournot-Nash theory will correctly describe the outcome of their interactions, and even if the theory can be made to single out a unique outcome, how confident can we be that the agents can carry out the computations necessary to characterize the equilibrium?

1.3.5.2 The one-shot Prisoners' Dilemma

A great deal of the work relating game theory to larger social theory issues has centered on a particular game situation, the Prisoners' Dilemma.. This game poses particularly sharply the classic social dilemma of opportunism and the paradoxes of the pursuit of self-interest. In its simplest form the Prisoners' Dilemma involves two players, each of whom has two strategies, often called *cooperate* and *defect*. If both agents cooperate, they share a reward. But if one cooperates and the other defects, the defector gets a larger reward, while the cooperator suffers a penalty. If both defect, they share a smaller penalty. Thus regardless of what the other player does, it is in the direct individual interest of each player to defect: defection is a dominant strategy. The only Cournot-Nash equilibrium of the Prisoners' Dilemma is mutual defection. But this is disturbing because both players would be better off if they avoided the temptation of defection and cooperated. In economic terms the "invisible hand" that supposedly guides individual competitors pursuing their own self-interest to a socially desirable outcome misguides them in the Prisoners' Dilemma.

The Prisoners' Dilemma can be seen as an abstract model of a huge range of human interactions. Hobbes's state of nature can be viewed as a Prisoners' Dilemma, and Hobbes's proposed solution in the form of a coercive external force a major rationalization of institutions of power. Thoughtful economists from Adam Smith on have recognized that the benefits of the invisible hand depend on the existence of a stable institutional structure (such as property rights) supported by political power which can prevent competition from destroying itself. Wherever the development of property rights lags behind the emergence of economically important interests, as in the area of environmental pollution, a social space emerges where the opportunism modeled by the Prisoners' Dilemma has a free run.

Hobbes's Leviathan may be the explanation for the absence of private armies in modern industrial societies, but there are lots of other spheres of life where cooperative behavior survives without the support of the organized violence of the state. People manage to function in families, neighborhoods, clubs, bureaucracies, and firms where cooperative behavior is essential and the direct police power of the state weak or absent. There is a need for a theory of what Robert Axelrod (1984) has called the "evolution of cooperation," the spontaneous maintenance of cooperative behavior in the face of the strong temptations modeled by the Prisoners' Dilemma.

1.3.5.3 Repeated games

The argument that agents caught in a Prisoners' Dilemma will fall into the mutual defection equilibrium is strongest when we imagine them to be playing the game just once. If agents know they are going to interact many times, it may be easier for them to establish a pattern of mutually advantageous cooperation. This consideration leads to the model of a *repeated game*, which is a major focus of the essays in this volume. The agents in a repeated game know that they will encounter each other many times in situations structured the same way. Each agent can condition her strategic choices on the past behavior of the other player.

The structure of repeated games is inherently much more complex than the structure of the corresponding one-shot games. If each player has just two strategies available in each one-shot game (like cooperation and defection in the Prisoners' Dilemma) the record of a player's behavior in a game repeated n times consists of a vector of dimension n, each component recording the player's strategy choice on one round. There are 2^n such pairs of vectors. In principle an agent's strategy in the $n + 1$st round

1.3. ECONOMIC MODELS

of the repeated game could be conditioned on this full information, giving rise to a game with 2^{n+1} strategies for each player on the nth round. As n increases, the number of strategies becomes very large indeed. A full strategy for the entire repeated game, would be a plan telling what the player will do on the first round, then what she will do on the second move depending on what the opponent did on the first round (two possibilities), then what she will do on the third round depending on what the opponent did in the first two rounds (four possibilities) and so on. Even if the player knows the game will be repeated a finite number of times, and were to be fortunate enough to know the exact strategy chosen by her opponent, the examination of her own enormous strategy set in a search for a best response, the core of the Cournot-Nash concept, is a daunting prospect.

Once again we see the issues of computational feasibility and costs arising naturally and centrally in the development of a theory of completely rational action. The difficulties of computation strongly suggest truncating the strategic choice problem in some plausible way. The full strategy problem, for example, requires the player of the game to remember the behavior of her opponent on every previous round; in a game repeated N times, she would need N memory cells to devote to this task. Since memory (either human or machine) is expensive, we might reasonably restrict her strategy choices to those that could be implemented with a smaller number of memory cells. This is a practical and plausible, but not strictly rational strategy. Strictly rational logic would require the agent to consider whether she would be better off allocating $1, 2, \ldots, N$ memory cells to this game. Of course, to decide how many memory cells the game is worth, the agent would have to solve an even much more complex problem, and spend even more computing resources to do it. In the essays in this book the cost of computation is often represented, crudely to be sure, by limitations on the computing power of the agent.

Suppose that the agent can devote only 1 memory cell to a repeated game, for example. Then she is restricted in her strategy choice to those strategies that are sensitive only to whatever statistic she chooses to record. If she remembers only the last choice of her opponent, she has reduced the size of her strategy space from $\sum_{n=1}^{N} 2^n$ to 4 (since she has two strategy choices on the $n+1$st round of the game for each of the two possible plays of her opponent on the nth round). In this much reduced strategy space it may be easier to evaluate strategies.

1.3.5.4 The repeated Prisoners' Dilemma

The specific case of the Prisoners' Dilemma has been the subject of considerable theoretical attention. A moment's thought shows that even in a repeated Prisoners' Dilemma of known finite length N, defection is still a dominant strategy. On the last round, it is clear that defection dominates, since both players know that this is the last episode of interaction. But if each knows the opponent will defect on the last round, there is no point to cooperating on the next-to-last round, and so forth back to the very first round. To get around this analytical hurdle, it is common to assume that the players face a positive probability of the game continuing on every round, so that there is at least the possibility that the prospect of future cooperation can influence their behavior at all times.

The full analysis of the repeated Prisoners' Dilemma on rational grounds remains a major research area. There may be a very large set of Cournot-Nash equilibria for the metagame, but we do not know very much about this set. Mutual defection is always a Cournot-Nash equilibrium, since if you know your opponent will defect there is no point in your cooperating. One equilibrium that seems to be capable of sustaining cooperation is a trigger strategy: the player cooperates on the first round, but shifts to permanent defection if her opponent ever defects. If the game will continue a long time with high probability, the prospective losses from facing permanent defection can outweigh the one-shot gain from defection against a cooperator, making the trigger strategy a best responses to itself, and therefore a Cournot-Nash equilibrium. The trigger strategy requires only one bit of information to implement, a record of the opponent's worst behavior in the game up until the present. Thus it has the advantage of computational cost-effectiveness. Everyone has probably encountered people who adopt trigger strategies in life, but they are notoriously difficult people to get along with. The trigger strategy is too unforgiving of errors in perception or execution, for example, to be a very good method for sustaining cooperation in real human interactions.

Considerable attention has been given to another low-computation cost strategy, tit-for-tat. An agent playing tit-for-tat cooperates on the first round of play, and thereafter plays whatever strategy the opponent played on the last round. In effect, tit-for-tat punishes defection by defecting just once, as long as the opponent returns to a policy of cooperation. Tit-for-tat defends itself better against unconditional defection than unconditional cooperation does, since it shifts promptly to defection on encountering a defecting opponent. It also requires only a single memory cell to implement, a record of the opponent's play on the last round. But it is not a best response to itself, and therefore not a Cournot-Nash equilibrium.

1.3.5.5 Repeated local interaction multiperson Prisoners' Dilemma on the torus

The complexity of the Prisoners' Dilemma even in the two-person repeated game model is high, but plausible and interesting extensions of the two-

1.3. ECONOMIC MODELS

person game lead rapidly to even more complex situations. Peter Albin in Chapter 6 below proposes such a generalization, which reveals close links between game theory and cellular automata: the local interaction multi-person Prisoners' Dilemma played on a lattice. In this model each player occupies a node of a lattice in two dimensions. The upper and lower boundaries of the lattice are identified, as are the right and left boundaries, so that in effect the players find themselves on the surface of a torus. The payoffs to an agent depend on the number of her neighbors (including herself) who cooperate in the game. The payoff structure generalizes the Prisoners' Dilemma in that defection is a dominant strategy (no matter what your neighbors do, your one-shot payoff is higher if you defect than if you cooperate), but the payoffs to uniform cooperation are higher than to uniform defection. As in the original Prisoners' Dilemma, private incentives are at sharp variance with social goals.

This is a simple and plausible abstract representation of social interactions and the collective action problem. In real societies neighborhood effects (or small group effects) are extremely important to the welfare of individuals. The externalities modeled by the Prisoners' Dilemma correspond to a wide range of real social problems. The cleanliness of the street depends on the actions of the relatively small number of users; the psychological health of an office depends on the resistance of fellow workers to rumormongering and scapegoating; the effectiveness of education depends on students' reluctance to cheat. But an agent's neighbors in one interaction are involved in turn with other agents with whom the first agent has no direct contact. Just as we are exposed to disease by the behavior of people we do not know through people we do know, our social environment can be influenced by the behavior of strangers who interact with our friends.

Despite its simplicity and appeal as an abstract model of social interaction, the complexity of Albin's local interaction multiperson Prisoners' Dilemma considered from the point of view of rational choice theory (say, Cournot-Nash equilibrium) is staggering. Strictly speaking, the relevant state of the repeated game at any moment from the point of view of one of the agents depends not just on her own and her neighbors' past behavior, but on her neighbors' neighbors' past behavior as well, in fact, on the behavior of all the agents indirectly linked through the neighborhood structure. Since each agent's strategic choices can in principle depend on her neighbors' past behavior, which in turn may be conditioned on the neighbors' neighbors' past behavior, all of the agents in the whole society are indirectly linked. A full Cournot-Nash equilibrium has to consider the best response of each agent to the strategies, not just of her neighbors, but of all the agents in the society. The problems of computational cost and feasibility obtrude immediately and unavoidably.

As Albin shows in his essay, there are actually two levels of computational complexity problems in this kind of situation. On the one hand it may in principle be feasible to set up algorithms to predict the detailed evolution of the system in response to a particular action of one agent (say, a change in her strategy choice), but very expensive because of the chaotic nature of the ramifications. The cost of the computation constitutes a bound to rationality, and suggests limiting the strategic plans of agents to a subset of all those that are in principle relevant. For example, we might limit the agent to strategies that are conditioned on the past behavior of her neighbors (since she may have difficulty even observing the behavior of her neighbors' neighbors and further degrees of separation). Even here, as the discussion of the two-person Prisoners' Dilemma shows, the complexity of the strategy space is quite high, and may exceed reasonable estimates of the computing power available to an agent. These considerations lead us to study boundedly rational agents who pursue their self-interest within limits imposed by computational costs.

But Albin's analysis also reveals a further remarkable problem implicit in the multiperson Prisoners' Dilemma. Albin shows by construction that there are bounded rationality strategies (one, e.g., which is mathematically equivalent to John Conway's cellular automaton Life) which will lead to a level of complexity in the social interactions represented that is equivalent to that of a general-purpose computer or Turing machine, or to an unrestricted formal language. In this context the computational issues that arise when an agent tries to work out the consequences of a change in her strategy are not just those of cost, but include issues of feasibility. If the society as a whole has the complexity level of a general-purpose computer, it will be impossible for any other general-purpose computer to work out its evolution except by direct simulation. To carry out the program of rational explanation of behavior in this context would require positing that each individual agent in society had some way of simulating the potential evolution of a system of interlinked Turing machines. At this point the rational explanation program runs into deep paradoxes of self-reference. Albin explores these paradoxes in Chapters 2 and 6 of this volume.

1.4 Definitions and measures of complexity

We can see that issues of complexity arise inexorably in social and economic theory once we contemplate seriously the possibility of nonlinearity in the underlying lawful behavior of agents. The development of economic theory in particular has managed to finesse these issues by focusing attention on idealizations like perfect competition, which abstract from the interactions of individual agents, and on situations in which the structure of equilibria is relatively simple, like the saddle-point stable trajectories of intertempo-

1.4. COMPLEXITY

ral accumulation models. Some such maneuver was probably functional to the progress of social science, especially during periods in which the mathematical and philosophical understanding of complexity issues was relatively undeveloped. But if complex interactions indeed play a fundamental role in the evolution of social reality, this abstraction may have imposed a high price on the relevance of accepted economic and social theory.

The emergence of computers and of a mathematical theory of language has transformed our understanding of these issues at an abstract level. Albin's work in this volume shows how central these concerns are to the further development of social theory. One of the key achievements of computational and linguistic theory has been to propose explicit definitions of system complexity, and to provide a qualitative classification and quantitative measures of complexity. A brief review of these developments can help put the essays in this volume in context.

The intuitive concept of complexity that lies behind most measures is that simple systems are easy to describe with a small amount of information, while the description of a complex system requires a large amount of information. This idea can be unpacked in several different contexts, which turn out to be closely related. We can, for example, measure the complexity of a system by the size of the smallest computer program capable of describing it. More complex systems require larger programs. Or we could measure the complexity of the system by the computer resources required to represent it, in time and memory. A more complex system requires more time and memory to describe than a simple one. Or we could measure the complexity of a system by the richness of the language required to describe it. A simple system can be described by a minimally structured language, while a complex one requires a language rich in possibilities.

1.4.1 Computational complexity

Mathematicians have always been interested in solving problems, that is, developing algorithms that allow a computing system (up until 1940 usually a human equipped with pencil and paper) to transform one description of a situation (the problem) into another description in a more functional and usable form (the solution). Mathematics has also from its earliest beginnings recognized a relation between the computational tools available and the range of problems that can be solved. Greek geometry, for example, stipulates constructions with straight-edge and compass as a computational limit: the trisection of an angle is not possible with these tools, though it is possible with the addition of more powerful computational devices. Those mathematicians who pursued the practical solution of real problems, such as the computation of artillery trajectory tables, or the compilation of ephemeridae describing the motion of heavenly bodies, became acutely aware of the wide gap between the discovery of methods that in principle are capable of solving certain problems, and the implementation of these methods in practical situations.

Our understanding of the relation between systems and the sophistication of the machines needed to describe or represent them has been most completely developed for *formal languages* (see Hopcroft and Ullman, 1979, and Révész, 1983, for thorough surveys of these results). The next two sections summarize these accounts. This theory establishes the existence of parallel four-level hierarchies of complexity for machines and languages. A similar four-part hierarchy appears in the study of nonlinear dynamical systems, such as cellular automata as well, and plays a central role in Albin's theory of the complexity of social and economic systems.

1.4.2 Linguistic complexity

Noam Chomsky (1959, 1963) defines a formal language as a set of rules for producing strings from a finite alphabet of symbols. These rules establish certain strings as words (or sentences) in the language and define procedures for producing new words by substitution in existing words. The complexity of a language in Chomsky's hierarchy corresponds to the restrictions imposed on the procedures for producing new words.

A brief sketch of this theory and its main results can help to clarify the mutual relationship of linguistic, computational, and nonlinear dynamical system complexities that informs Albin's work.

A formal language is defined by a *grammar*, which is defined by a finite *alphabet* T of terminal symbols, a finite set V of *intermediary variables*, a finite set P of *productions*, rules for substituting new strings of symbols and variables in existing strings, and a *distinguished variable* S, which serves to start the productions of the language. The productions take the form $P \to Q$, where P is a string composed of one or more variables together with zero or more terminals, and Q is a string composed of any combination of variables and terminals. The terminal symbols are analogous to the words of a natural language (nouns, verbs, and so forth); the variables are analogous to grammatical forms (sentences, clauses, parts of speech); and the productions are analogous to the grammatical rules of a language. The productions of a natural language like English might take such forms as: <sentence> → <noun phrase> <verb phrase>, and <noun> → "car," indicating that the variable <sentence> can be replaced by a noun phrase followed by a verb phrase, and that the variable <noun> can be replaced by (among many other things) the terminal "car" to produce grammatical (but not necessarily meaningful) English expressions.

The potential complexity of the language generated by a grammar depends on what restrictions, if any, are placed on the production rules.

1.4. COMPLEXITY

The languages produced by grammars satisfying the preceding definition with no further restrictions on the production rules are called *unrestricted languages*. The unrestricted languages include the most complex formal languages (and all the simpler ones as well).

The first step in establishing Chomsky's hierarchy of complexity of languages is to consider the subset of grammars for which all the productions $P \to Q$ have the length of Q at least as long as the length of P. The languages generated by such grammars are called *context-sensitive languages*, because it is possible to prove that all their productions have the form $P_1 P P_2 \to P_1 Q P_2$, where Q is a nonempty string. This kind of production rule allows the substitution of Q for P in the context $P_1 \ldots P_2$, but not necessarily in other contexts.

Note the monotonicity inherent in derivations arising from context-sensitive languages: each application of a production to a word must result in a word no shorter than the one we started with. This need not be true for an unrestricted grammar: in general the application of productions might first lengthen and then shorten the words produced. This monotonicity greatly reduces the complexity of the languages generated. For example, if we are trying to "parse" a word, that is, decide whether or not it could have been generated from a given grammar and by what sequence of applications of production rules, we know that a given word from a context-sensitive language can have as its antecedents only expressions of the same length or less, a finite set. Thus we can be sure of reaching a definite answer in parsing context-sensitive languages, since we have only a finite number of possible paths by which the word could have been generated. But if an unrestricted grammar is not context-sensitive, a word of a given length could be generated by intermediary expressions of any length whatsoever, thus raising the specter that any parsing procedure might have to run for any length of time before reaching a conclusion. It might even be impossible for us to design a parsing procedure guaranteed to return an answer for any word of such a noncontext-sensitive language in finite time.

The next subset in Chomsky's hierarchy consists of languages generated by grammars whose productions take the form $P \to Q$, where P is a string of variables (and Q a string composed of terminals and variables), without contextual restrictions, called the *context-free languages*. The not immediately obvious fact is that the context-free languages that do not contain the empty string are a strict subset of the context-sensitive languages, so that they share the monotonicity property of the context-sensitive languages, and have further complexity-reducing structure as well.

The final subset in the Chomsky hierarchy consists of languages generated by grammars with production rules of the form $P \to T$ or $P \to TQ$, where P and Q are variables and T is a string of terminal symbols, called the *regular languages*. The regular languages are a strict subset of the context-free languages, and exhibit a further reduction in complexity.

The Chomsky hierarchy of complexities of formal languages is a key to the characterization and analysis of the complexity of social and economic systems because of its close relation to the complexity of computational devices, on the one hand, and to the complexity of nonlinear dynamical systems (e.g., cellular automata), on the other. As we have seen, we are led to represent social and economic systems by nonlinear dynamic models, and forced to consider the agents in social and economic interactions as operating with meaningful costs of computation. Thus, as Albin's work shows, we must come to grips with the complexity hierarchy of social and economic systems through the same methods and tools that have been developed to analyze linguistic and computational complexity.

1.4.3 Machine complexity

A hierarchy of abstract models of computing devices parallels the Chomsky hierarchy of formal languages. The simplest of these models, the finite automaton, has a finite number of internal states, and can read input symbols from a tape. The automaton makes a move by reading a symbol from the tape and entering a new state which depends on the symbol read and its current state. The automaton is defined by stipulating its starting state, its allowable moves, and a particular subset of states which signal that the automaton has accepted the input. A pocket calculator is a finite automaton. It reads the alphabet of symbols present on its keyboard, and processes them. If it encounters a sequence of symbols that are uninterpretable, it enters an error state. In all states except the error state the calculator has accepted the input stream. It is plausible to regard the finite automaton from the economic point of view as the cheapest form of computational capacity available to a decision maker.

The languages accepted by finite automata are precisely the regular languages that occupy the lowest rank in the Chomsky hierarchy. Conversely, a finite automaton can be constructed to accept any regular language as well, so that the correspondence between finite automata and regular languages is exact.

A consequence of this exact correspondence is that it is impossible to construct a finite automaton to recognize a context-free language which is not a regular language. We can, however, supplement the computational capacity of a finite automaton by adding an unbounded pushdown stack on which the automaton can store and retrieve symbols on a first-in, last-out basis. The resulting pushdown automata can recognize all context-free languages (including, of course, regular languages). Conversely, given any context-free language, it is possible to construct a pushdown automaton that will recognize it, so that the correspondence between pushdown

1.4. COMPLEXITY

automata and context-free formal languages is exact. The pushdown automaton still represents a relatively primitive form of computing machine, since its access to the information stored on the pushdown stack is highly restricted: only the last stored symbol is available to influence the course of the computation at any stage; the automaton can access symbols deeper in the stack only by discarding those stored later above. A decision maker equipped with a pushdown automaton, however, is in a position to recognize and respond to a much larger and more complex set of patterns in the world than one equipped only with the computational capacity of a finite automaton.

A logical next step in extending the computational capacity of an automaton is to add a second pushdown stack, thus creating a two-pushdown automaton. A two-pushdown automaton has access at any stage to all of its stored information, since it can shift the symbols from one stack to the other without losing any. The second pushdown stack provides the automaton with the ability to recognize languages of any complexity: a two-pushdown automaton can be constructed to recognize any formal language and, conversely, so that the two-pushdown automata correspond exactly to the Chomskian unrestricted formal languages.

The two-pushdown automaton is equivalent in its computational power to the abstract Turing machine, the generally accepted abstract model of a general-purpose computer capable of implementing any conceivable systematic problem-solving procedure. The Turing machine is an automaton which operates by reading and writing symbols on a single one-sided infinite tape, with the possibility of moving forward and backward on the tape depending on its state and the input stream. The class of Turing machines also is equivalent to the class of unrestricted languages in complexity.

As we might expect, there is an intermediate level of computing power between the pushdown automata and the two-pushdown automata corresponding to the context-sensitive languages. This class of automata includes two-pushdown automata with bounded storage (where the bound on storage may depend on the length of the input word), called *linear bounded automata*. Intuitively, an automaton reading a word from a formal language is inverting the production rules that govern the language, thereby replacing parts of the word with the expressions that might have produced it. The monotonicity of context-sensitive language production rules assures that an automaton applying their inverse can never lengthen the word, so that the space necessary for the work is bounded by the size of the input word itself. Since the context-free languages without the empty string are a strict subset of the context-sensitive languages, a linear bounded automaton can also recognize all of the context-free languages.

From an economic point of view, the bounded storage of the linear bounded automaton represents a qualitatively different computation cost from the unbounded two-pushdown automaton. A decision maker using a linear bounded automaton to analyze a problem can confidently budget the cost of the computational resources required, while a decision maker using a general two-pushdown automaton can never be sure how large the computational costs of any given analysis might grow to be. This difference in computational costs represents an economic trade-off in computational capacity as well, since the costly general two-pushdown automaton can carry out all the analyses possible for the linear bounded automaton and many others as well.

1.4.4 Decidability, computational complexity, and rationality

A fundamental question about any problem is whether there exists a computational procedure for solving it that will eventually come up with an answer. This question can be rigorously formulated as whether or not a Turing machine (or equivalently, a two-pushdown automaton) exists which, presented with the problem as input, will halt in finite time with the answer. Problems of this type are *decidable*. One of the central mathematical discoveries of the century is that undecidable problems exist (an idea which can be expressed in a variety of forms, including formal language and automaton theory).

A second practical question about any decidable problem is how much resources (e.g., time and machine memory) its solution will require. A decidable problem may still become intractable if it requires computational resources that grow rapidly with the size of the problem itself.

A decision maker trying to carry out the rational choice paradigm in a complex environment faces the fundamental problem of the computational cost of predicting the consequences of her various actions so as to choose the best action in the situation. The theory of computability and computational complexity suggests that there are two inherent limitations to the rational choice paradigm. One limitation stems from the possibility that the agent's problem is in fact undecidable, so that no computational procedure exists which for all inputs will give her the needed answer in a finite time. A second limitation is posed by computational complexity in that even if her problem is decidable, the computational cost of solving it may in many situations be so large as to overwhelm any possible gains from the optimal choice of action.

1.4. COMPLEXITY

1.4.5 Dynamical systems and computational complexity

A rational decision maker confronting a dynamical system needs a machine that can evaluate the consequences of her actions to carry out the program of rationality. The analysis of the computation power required of the machine is thus closely connected with the cost the rational agent must sustain.

Albin approaches this problem by associating the economic cost of computation to the hierarchy of computing complexity: finite automata, pushdown automata, linear bounded automata, and two-pushdown automata (Turing machines). These classes of computation can also be linked to the character of dynamical systems.

A dynamical system with a unique globally attracting equilibrium state from this point of view corresponds to a finite automata and to regular languages. A finite automaton needs no memory to record any of the data it has read, and is therefore very cheap. A rational agent confronting a single-point attractor dynamical system needs, therefore, only very primitive computational resources.

Dynamical systems with a periodic attractor correspond to pushdown automata and to context-free languages. The memory needed here, and thus the cost of the device, is proportional to the length of the repetitive patterns the dynamical system will generate. It is notable that most human beings can implement programs representing only very short periodic attractors without becoming confused and losing track of the problem they are working on. Most human beings can work out the dynamics of a two- or three-state system (e.g., what happens if their spouse is angry at them or is friendly with them), but very few can carry on chains of recursion of even ten periods, not to speak of the hundreds or thousands that easily arise in complex financial transactions or complex diplomatic or military confrontations. Even periodic systems, if they involve a large number of degrees of freedom, can challenge the computational resources built into our brains by evolution.

Context-free languages can exhibit a long-distance correlation in data strings: an opening parenthesis requires the eventual appearance of its matching closing parenthesis, but an indeterminately large amount of material (including many more parenthesis pairs) may intervene. This type of long-distance correlation has not received much attention in economic models, though in principle it may play an important role. For example, the settling of debts has this recursive character. Agent B may borrow from agent A, opening a parenthesis that will be closed by the eventual repayment of the debt. But agent B may then turn around and lend to C, opening a second parenthesis. C's repayment of B is the precondition for the resolution of the original loan by B's paying A.

Dynamical systems with a chaotic attractor correspond to linear bounded automata and to context-sensitive languages. Small deviations in a trajectory at one time ramify indefinitely over time and space, and are never resolved by a closing parenthesis. This spreading out of chaotic trajectories corresponds to the monotonicity property of production rules for context-sensitive languages. While problems in this complexity class are typically decidable in principle, they are often computationally intractable because of rapid increases in computational cost associated with increases in the complexity of the problem, the time horizon of interest, or the accuracy of solutions required.

As Albin points out in his essay on the metalogic of economics (Chapter 2) if we regard human beings as having a complexity at the least equivalent to that of Turing machines, then economic and social systems composed of interacting human beings are in principle more complex than the context-sensitive languages that correspond to linear bounded automata, corresponding at least to the complexity of unrestricted formal languages. The distinguishing characteristic of these systems is the nonmonotonicity of the derivations of their states. If we choose some measure of complexity (such as the length of a word generated, or the number of transactions we observe in an economic market) to characterize the state of the system, we cannot rule out the possibility that it evolved from an even more complex state. Human beings, for example, may adopt apparently simple modes of behavior on the basis of extremely complex and involuted reasoning that considers much more subtle possibilities.

The representation of dynamical systems as a part of the rational choice program thus raises two important questions involving computation. The first is the more important from a practical perspective: how much will the effective computation of the behavior of the system cost? This question, as we have argued, poses a bound to the degree of rationality achievable in any given situation. The second is the more important from a theoretical point of view: is it possible in principle to compute the functions posited by the rational choice program? This question, when answered in the negative, poses an absolute barrier to the rational choice program.

The essays in this volume address these two questions in a variety of economic modeling contexts.

1.5 Complexity in cellular automata

Cellular automata are, as we have seen, a simplified representation of general nonlinear dynamical systems. Because they are defined by very simple

1.5. CELLULAR AUTOMATA

rules, it is possible to investigate a substantial subset of the possible cellular automata in some detail by simulation, even within the limits posed by the power of contemporary computers.

Stephen Wolfram's studies of cellular automata are the foundation of the economic and social models in this book.

Wolfram proceeds by classifying cellular automata in terms of the dimension of the lattice on which they exist, the number of states, k, each site can occupy in each step, the radius defining the limits of one-step influence of sites, r, and the rule of evolution governing the evolution of the automaton. One-dimensional cellular automata are the cheapest to simulate and the results of the simulation can be visualized in two-dimensional plots, with the sites of the automaton arrayed horizontally and time represented vertically. Wolfram and others have also looked intensively at two-dimensional cellular automata. As the dimension of the lattice increases, the number of rules possible increases enormously, so that exploration by simulation becomes an increasingly difficult program to carry out.

In general a cellular automaton rule can allow the next-step state of each site to depend in an arbitrary way on the states of the cells in its neighborhood. For example, in a one-dimensional cellular automaton with $k = 2$ and $r = 1$ the next state of each site depends on three bits representing the current state of itself and its left- and right-hand neighbors. The state of this neighborhood can take on eight configurations. In an arbitrary rule, each of these configurations is mapped onto a 1 or a 0 representing the next state of the center cell, so there are 256 possible cellular automaton rules. Wolfram cuts down the number of possibilities by restricting his attention to subsets of the possible rules that reflect natural physical assumptions. In physical systems, for example, there is no reason to think that influences on one side of a site are any different from influences on another side, so that it is natural to concentrate attention on *symmetrical* rules. In many physical systems the influences of neighbors are at least approximately additive, so that it makes sense to look at *totalistic* rules, in which the next state of the cell depends only on the total number of neighbors (including itself) in each state, or to *outer totalistic* rules, in which the next state of the cell depends separately on the total number of neighbors (not including itself) in each state and the state of the cell itself. In many physical systems the 0 state represents a minimum energy state of a cell, so that it is plausible to require that when the neighborhood is all in the 0 state, the next state of the cell is 0 (*legal* rules).

These restrictions are plausible physically, there is no strong indication that the behavior of the totalistic, legal, or symmetric class of cellular automata is unrepresentative of the behavior of the general case, and the restrictions greatly increase the efficiency of the simulation exploration program by restricting the parameter space it must examine. But it is worth noting that each of these physically plausible restrictions on cellular automaton rules is less compelling in a social than a physical context. If we think, as Albin does in some of the essays in this volume, of the cells as representing firms, then the concept of "neighboring firm" might be thought of as "suppliers" and "customers." In this interpretation the next state of firm might be thought of as depending on the current state of its suppliers and customers, since they determine the availability of inputs and the demand for output from the firm. If we were to array the firms on a line with suppliers to the left and customers to the right, the assumption of symmetry in the cellular automaton representation would not necessarily hold, since the impact of the state of its supplier on the future state of the firm could be quite different from the impact of the state of its customer.

Similarly, totalistic rules make considerable sense in some social and economic contexts, but are less attractive in others. In the exchange model of Chapter 5, for example, an agent's decision to undertake costly advertising to enter the market depends on her estimate of the exact offer prices of her neighbors, information which cannot easily be summarized by a single statistic derived by addition. Even the restriction to "legal" rules, in which the state of all 0s in a neighborhood determines a 0 for the next state of the cell, might not be attractive in some economic models. If the cell represents a possible production activity, and the neighborhood similar production activities, 0s in neighboring cells might represent a competitive opportunity, and lead to spontaneous generation of activity in a particular location.

Since the rules governing the evolution of cellular automata are so simple, one might hope that it would be possible to derive simple and general algorithms to predict the evolution of cellular automata from initial conditions. Wolfram's study is motivated largely by exploring the limits of this program. His method is to look through simulation at the evolution of a large number of cellular automata from either simple seeds (single nonzero sites) or random seeds, to see what patterns emerge over time. His striking findings are the basis for a number of the essays in this volume.

1.5.1 Complexity types

Wolfram finds that one-dimensional cellular automata can be classified into four basic complexity levels. (He conjectures that these same four levels also suffice for higher dimensional cellular automata.) The first three levels of complexity are analogous to various types of attractors in nonlinear dynamical systems.

Type 1 cellular automata evolve to uniform states from arbitrary initial conditions. Alteration of the initial conditions leads to changes that die out

1.5. CELLULAR AUTOMATA

over time as the system seeks out the uniform state. They are analogous to dynamical systems that have a unique stable equilibrium.

Type 2 cellular automata evolve to periodic patterns of states from arbitrary initial conditions. Small change in initial conditions may change the phase of the periodic limit, but not its basic pattern. They are analogous to dynamical systems that have periodic attractors.

It is not difficult to predict the evolution of type 1 and type 2 systems: once we have seen the pattern that evolves for a few initial conditions, we pretty well know what is going to happen in any further experiment we do on the system. Small errors in the measurement of the initial conditions lead to errors in prediction which decrease over time.

Type 3 cellular automata evolve to nonrepeating, complicated patterns from arbitrary initial conditions. A small change in initial conditions changes features of the evolutionary pattern on a larger and larger scale with time. They are analogous to dynamical systems with chaotic behavior and chaotic attractors. While it is difficult to predict the evolution of type 3 cellular automata in detail, it is possible to find statistical regularities in the patterns that evolve, such as the average number of cells in each state, and entropy measures of the diversity of patterns developed. In some cases it is possible to identify types of patterns that can never evolve in the automaton, despite the large and constantly changing patterns that do evolve. Type 3 cellular automata, like the context-sensitive languages, exhibit a monotonically increasing range of changes emanating from a local perturbation of initial conditions.

Type 4 cellular automata produce propagating irregular structures from arbitrary initial conditions. A change in initial conditions can lead to changes that propagate coherently for large distances. The structures that evolve from similar initial conditions may be quite different. In type 3 cellular automata the effects of changes in initial conditions spread out constantly in space over time, but in type 4 systems the effects may spread and then contract. As a result there is no way to tell in a type 4 system how large the intermediate structures leading to a particular configuration might be: a relatively simple final configuration of the system may be the result of the distillation of immense and very complex intermediate structures. The type 4 cellular automata are thus analogous to formal languages produced by unrestricted grammars.

From the dynamical systems point of view, type 4 cellular automata lie on the boundary between types 2 and 3. A disturbance in the initial conditions of a type 2 cellular automaton monotonically subsides into the periodic attractor, and a disturbance in a type 3 system monotonically explodes through the whole space. A disturbance in a type 4 system neither implodes nor explodes, but propagates irregularly through the system.

Type 4 cellular automata are thus models of "complexity on the edge of chaos," systems just on the boundary between subcritical stability and supercritical instability.

1.5.2 Computability, predictability, and complexity in cellular automata

Type 3 and type 4 cellular automata represent the boundaries and barriers to rationality that are the theme of the essays in this book.

Type 3 cellular automata produce the propagating, irregular patterns characteristic of chaotic dynamical systems. A small change in the initial conditions of the system leads to ever-widening changes in its eventual configuration. Thus the computational cost of predicting the effect of a change in a type 3 system rises with the length of the horizon and with the accuracy of prediction required. An agent attempting to carry out the program of rational action in a type 3 environment faces these costs. For even fairly simple representations of real social and economic interactions, the costs of implementing a fully rational strategy become unreasonably large. In such a situation the agent has to accept limited computation as a bound on her rationality. She may, like the agents in some of the papers below, deploy limited computational capacity to improve her strategy by adopting one of a number of boundedly rational strategies, but she cannot reasonably be supposed to carry out the full computations presupposed by the hypothesis of full rationality.

Type 4 cellular automata pose even more fundamental paradoxes for the conception of rational action. Type 4 cellular automata are conjectured to be capable of general computation, that is, of simulating a Turing machine. Systems of this level of complexity pose difficult problems for a decisionmaker. A given small change in initial conditions (e.g., representing a change in the behavior of the rational agent) may lead to a series of ramifying consequences which simplify over time into the emergence of a particular state (perhaps a state very much desired or disliked by the agent). But there is no way for the agent to find out whether or not this is true except to simulate the whole system in all its complexity. In undertaking this computation, the agent will run into frustrating barriers to her carrying out the program of rational choice. There is no way for her to tell whether the simulation in question will arrive at the desired answer in a finite time, or indeed any answer in finite time. She may let her computer run for a long time; at any moment she has no way of knowing whether it is just a few steps away from resolving the question or is caught in an enormous loop from which she can never garner any useful information.

One of the main themes of the essays in this volume is how easy it is for type 4 environments to appear in relatively simple and standard models of human social and economic interaction.

1.6 Modeling complex social and economic interactions

1.6.1 Self-referencing individual agents

In "The metalogic of economic predictions, calculations and propositions" (Chapter 2), Albin addresses the paradoxes of computability in the context of rational economic decision making at the most abstract and general level.

The central point is that economic agents are at least as complex as Turing machines, and the economy (or any subsystem of the economy, such as a firm or an industry or a market) is a system made up of agents with this complexity level. An agent (or indeed, an economist) trying to predict the behavior of such a system in relevant dimensions faces a problem exactly equivalent to the problem of calculating the value of an uncomputable function. The difficulty arises because there is no shortcut available to simulate the behavior of the complex agents who make up the system. The consequences of a change in initial conditions (say, the behavior of an agent herself) can be worked out only by predicting the complex reactions of the other agents in the system, and there is no way to do this except by a complete simulation of these other complex systems. In this chapter Albin establishes the necessary logical mapping from a general social system to the theory of computable functions, and shows that the undecidability propositions of computation theory translated into the economic sphere imply the impossibility in general of computing the economic outcome of a change in initial conditions.

One might hope that this difficulty is essentially a problem of approximation, and that the agent might, with finite computational resources, reach an acceptable approximation to the true consequences of the change in initial conditions in finite time. But Albin shows that the same logic that applies to the computation of the consequences of an action themselves applies to the problem of determining how good an approximation any particular feasible computational method will produce.

For example, economists have often based policy prescriptions on their evaluation of the social welfare implications of changes in taxes or subsidies. But in the general case, the computation of the allocation that will result from a given change is undecidable; the economist could carry out her analysis only by simulating the economic system in detail, a task she could not accomplish with finite resources.

For another example, the manager of a firm considering the consequences of a pricing decision, would in principle have to simulate the full reactions of all the other agents in the economy to a contemplated price increase, taking into account the reactions of her customers to the change, and the rippling effects of their changed actions on other related sectors of the economy.

It is important to appreciate the fundamental nature of this result, as well as some of its limitations and qualifications. What is at issue here is not the quantitative efficiency of computers or information collection systems. The problems of undecidability in computational theory arise not from the specific limitations of particular machines, but from the self-referential character of certain computations, a logical difficulty that raw computing power cannot overcome. Nor should we regard this result as a kind of special case: it is in fact the general situation of interacting social actors. The key characteristic of these social systems is that they are made up of linked actors each of which has a complexity level at least as great as that of a Turing machine.

The apparent nihilism of this result also needs to be put into perspective. Albin's analysis does not claim that it is always impossible to forecast the consequences of an action in finite time, only that it is impossible in general and impossible to find out except by trying. It may be that the ramifying consequences of a price increase by a particular firm are limited and can be simulated in finite time by a sufficiently sophisticated computer. But the manager of the firm cannot be sure whether this particular instance of a price increase will lead to consequences in the computable category. She has no way of finding out except to start to compute the consequences; if her program stops after a minute or a year, she will know the answer, but if the program is still running after a minute or a year, she has no way of knowing whether it will continue to run forever, or for ten thousand years, or is just one cycle away from stopping with the answer she wants. The computational complexity inherent in a social or economic system does not prevent agents from carrying out the rational decision program in some (perhaps in a large number) of contexts, but it does prevent us from accepting the logical adequacy of the rational program as a general account of what might happen.

Economists have been aware of this paradox to a certain extent since the early beginnings of the discipline. It is instructive to see how economics has attempted to cope with the challenge of complexity. The critical maneuver is to replace the computationally intractable problem of forecasting the behavior of many other complex decisionmakers and their interactions with the computationally simpler problem of calculating a posited equilibrium of the economic system. Thus the classical British political economists, Smith, Malthus, and Ricardo, employed the concept of *natural*

1.6. MODELING SOCIAL INTERACTIONS

prices, around which day-to-day market prices of commodities fluctuate (or *gravitate*.) The implication is that the natural prices are equilibria subject to logical analysis and prediction despite the fact that the fluctuating market prices may be the result of detailed interactions too complex to predict or explain. Contemporary neoclassical economic theory rests on a similar epistemological postulate, which claims that the equilibrium of the economy is computable, even if the disequilibrium paths of the economy are not. From this epistemological viewpoint the rational economic actor need not consider the detailed reactions of other actors in all their potential complexity, since the equilibrium market prices convey enough summary information to allow her to make a rational plan. This program has had a certain amount of success, but clearly rests on a leap of faith that somehow the complexity level of the economy as a whole is lower than that of the agents who constitute it.

The study of cellular automata can throw some light on this epistemological puzzle. Complexity in cellular automata arises through the ramifications of linked local interactions. Equilibrium market prices, on the other hand, summarize information about the global state of the economic system, since they depend in principle on the states (say excess demand functions) of all the participants in the market. The traditional economist effectively assumes that this global information dominates local interactions in influencing the behavior of the agents in the system, and thus suppresses the complexity latent in the local interactions. There is surely some truth in this point of view, but it raises other serious and interesting questions that have hardly been addressed in any rigor by economic theory. The most central of these questions is where the resources come from to diffuse the information contained in market prices. The weakest aspect of economic equilibrium theory is its implicit assumption that information diffusion in the market is costless and instantaneous.

1.6.2 Organizations

The interplay of information and the complexity level of individual agents in an economy is the theme of "The complexity of social groups and social systems described by graph structures" (Chapter 7), which reveals the interplay of whimsical humor and mathematics in Albin's thought. Here Albin lays the conceptual foundations for the measurement of the complexity level of an organization, modeled as a directed graph. The nodes of the graph represent information processing units in an organization (e.g., a production unit or an accounting office) and the graph connections the communication links between them, which may be one- or two-way.

Albin proposes an extension of the concept of algorithmic complexity to measure the complexity of such directed graphs. He asks us to consider the organization as a *rumor mill*, devoted entirely to the spreading of bits (or tidbits) of information. Each node of the organizational graph has a certain number of input and output channels along which this information must flow. The requirement that each node keep track of the rumor's path ("I heard it from Z who heard it from Y ...") for the largest possible rumor the graph can generate establishes a measure of the algorithmic complexity of each node. The sum of these algorithmic complexities over the whole organization (or graph) is a useful measure of the complexity of the organization.

Albin is able to link this measure of complexity with observable organizational phenomena, including the effectiveness and the functionality of the organization. This line of thinking raises sharply the question of whether real organizations can reasonably be supposed to reach the complexity level assumed in rational choice theory. If in most situations resources limit the complexity levels that can be sustained by organizations, they will also limit the type of prediction and projection the organization can undertake in making decisions. Under these circumstances the systems modeler may get further by identifying the particular algorithms of bounded complexity the organizations are actually using than by positing full rationality.

1.6.3 Industries and economies

Since cellular automata are a mathematically economical representation of the full range of potential system complexity, it is tempting to use them to model whole interactive economic systems, indeed, whole economies.

Albin's "Microeconomic foundations of cyclical irregularities or 'chaos'" (Chapter 3) is a pioneering effort in this direction. Here Albin seeks to map Richard Day's model of chaotic economic growth paths onto a cellular automaton. Day's aim was to show that a plausible modification of Robert Solow's model of economic growth could lead to a dynamical system with a chaotic attractor. In Solow's model the state variable of the economy is taken to be the capital stock per worker, which follows a dynamical law representing the productivity of the economy and its saving/investment behavior. Solow's original examples were carefully constructed so as to yield a system with a single equilibrium point attractor. Day showed that the addition of a plausible assumption lowering investment or output at high levels of capital per worker (which could be the reflection either of wealth effects on saving or of external pollution effects on productivity) gives rise to a dynamical system with a chaotic attractor.

Albin takes this line of thinking one step further. He disaggregates the Solow/Day analysis by considering the economy as a large number of separate firms, each with its own production function and investment decision.

1.6. MODELING SOCIAL INTERACTIONS

The aggregation of these firms constitutes the macroeconomy; the aggregation of their investment plans corresponds to the economy-wide levels of investment in the Solow/Day setup. Albin then regards each of these microlevel firms as cells in a one-dimensional cellular automaton. In order to simplify the simulations, he restricts the investment levels for each firm to "high," "normal," and "low," leading to a three-state cellular automaton. The geometry of the line can be seen as an ordering of firms by industries, with supplier industries on the left and customer industries on the right. A cellular automaton rule in this context represents a pattern of local interaction in which each firm chooses its next period investment policy conditional on the current investment policies of its suppliers and customers. Aggregate fluctuations in investment arise from the individual fluctuations of the firms' policies. There are clearly a large number of possible rules, each corresponding to a different pattern of behavioral interactions on the part of the firms.

Albin uses this model to make two fundamental and compelling points. First, for a large class of rules, the resulting cellular automata are chaotic. In these economies there are ceaseless fluctuations of investment and growth both at the microeconomic level within industry groupings (neighborhoods), and in the economy as a whole. These chaotic fluctuations pose a serious challenge to modeling the behavior of any one firm as fully rational, that is, based on a correct prediction of the behavior of the economy or its neighbors. The problem is that a full projection of the evolution of the economy, or any piece of it, will require computational resources that grow at the same rate as the horizon of the projection. Under these circumstances the implicit assumption in rational choice models that the computational costs of projecting the consequences of behavior are negligible is unsustainable.

Second, as we have seen, one-dimensional, three-state cellular automata can produce not just type 3 chaotic patterns, but also type 4 behavior, which is conjectured to be at the same complexity level as a general-purpose computer, or an unrestricted formal language. We have no reason to believe that the interactions of the real economy exclude type 4 behavior (though by the same token we have no reason to believe that the real economic interactions lead to type 4 behavior, either). If the economy as a whole or subsystems are governed by interactions that lead to type 4 behavior, the barriers to rationality established by the paradoxes of self-reference come into play as well.

Albin's modeling of firm interaction as a cellular automaton breaks new ground in cellular automaton theory as well. Once we interpret the cells of the automaton as firms and the relation of neighbors as members of the same industry or suppliers or customers, some of the physically motivated assumptions of cellular automata theory need to be rethought. In physical models, as we have seen, it is very natural to assume that neighbor effects are symmetrical, but if the geometry of the lattice represents asymmetric economic relations (such as supplier and customer), this assumption is no longer strongly compelling. Albin's simulation of asymmetric rules thus also extends the cellular automaton model in interesting ways.

The fluctuations that arise from the local interactions of investment policy in this model raise the question of whether some weak global information could stabilize the economy. In "Qualitative effects of monetary policy in 'rich' dynamic systems" (Chapter 4), Albin extends the model of local firm investment interaction to include a simple representation of monetary policy. The idea is to append to the set of firms a single site which is a neighbor of all of them. The state of this site represents a systemwide monetary policy (+1 corresponding to an expansionary policy, 0 to a neutral policy, and −1 to a contractionary policy). A procyclical monetary policy takes the value +1 when a majority of the firms in the economy are also in state +1, and therefore investing at a higher than average rate, and −1 when a majority of firms are in the −1 state and therefore investing less than average. A countercyclical monetary policy "leans against the wind" by assuming the value −1 when a majority of the firms are in state +1, and +1 when a majority are in state −1, thus offsetting the aggregate tendency of the system.

Albin uses simulation to investigate the impact of these monetary policies on the evolution of the cellular automata representing the economy of firms. His analysis is aimed not so much at measuring the effectiveness of policy in actually stabilizing the aggregate behavior of the economy as in observing the impact of the policy on the complexity level of the resulting automaton. He finds that turning on the policy interaction can result, depending on the rules governing the local interactions of the firms, in any possible change in complexity levels: type 1 point attractor systems may be transformed by the weak global interaction of the policy variable into type 2 or 3 or 4 systems, and similarly for the other complexity levels.

In his investigations of the metalogic of economic forecasts, Albin already raised the possibility that the impact of policy on economic outcomes and hence on social welfare might be unpredictable. The monetary policy model complements this point by posing an abstract but not implausible model of the economy in which policy intervention may itself move the system from one level of computational complexity to another.

1.6.4 Markets

In "Decentralized, dispersed exchange without an auctioneer" (Chapter 5), Albin and Foley begin to attack the problem of representing canonical economic exchange as a cellular automaton. The basic economic setting is

1.6. MODELING SOCIAL INTERACTIONS

chosen to be as simple as possible: 100 agents arrayed in a circle trade endowments of two goods. The agents have identical preferences, represented by the utility function $x_1 x_2$, so that the marginal rate of substitution, (or willingness to pay) of good 2 for good 1 for an agent currently owning $\{x_1, x_2\}$ is just x_2/x_1. Trade is motivated by differences in initial endowments of the agents. The total endowment of the two goods in the economy is arranged to be equal (though the agents do not know this), so that the Walrasian market equilibrium relative price will be unity. The agents' endowments are diversified subject to the constraint that their wealth at the Walrasian equilibrium price is the same. Thus agents start with the same total $e_1 + e_2$ of the two goods, but in different proportions. As a result, the initial offer prices differ, so that agents typically have a motive to make a mutually advantageous exchange.

The model puts stringent restrictions on the information available to the agents and their economic strategies. Each agent can communicate and trade only with her neighbors within a given radius, which is a parameter of the model. When the model starts, she does not know the total endowment of the two goods, or the Walrasian equilibrium price, so that she does not know whether her endowment is typical of the whole economy or skewed in one direction or another. As a result she does not initially know whether she would be a net buyer or seller of good 1 in the Walrasian equilibrium. Each agent must inform herself about her trading possibilities by actually trying to trade with her neighbors. To do this she must pay a cost to advertise her willingness to buy or sell good 1. This advertising puts her in contact with those neighbors who advertise on the other side of the market (buyers with sellers and vice-versa). Each such pair meets and reveals its current willingness to pay. If the buyer's willingness to pay is higher than the sellers, they exchange a small amount of the goods at a price that is the geometrical average of the two marginal rates of substitution, thus accomplishing a mutually advantageous exchange. Each agent remembers the most recent willingness to pay for each of her neighbors with whom she has actually bargained, and uses this to construct a simple model of the distribution of offer prices in her neighborhood, which she uses to decide whether it is worth her while to incur the cost of further advertising.

From an economic point of view this is a model of bounded rationality. In principle, each exchange an agent makes will influence the whole future course of exchanges in the whole market. From a game-theoretic point of view, for example, we could try to work out the best strategy (in terms of advertising and revelation of prices) for an agent, supposing that all the other agents continued to follow the rules set out in their programs. It is unlikely that the program we have proposed would be the best response to itself, though it is not clear how one would even establish this proposition, since the consequences of a given change in the behavior of one agent involve a complicated ramifying sequence of events which depend critically on facts, such as the exact or even the average endowments of the other agents, which the agent does not know. One Nash equilibrium of this economy is easy to spot, but not very interesting, in which all the agents refuse to advertise or trade at all. (If an agent knows that none of her neighbors will advertise, there is no point in her incurring the costs of doing so.) Despite the fact that the agents are not trying to be anything like fully rational, their behavior is a reasonable way to pursue the end of trading to mutual advantage. Simulations of the model reveal that it works rather well to achieve an approximation to a Pareto-efficient allocation of the goods (in which no further mutually advantageous trades exist) at a relatively low advertising cost. The main difficulty is a halting problem: occasionally two agents in a neighborhood who do not know each other's willingness to pay get caught in an endless loop, in which they both alternate between advertising as buyers and sellers in the hope of advantageous trade with each other.

A further striking feature of the simulations is that while the market, as it is supposed to, efficiently redistributes the initial endowments around the circle and evens out the relative proportions in which agents hold the two goods, it also systematically introduces inequalities of wealth into the economy. This is a manifestation of a point long acknowledged but little investigated by economic theory: when agents trade at disequilibrium prices they effectively redistribute wealth at the same time that they narrow the differences in willingness to pay. In this particular model it is not hard to see that agents who start with endowment proportions far different from 1:1, and therefore with very high or very low willingness to pay good 2 for good 1, will make most of their transactions at unfavorable prices, effectively transferring their wealth to the lucky agents whose endowment proportions are close to the average.

This model is a cellular automaton, but the states each cell (or agent) can occupy are more general than those typically studied in the cellular automaton literature. The full state of an agent at any round of trading includes her current holdings of the two goods (effectively a continuous state variable), and the record she keeps of the willingness to pay of those neighbors she has met in attempts to trade. The neighborhood structure, and locality of interactions, on the other hand, keep strictly to the cellular automaton format.

The emergence of a close-to-Pareto-efficient allocation in this model is an example of the self-organization of a complex system based solely on local interactions undertaken with no information about the global state. Because no agent can ever make a trade that leaves her worse off, the opportunities for mutually advantageous exchange are gradually exploited in the evolution of the system. The market effectively computes a Pareto-

1.6. MODELING SOCIAL INTERACTIONS

efficient allocation (though not the one that is generated by Walrasian *tâtonnement*, in which each agent makes all her transactions at the same, market-clearing, price) and a corresponding almost-uniform willingness to pay. The simultaneous emergence of a definite wealth distribution as the consequence of market transactions at nonequilibrium prices is a further example of such self-organization.

1.6.5 The local interaction multiperson Prisoners' Dilemma

In "Approximations of cooperative equilibria in multiperson Prisoners' Dilemma played by cellular automata" (Chapter 6), Albin proposes an elegant generalization of the two-person repeated Prisoners' Dilemma game that social scientists have come to take as the paradigmatic representation of the paradoxes of rationality and social interaction. The society is represented as a cellular automaton in two dimensions with $k = 2$ states, and the "Moore" neighborhood, consisting of the eight adjacent sites in the lattice. Each cell represents an agent. The kernel of the model is a one-shot game in which each agent chooses one of two strategies, cooperation or defection. The payoff to each agent depends on her strategy and the total number of cooperators in her neighborhood. The payoffs, as in the two-person Prisoners' Dilemma, are structured so that defection dominates cooperation: no matter what the neighbors do, the payoff is higher to a defector than to a cooperator. But also, as in the two-person Prisoners' Dilemma, the payoff to a neighborhood where everyone cooperates is higher than to a neighborhood where everyone defects. From a social point of view everyone will be better off if everyone cooperates (the Pareto-efficient solution), but everyone has an incentive to increase her individual payoff by defecting.

Many interpretations could be given to this model. The quality of life in city neighborhoods, for example, depends to a considerable degree on the willingness of residents to incur real costs to maintain their property. There are considerable joint benefits to be had from uniformly high levels of property maintenance, and considerable joint costs imposed if everyone lets their property go unmaintained. Local industrial pollution poses a similar scenario, in which all the producers may enjoy lower costs if they all control their pollution, but any individual producer is tempted to pollute.

Although this model is a minimal and simple extension of the Prisoners' Dilemma, and, given the level of abstraction, plausibly represents a wide range of important social interactions, its structure poses a severe challenge to standard noncooperative game theory. The relevant strategy set would allow each agent to condition her strategy in any one play of the game on the whole past history of her and the other participants' actions. But she is linked indirectly to all of the agents in the game by the neighborhood structure. Is it plausible to assume that the agent can even observe the actions of agents far away from her geographically? If she cannot, must she undertake to infer their behavior from the behavior of her neighbors? Even if we assume the agent can observe the whole history of the global game, the problem of calculating best responses is formidable. Of course, some game theoretic results are fairly immediate. Uniform defection, for example, is a Nash equilibrium, but not a plausible or interesting one. A "trigger" strategy that cooperates until some agent anywhere in the game defects, and then shifts to uniform defection might sustain uniform cooperation and be a best response, but most people would not view it as particularly practical in the contexts where some level of defection is almost certain, but it still pays collectively to maintain high average levels of cooperation.

Albin approaches these difficulties by restricting attention to a subset of possible strategies, those conditioned simply on the last action of the immediate neighbors. He adopts, in other words, a bounded rationality perspective on the grounds that computational complexity problems that arise in this limited setting cannot be presumed to get any better when the strategy space is expanded and the model thereby made even more complicated. This limitation also has the appealing feature of creating a strict equivalence between strategies and the rules governing the evolution of a two-dimensional cellular automaton with the Moore neighborhood. The current state of each cell is the decision of the agent to cooperate or defect, and the next state, given the strategy of the agent, will depend only on her current strategy and the current strategies of her neighbors. Thus holding the strategies of agents constant, the game evolves as a cellular automaton, about which we have considerable knowledge from earlier research.

In the context of this model Albin raises a subtle but extremely interesting question. If there were a Nash equilibrium in this subset of strategies different from universal defection, in other words, a Nash equilibrium that could sustain social cooperation, what would the complexity type of the resulting cellular automaton have to be? Consider a society in which all the agents have adopted a uniform strategy that leads to a cellular automaton evolution of types 1, 2, or 3. Suppose that a particular agent now considers changing her strategy. To work out the exact consequences of such a change assuming that the other agents continue with their existing strategies is in general computationally infeasible. Albin supposes that the agent, in the spirit, if not the letter, of Nash equilibrium reasoning, assumes that the complexity type of the society will not change when she changes her strategy. If she confronts a predictable type 1 or type 2 cellular automaton, she will do better shifting to uniform defection. Even if she confronts a type 3 situation, in which the behavior of her neighbors appears to be chaotic, it is plausible to suppose that she will view her environment as stochastic,

1.6. MODELING SOCIAL INTERACTIONS

and realize that uniform defection is also her dominating policy against any randomized strategy of her neighbors. Thus it is implausible to imagine that even boundedly rational agents would maintain a strategy that could sustain cooperation if this strategy resulted in a social environment of complexity level lower than type 4.

An agent who lives in a society corresponding to type 4 complexity, however, might not choose to shift to uniform defection. She might perceive her neighbors as at least potentially reacting thoughtfully and predictably to defection, and punishing it selectively in such a way that uniform defection would lead to a lower average payoff. Despite the difficulty of proving the stability of a type 4 strategy, Albin conjectures that strategies which implement the game of "Life" may have this property. "Life" is known to support type 4 complexity, and is known to be capable of emulating a generalized Turing machine. In support of his conjecture, Albin presents simulations showing the ability of "Life" to generate systematic and selective punishment of uniform defectors.

Whether or not "Life" turns out to be a stable equilibrium strategy for the local interaction multiperson Prisoners' Dilemma, Albin's investigation underlines the philosophical theme that runs through his work. We live in a social environment created by human beings, who are, considered as systems, highly complex. Albin does not believe that there is any way to reduce this essential complexity to produce a simple theory of social interaction that is also robust. Despite occasional apparent successes of economic theory in using the assumption of competition to simplify the rational choice problem of individual agents, Albin argues that there remains an irreducible kernel of latent complexity in even the most stylized and abstract models of society, such as the local interaction multiperson Prisoners' Dilemma. This is probably not news to human beings who are living their way through social interactions, but it poses some fundamental challenges to social and economic theory.

In this perspective, the questions Albin poses about the complexity of social institutions, despite the difficulty or perhaps the impossibility of answering them with currently available conceptual tools, involve fundamental issues of method and metatheory. They suggest that the kind of knowledge we can hope to have about complex social systems is different in kind from the kind of knowledge we have gained about physical systems. The program of reducing complex physical interactions to computable models, which has had such striking success in the physical sciences, has much narrower conceptual limits in the context of social interactions, precisely because the constituent subsystems of societies, human beings, are themselves emergent, complex adaptive systems.

These implications of Albin's work need not lead us to nihilism about the possibility of some important and powerful kinds of knowledge of social interactions. The ability to recognize, name, and classify the complexity levels of particular social interactions, as Albin argues, is valuable in itself. Furthermore, a rigorous ability to recognize the limits of what is knowable, which is what the complexity analysis of social systems offers, is the starting point for scientific advance.

1.7 Complexity, rationality, and social interaction

Peter Albin's investigations establish a strong presumption that the bounds to rationality constituted by computation costs in chaotic environments and the barriers to rationality raised by the self-referential paradoxes of complex environments are inherent in our conception of social systems as interactions of rational individuals. The systematic analysis of complexity reveals an internal conceptual contradiction in the program that seeks to reduce social phenomena to the interactions of self-interested individuals. This challenge to the dogmas of rationality takes a new and unexpected form. The rational choice/social interaction paradigm has often been criticized on various grounds: that human beings are in fact not motivated by individual self-interest; that individual personality is a social construct which cannot be posited independent of the social context in which it develops; that social interaction leads to the emergence of specifically social interests and forms that cannot be reduced to individual actions. These external critiques question the premises, relevance, and explanatory power of the rational choice paradigm.

The issues raised by the consideration of computational costs and complexity, on the other hand, are fundamentally internal to the rational choice paradigm. The complexity analysis accepts the premises of rationality, and pushes them rigorously to their limits. This process first of all revealed what might appear to be a gap or oversight in the rational choice theory. In assuming that agents could map their actions onto consequences, rationality implicitly abstracts from computation costs. This abstraction, like many others, would do no harm if it were appropriate, in the sense that ignoring computation costs made little practical difference to the predictions and explanations of the theory. In many familiar human situations, after all, computation costs seem negligible. We are automatically provided with a powerful general-purpose pattern recognition and computation device in the form of our brains, which typically have plenty of spare capacity to deal with day-to-day decision making, like finding the nut-bearing trees or the boar hiding in the forest, with enough left over to write epic poetry, speculate on the nature of the universe, and devise elaborate insults for

1.7. COMPLEXITY AND RATIONALITY

each other. It is easy to see how theorists slipped into the universal presumption that the human brain could solve the problems predicting the consequences of actions. Rational choice theory inherits from theology a preoccupation with issues of will, morality, and efficacy: what is the right decision in a given context.

One response to the criticisms of rationality based on complexity and computation costs might be to see them as requiring simply an extension of the field of rational choice. The rational decisionmaker must decide not just what action to take, but how much scarce computational resources to devote to working out the consequences of actions, presumably balancing the costs and benefits of future computation at the margin. As we have argued, this easy fix is untenable, because it leads to an infinite regress: the problem of estimating the costs and benefits of computation at the margin is itself just as complex as the original problem, and just as intractable.

A second response would be to argue that there are at least some contexts where the complexity levels of the environment are low, so that individual agents can plausibly be assumed to bear the costs of complete computation. For example, some economists believe that competitive economic systems are well represented by Walrasian equilibrium systems that have a relatively simple dynamic behavior, for example, unique point attractors. One of the major thrusts of Albin's work is to show how quickly even very simple models of local interaction in fact develop highly complex dynamic behavior.

1.7.1 How complex are social systems?

This line of thinking raises an important research issue, which is to find methods to measure the actual complexity of real social systems. Albin's proposed complexity measures for social organizations are a first step in this direction.

As Albin argues, human social systems are composed of agents, human beings, each of whom has a complexity level at least as high as a general purpose computer, a Turing machine. As a result it is impossible to rule out a priori, similarly complex behavior on the part of the social system as a whole. Social theory and economic theory in particular, however, have developed without explicitly addressing the level of complexity of the social system. Some of the most apparently successful social theories, such as economic equilibrium theory, picture the social environment as having limited complexity.

Two possibilities suggest themselves to reconcile these points of view. First, something may mitigate the potential complexity of social interaction, leading to a social system that has lower complexity than its component subsystems. In economic equilibrium theory we see an embryonic argument along these lines, resting on the effects of competition and weak global interactions to suppress potential complexity in the behavior of the economy as a whole. We need to understand these claims better, and to analyze them carefully with the tools of complexity theory. Albin's model of monetary policy, in which the central bank is represented as a neighbor of all the firms in the economy, shows one way to approach this issue. The results of his simulations are ambiguous, since he finds that the addition of the weak global interaction represented by the central bank can, depending on the complexity level of the economy without intervention, lead to any possible shift of complexity level, from type 4 to types 2 and 1, to be sure, but also in the other direction. Thus it seems unlikely that there is a general principle that any kind of weak global interaction will simplify complex interactions.

One difficulty in pursuing these investigations in economic theory is the absence in received economic equilibrium theory of a generally accepted account of how market prices emerge from the decentralized interactions of competitive economic agents. Economic theory has relied on parables like Walras's auctioneer, a centralized agent who is imagined to "cry out" trial price systems in order to discover the equilibrium, to cover over this lacuna.

A second possibility is that we as human beings have difficulty in perceiving the complexity level of real social and economic interactions. The world of social interactions might seem less complex than it is, or indeed than we ourselves are. Albin's reflections on the metalogic of economic prediction suggests why this might be so. The only way to grasp a system of type 4 complexity is to simulate it on another system of equal complexity. If the interactions of a large number of complex subsystems like human beings leads to a system of even higher complexity than ourselves, our own complexity level may not be high enough to represent the interacting system as a whole. Just as two-dimensional creatures would experience a third dimension only as an abstract conception, we may be capable of direct contact with the complexity of our own social existence only through abstractions like complexity theory itself.

In this kind of situation, where a subsystem of given complexity, a human being, confronts a system of higher complexity, the society, how will things work out? The individual agent will have to find some way of representing the social system with a less complex surrogate. There may, in fact, be many such surrogates, many forms of imperfect representation of the complex social system.

Social theory based on the rational choice paradigm seeks to explain agents' representations of their social world as more or less accurate reflections of its true nature. Agents in this perspective believe the society to work in a certain way because it actually does work that way. The rational

1.7. COMPLEXITY AND RATIONALITY

economic actor believes that market prices reach an equilibrium because they actually do, that democratic political regimes somehow make policy choices by aggregating the preferences of the citizens, and so forth. But if complexity intervenes to prevent agents in principle from representing the system to themselves faithfully, there is another level of social explanation that must be developed. We need an explicit theory of the ways in which agents achieve simplified representations of complex social interactions. This is the program of which studies of bounded rationality form a part; Albin's work contributes to its first tentative stages of development.

1.7.2 How smart do agents need to be?

To carry out the rational choice program, agents have to be smart enough to figure out the consequences of their actions in the relevant context. As Albin's work shows, in a wide variety of plausible social and economic contexts this requirement is far too demanding to be plausible. The complexity of the social environment reflects the complexity level of the agents who interact in it, creating an unresolvable self-referential paradox.

There is, however, reason to think that the rational choice program demands far too much of agents. The rational choice program commits an agent to expending arbitrarily large computational resources to achieve a better outcome, no matter how small the potential gain may be. Ordinary experience suggests that human beings, at least, sensibly reject this counsel of perfection. In many situations algorithms with relatively low computation cost achieve quite good, if not optimal results. An example is the trading algorithm in "Decentralized, dispersed exchange without an auctioneer" (Chapter 5), which requires quite limited computational resources, does not commit agents to pursuing elaborate chains of inferential reasoning, but achieves approximately efficient allocation at a moderate resource cost.

Furthermore, in many human social contexts optimization of an objective function may be less important than avoidance of disaster. There may be computationally simple strategies that lead to high rates of survival even in complex environments. In human contexts where imitation and learning play a major role in diffusing strategies, such low-cost, high-survival probability behavior may have a considerable evolutionary advantage.

Strict rationality, on the other hand, may be evolutionarily disadvantageous in some contexts. Certainly rational strategies that commit an agent to incurring extremely high computation costs impose a resource overhead burden that may offset the small gains in performance they secure. One way out of the paradoxes of self-reference created by the presupposition of rational behavior is to generalize Simon's concept of bounded rationality to consider behavioral strategies primarily in terms of their survival and evolutionary effectiveness in relation to their computational cost, rather than in terms of their ability to approximate abstract standards of optimality.

The methodological criticism most often leveled at the program of bounded rationality is that of inherent indeterminism. The set of boundedly rational behaviors is huge, and there seems to be no systematic way to explore it, or to discover those parts of it most relevant to the explanation and prediction of particular social interactions. Rational behavior, on the other hand, appears to be generically unique, since there must be one best way to solve any given problem. Albin's work strongly challenges this methodological presumption by suggesting that in many relevant contexts the set of strictly rational behaviors is either empty or effectively beyond our knowledge because of the paradoxes of self-reference.

1.7.2.1 We are what we compute

In positive terms, the contemplation of the paradoxes of self-reference and unbounded computation cost suggests a reconceptualization of human beings as algorithms rather than preferences. Axel Leijonhufvud (1993) proposes to substitute *algorithmic man* [sic] as the protagonist of twenty-first century social theory in place of the eighteenth century's *homo economicus*.

What is characteristic of human beings as actors, in this perspective, is the computational resources and methods they deploy in decision making, rather than their pursuit of particular goals by rational means. The regularities to be discovered by social science, then, are reflections of these computational capacities rather than reflections of the rational action of the individuals. The First Welfare Theorem of economic theory, for example, shows that Walras's concept of market equilibrium logically entails Pareto's concept of efficient allocation (a situation in which it is impossible to improve any agent's state without harming some other agent). This is a paradigmatic example of a global social property derived from the presumed rationality of individual agents. From a computational point of view the analogous insights are those of Albin's local interaction multiperson Prisoners' Dilemma, in which the complexity level of the resulting social interaction reflects the algorithmic constitution of the individual agents.

1.8 Toward a robust theory of action and society

From a computational cost point of view, the rational choice paradigm's most serious weakness appears to be the lack of robustness of its predictions. Small changes in the environment or in the informational situation of

1.8. ACTION AND SOCIETY

the rational actor tend to lead to large changes in rational actions, or radical alterations of basic patterns of behavior. In some situations even the formulation of a rational strategy becomes impossibly difficult in response to what appear to be relatively small changes in the posited environment.

Take, for example, the fundamental economic problem of an economic agent confronting a market. Traditional economic theory assumes that a competitive market appears to the agent as a set of established market prices at which she can exchange arbitrarily large amounts of commodities. The market prices establish a well-defined budget set of alternative combinations of commodities the agent can afford, and rational choice theory recommends that she choose that combination of commodities she most prefers among those in her budget set. Consider now the slightly altered representation of the market in Chapter 5, "Decentralized, dispersed exchange without an auctioneer." Agents still have well-defined preferences over commodity bundles, and still face the problem of organizing social exchanges when there are strong motives to trade due to differences in endowments. The agents, however, lack the convenience of a central information source, like Walras's auctioneer, to communicate uniform market prices to the market as a whole. The individual agents have to elicit this information by advertising and probing the willingness to trade in their local neighborhood.

One might suppose that this relatively small change in informational assumptions should not lead to drastic changes in the theory of rational agent behavior in the market. A robust theory would adapt smoothly to the reduction of centralized information and the rise in costs of discovering real trading opportunities. But it turns out to be very difficult even to conceptualize the fully rational behavior of an agent in the decentralized, dispersed market setting. Her final consumption plan is the result of a large number of individual trades strung out over time, each one made with slightly different information. Her own actions in advertising and announcing willingness to pay have potentially global consequences which it is impossible for her to calculate accurately. As a result it is very difficult to map her well-defined preferences for the commodities into a ranking of her available trading strategies. What appears to be a clear-cut, unambiguous application of the rational choice principle to the problem of market demand in the Walrasian setting dissolves into a maze of competing modeling strategies when we eliminate the central information.

The welfare economist or policy maker confronting this kind of decentralized market must consider possible interventions in the informational infrastructure defining the market interactions in addition to the classical economic tools of taxes and price control. The introduction of institutions that alter the flow of information in the market, and the provision of new technologies to implement this flow, can have powerful impacts on the equity and efficiency of the final outcome.

A similar methodological problem arises in the repeated Prisoners' Dilemma. The two person one-shot Prisoners' Dilemma seems to pose no serious difficulty to the rational choice paradigm, since there is a unique Nash equilibrium in which both players choose dominant strategies. Even the elementary generalization of this model to the case of repeated plays poses serious problems for the rational choice approach, though it is possible to make some headway in defining Nash equilibria. When we take the further step, which appears modest and natural in commonsense terms, to Albin's local interaction multiperson Prisoners' Dilemma played on the lattice, however, the fundamental tasks suggested by rational choice theory, such as calculating the best response of an agent when the strategies of her neighbors are given, become computationally infeasible.

Historically rational choice theory developed in tandem with a particular method of analyzing economic behavior on markets. The tendency to represent markets as given systems of price that establish computationally trivial budget sets strongly reinforced the tendency to argue that human beings will act so as to maximize their utility given their constraints. In the abstract market setting the rational choice prescription is both feasible and plausible, and the combination of the two abstractions reinforce each other powerfully. In the other social sciences, including politics, sociology, and anthropology, rational choice methods have played a much less dominant role because the paradigmatic institutional settings—for example, elections and diplomatic negotiations, the establishment of social networks, and the evolution of human cultures—are inherently more complex. The rational choice paradigm can be imported into the other social sciences only at the cost of drastically simplifying the abstract representation of their characteristic institutional problems. Albin's application of complexity methods to economic scenarios has the important consequence of revealing the fragile interdependence of method and institutional abstraction on which traditional economic theory is based.

We are far from the point where we can propose anything like a complete computationally robust alternative to the rational choice program for economics or other social sciences. But Albin's reflections on the interplay of individual action and aggregate outcomes in complex economic interactions offers us some vital clues to the nature of such alternatives.

A more robust conception of human action in complex social contexts must explicitly address the computational resources available to and deployed by the agents. Recent advances in abstract modeling of language and computation provide the tools for at least a qualitative categorization of models in terms of their complexity levels. We ought to be able to make some progress in understanding social interactions where the complexity level of individual strategies is limited, say to the equivalent of regular lan-

1.8. ACTION AND SOCIETY 71

guages or pocket calculators. These investigations will naturally lead to a systematic exploration of models with higher assumed complexity levels.

A robust alternative to the rational choice program must also be more explicitly context-dependent. The rational choice paradigm itself, of course, is already context-dependent, in that the conception of self-interest that operates changes from context to context: a single human is imagined to maximize quite different functions in the roles of corporate executive and mother, for example. But the rational choice program posits the pattern of explanation of action in terms of maximization subject to constraints to be universal. It seems likely, however, that in reality humans deploy very different modes of action in different contexts, and that these modes of behavior differ in their computational complexity. There is good reason to believe that the stock market, for example, is in effect a system of type 4 complexity, capable of universal computation (though it is not at all obvious what function it might be working out). But many participants in the market appear to model it at lower levels of complexity: as a periodic type 2 system in some cases, or as a chaotic type 3 system subject to statistical regularities in others.

We can also see the centrality of concepts of imitation, learning, adaptation, innovation and evolution to robust approaches to explaining human action. The rational choice program is rooted in seventeenth- and eighteenth-century conceptions of natural law, property rights, and individual autonomy. The notion of individual sovereignty is deeply bound up in its structure with the postulate that preferences are given, exogenous parameters in social theory. During the last half of the nineteenth century, and the first half of the twentieth century, while other life and human sciences were revolutionized to incorporate evolutionary ideas, economics turned increasingly to an axiomatization of rationality that is indifferent if not hostile to evolutionary ideas. But one promising path to discovering a knowable orderliness in human behavior that is context-dependent and computationally bounded is to ask whether and when the social environment favors some behaviors over others and why. Evolutionary models, in which the distribution of strategies in a population change in response to their success, and in which mutation and innovation lead to new behaviors, are a logical way to attack these issues.

Peter Albin's foray into the intersection of economics and complexity theory reveals puzzling and perhaps even insurmountable problems for the rational choice paradigm. But the rational choice paradigm is not the only theoretical path to a scientific understanding of human behavior. Albin's work also provides crucial hints to the construction of fertile alternative explanatory methods.

The role and significance of complexity theory in the physical and biological sciences are at the moment highly controversial subjects. Critics question whether the methods and insights founded on simple and highly abstract models like cellular automata can be applied successfully to real-world systems and problems. The same questions and doubts arise legitimately in considering the application of complexity methods to social and economic interactions. There is a long step between exhibiting the possibility of interesting regularities or categorization of behaviors in abstract models and the explanation or prediction of real phenomena. But the essays of Peter Albin in this book serve economic and social theory discourse unambiguously at another level as well. In clarifying the role of implicit computational complexity assumptions in received social theory, this work poses fundamental and inescapable methodological questions to theories based on rational choice axioms.

Chapter 2

The Metalogic of Economic Predictions, Calculations, and Propositions

2.1 Introduction

"This statement is false." The paradox inherent in self-referential statements has been puzzled over since Epimenides the Cretan announced that "All Cretans are liars." The nature of this and similar paradoxical statements has only been clarified with the propagation of Gödel's work on formal systems. In a capsule (and leaving a number of important terms undefined), Gödel shows that any formal system which is rich enough or comprehensive enough to contain descriptions of itself or its basic structure is subject to "incompleteness";[1] where incompleteness in the Gödel sense consists of the existence within the system of a nonempty set of propositions or system productions whose validity can neither be proven nor disproven.[2]

---
*Research supported by the National Science Foundation.

[1] See Gödel (1931, 1962) or one of several recent popular treatments, of which Hofstadter (1979) is best known. Others of merit include Nagel and Newman (1958), Kac and Ulam (1969), Bernstein (1980), and Davis (1965).

[2] Although originally presented as a proposition in abstract logic or metamathematics, the theorem in variant forms is crucial in a number of applied fields as well. Accordingly we see the Gödel theorem as the "halting problem" in abstract computer science where analysis of the "halting problem" in turn leads to a demonstration of the impossibility of programming mundane service routines and monitoring conveniences (e.g., general-

It is obvious that the "real world" which is studied by economists abounds with self-referential constructs (e.g., models of the system—which are data of participants in the system) and possesses a richness that suggests inherent logical incompleteness. For one thing, languages (e.g., English, French, . . ., Japanese) that produce paradox are used in the real world. For another, human beings are part of the system. A demonstration that the human mind is richer than a computational device which is Gödel incomplete is hardly necessary: human beings can change their minds; so, in effect, certain productions (e.g., predictions) of a system containing human beings can not be demonstrated to be either valid or invalid on prior grounds and no social scientist would be so foolish to assert otherwise. Nor should anyone claim that applying the adjective, "Gödel-undecidable," to a human system increases understanding of that system in any significant way. The matter is one of "inherent residual uncertainty" that can be ignored as a practical desideratum.

There is, however, the domain of theory in which simpler idealized forms are analyzed. Although men can change their minds in inscrutable ways; "economic men" are specified as finite devices whose calculations and optimizations are, on the face of it, determinate (read: "algorithmic"). Equal determinacy is conventionally assumed for collections of human beings such as firms and other decision-making units.

Indeterminacy is a matter of concern in the analysis of ideal forms and norms and I intend to show in this essay that Gödel incompleteness and undecidability directly pertain to the analysis of theoretical economic systems: that certain solution concepts such as "predictions of characteristics of policy outcomes guided by a social welfare function," "the existence of equilibrium," "the existence of welfare optima" are subject to Gödel undecidability and that concepts of what constitutes the universe of discourse pertaining to an economic model must be reexamined.

We begin by developing correspondences among models of equilibrium systems, the real-world referents of such systems, and composite forms including finite automata, "finite structural formations" and "generalized structural formations." It is shown that these forms are appropriate "metamodels" for decision systems in that they can embody all knowledge about information requirements of the system, dynamic information flows and interactions among participants. These features are summarized as the *structural* attributes of the referent economy and a model that specifies (actually or potentially) these attributes is designated a *structural model*.

---

purpose debuggers) that might otherwise seem plausible and constructible (Burks, 1970; Minsky, 1967). Other applications abound as well: counterpart theorems exist on the issue of constructing a numerical measure of "randomness" (Chaitin, 1975) and a large number of critical issues in modern linguistics (Hopcroft and Ullman, 1969).

2.1. INTRODUCTION

Corresponding to a structural model is a finite form here labeled the *surrogate formation* or *finite surrogate*. The surrogate formation in conjunction with narrowly restricted finite representations of the participants (e.g., firms, individuals, institutions, and policy makers) is itself a finite form and one that does not give rise to fundamental problems of computability or decidability. However, if one fits to the surrogate representations of participants who act according to conventional assumptions of decision rationality, computability and decidability problems begin to appear. The surrogate structure still explains the structural attributes of information flow and interaction; problems develop from what happens when unrestricted but reasonable demands for computation are placed on the system.

Calculation and computation as economic processes occur in a number of different contexts: (1) economic actors, individuals or firms, perform optimization-type calculations over variables under their control (e.g., a firm calculates a linear-program solution to a scheduling problem); (2) actors base behavior on calculations over variables outside of their control (e.g., a marketing or production decision is based on an econometric forecast; (3) certain equilibrating- or communications-type calculations are associated with market-making actors, institutions, or ensembles; (4) a policy maker bases actions on considerations within which are assumed calculations of the preceding types (e.g., based on econometric estimates of the macroinvestment function); (5) an economist outside of the system predicts or evaluates system outcomes for various assumptions on calculations of the first four types (e.g., the government expenditure or intervention decision is evaluated as to whether it leads to increased welfare or whether it leads to approximation of some other goal).

We will see that issues of Gödel undecidability must apply to the broader types of social decision or social evaluation. This is, in essence, a metatheoretic finding. The results here indicate the limits as to what the economist *qua* "welfare economist" or "pundit" can predict as to the qualities of system outcomes or the attainability of optima. In other words, Gödel undecidability amounts to a restriction on the generality of a priori general theories. A second type of undecidability applies in the policy context. Suppose that special information is available that a particular optimum or target position exists. It may still be true that the degree to which a system can approach the optimum is undecidable or, alternatively, that the time required to reach a target may not be predictable. A third type of undecidability applies to the predictability of microbehaviors conditional on forecasts of behaviors of other microactors. Here it is shown that by assuming the ability to forecast (i.e., by giving actors access to past data and permitting them to synthesize or simulate potential states) the essential quality of calculation is altered and system outcomes (the outcomes of mutual forecasts) become subject to undecidability.

The chapter proceeds from mathematical preliminaries to the specification of the meta model (Section 2.2) to consideration of rational forecasting and a first set of undecidability propositions (Section 2.3). Section 2.4 develops a set of undecidability propositions pertaining to social welfare evaluations in a still more general model.

2.2 Preliminaries: Automata and structural formations

An automaton is essentially a "black box" a form (or device) that generates a prescribed output for prescribed input.[3] For the cases of interest here we stipulate a clock that measures discrete time intervals. All automata in a system are synchronized to this clock, all inputs are received by automata in the system at one instant of time, and all outputs are uniformly emitted one tick of the clock later.

2.2.1 Finite automata

A finite automaton is a 5-tuple $< X, Y, Z, \delta, \omega >$. X and Y are finite sets of input and output symbols, respectively. Z is a finite set of internal states. δ is the output mapping $X * Z \to Y$ and ω is the next state mapping $X * Z \to Z$.

2.2.1.1 Semigroups

The sets and transition functions of a finite automata form a semigroup. An automaton is, in effect, a semigroup with the constraint and dynamic implications of clock synchronization. The description of an economy as a composition of specific finite automata is not a significant restriction on analysis since by free substitution of automata with identical semigroup structure it is possible to extend qualitative results to a broad class of economies of identical structure (the term "structure," is for the moment, undefined). Among the more obvious substitutions of automaton components are: the replacement of consumer j by consumer j', j' being a family unit with tastes (the mappings δ' and ω') that result in different goods orders for the same price signals and budget input; the replacement of enterprise n by enterprise n', a unit which maps the input set into the output

---

[3] The basics of automata theory are given in many graduate-level texts in computer science, in particular Minsky (1967). An excellent general introduction to the field is provided by Arbib (1980). Ginzburg (1968) codifies the algebra pertaining to the complexity measurement theory of Krohn and Rhodes (1965).

2.2. PRELIMINARIES

set "more efficiently"; the replacement of all units by units which calculate in price-deflated currency, and so forth.

2.2.1.2 Sequential machines

It is clear from the definition that automata $A_0, ..., A_n$ can be "linked" if there is appropriate matching of input and output sets. For example, $Y_j \subseteq X_k$ for $j < k$ permits the sequential linking of A_j and A_k with appropriate timing. The linked entities (sequential machines) are themselves finite automata satisfying the preceding definition. It is also established in computer science that any algorithm can be represented by a constructible sequential machine.

2.2.1.3 Measurement of structural complexity

Any finite automaton or semigroup machine can be represented by an equivalent machine which is formed out of simple, "group-type" devices and simple switches. Such devices include the building blocks of digital computers which perform the group type operation of mapping binary elements into binary elements. The simplest such devices which can produce the full Boolean algebra are termed "primitives," and it has been shown that any finite automaton can be given a complexity measure, constituting a count of primitives in an equivalent machine and an equivalence class corresponding to the "richest" primitive required in its construction. It suffices for present purposes that the complexity measures apply to the "structural-organization" of an automaton.

2.2.2 Finite formations

Automata, systematically combined, form a sequential machine, a higher-level deterministic automaton. However, actual, observable, socioeconomic configurations are rarely predesigned with engineered precision—hence the need for descriptive forms such as the "finite formation."[4] The finite formation is, in effect, a partially functioning machine. Its organization can be studied in isolation from its functioning. In this format, an observed or observable structure can be expressed in terms of *sets* of well-described

---

[4]The concept of "structural formation" is introduced in Albin (1980) and developed for economic theory in Albin (1981). 1 apologize for poor nomenclature in the first paper which labels the "formation" as a "finite structure." I apologize further for the many unfamiliar constructs which have been introduced to this point—I judge that patience has been strained. As will become clear these preliminaries are needed if we are to develop a metamodel for calculation and the communication of data that is free of restrictions due to the assumption of particular functional forms.

automata. Although a particular finite formation may not work, it is associated with *effective formations* which are, in principle, hypothetical complete machines that utilize the capacity of the automata sets of the finite formation.

2.2.2.1 Finite formation

A finite formation S is a triple $< E, A, F >$ consisting of: an element set $E = \{e_j\}$ of N elements, each of which is a finite automaton; a set $A = \{a_k\}$ of $N^L \leq N$ automata which represent the interface of some e_j to adjacent formations or the environment and F^i, a composite form describing the arrangement of parts.

2.2.2.2 Structural framework

A structural framework F^i is a 4-tuple $< G, SF^i, L, R >$.

G: G is the undirected connected graph of the structure consisting of the set of N nodes and the set of identified edge connections.

SF^i: SF^i is a set of N automata $\{sf_j\}^i$ produced under Sgc^i, the ith structure-generating convention. Sgc^i is an arbitrary design principle for machines which makes G into the circuit diagram of an automaton for relatively primitive, bit-dimensioned, information transfer.[5]

L: L is a set of N automata which when adjoined to SF inhibit or delay information to correspond to what is observed.

R: R is a set of N automata which when adjoined to SF augment the bit- dimensioned data flow of SF to the content level and rate observed.

Thus F^i emulates the data flow and interactions of an observed system in isolation from the elements E which are organized by F^i.

2.2.2.3 Effective formations

By the previous definition, a structural framework F^i, in isolation, executes the function in Sgc^i; it is *deemed effective* for that function. However, F^i in conjunction with E may not execute some arbitrary function or requirement: for example, F^i may not have sufficient complexity to realize the state potential in E or vice versa. In other words, they do not match— an excluded condition in machine design; a very possible condition in the socioeconomic context; where, for example, organizational infrastructure and individual departments or enterprises develop under distinct dynamic

---

[5] In combinatorial analysis one associates a graph with a given automaton. The convention here is to develop an automaton of standard form to associate with a given graph.

2.2. PRELIMINARIES

regimes. Mismatch as an essential cause of system failure, inefficiency, and uncontrollability is discussed in Albin (1980), where it is also shown that there exist counterpart, potentially realizable effective formations for any prespecified list of structural components. Our present concern is with performance problems that go beyond the assembly of consistent forms.

2.2.3 Generalized formations and finite surrogates

Consider the hypothetical substitution of an element $e_j^{()}$ into the position occupied by e_j in an effective formation S. $e_j^{()}$ may be variously: e^F, a finite formation; e^T a general type of nonfinite automaton labeled a Turing machine (with properties to be discussed in Section 2.2.4); or e^H, a human being subject to nondeterministic behavior.

2.2.3.1 Surrogate automata

It is not unreasonable to stipulate that any $e^{()}$ be restricted to finite sets of input and output symbols $X^{()}$ and $Z^{()}$. A surrogate automaton e^S is defined as a finite automaton which specifies $X^{()}$ and $Z^{()}$ and which when substituted in S (augmented to S' to maintain effectiveness) produces interactions comparable to those produced by $e^{()}$. Clearly e^S can be taken as identically equal to e^F, where e^F is the substituted element. In the case of e^T or e^H, e^S is any finite automaton which produces interactions in S which are judged by an observer to be appropriate, consistent with theory, approximating reality, approximating rationality, or meeting some other like criteria. Henceforth, a structure with component(s) $e^{()}$ will be referred to as a *generalized formation*, while the finite form with component(s) e^S will be referred to as the corresponding *surrogate formation* (or "finite surrogate" or "surrogate" where the context is clear).

2.2.3.2 Generalized formations

In one broad context the generalized formation could be any economy made up of small and large enterprises. The surrogate formation could be a model of that economy where each enterprise is represented by a finitized optimizing routine operating on the same input and output symbols as the generalized formation. Structural features of both might be well portrayed by attributes of the surrogate model—for example, the mechanics of a *tâtonnement* process could be specified with regard only to the surrogate formation. However, actual system outcomes depend upon the behaviors in $e^{()}$. (Thus the behavior of the system can be unusual if one $e_j^{()}$ departs from the rules of e^{S_j} and attempts to warehouse a year's output of precious metals.)

2.2.3.3 Modeling considerations

For reasons of convenience, most standard models are declared explicitly or tacitly to be finite or "effectively finite"—or, in present terms, representable by a surrogate formation. However, computational requirements are not usually examined with particular care; accordingly, several significant problems have been ignored in the literature. The most accessible problems concern the consistency of surrogate-formation representation with certain standard assumptions of decision rationality. In isolation, these assumptions seem harmless, although it will be seen that they have consequences which are anything but acceptable. To handle this case and prepare the ground for consideration of explicit generalized formations and still richer forms, it is necessary to introduce the concept of general computation and examine properties of the Turing machine automaton.

2.2.4 General computation and computability

A model to represent general computation, archival capacity, or the data bank expansion potential of a decision unit or enterprise is provided by the Turing machine.[6]

2.2.4.1 The Turing machine

The Turing machine is an abstract device consisting of a finite-state automaton (as defined earlier) which is linked to a tape on the following scheme: (1) the tape is divided into fields; (2) each field may be marked with symbols from a finite symbol set—the set includes a designated null symbol; (3) the finite "control automaton" has the capacity to read symbols on the tape and translate the symbol into an internal state; (4) the control has the capacity to "mark" the tape with a symbol according to an internal state; (5) the control can rewind or advance tape; (6) according to the requirements of calculation the control can order the manufacture of new tape. Requirement (6) provides for the archival characteristics of the Turing machine. It has also been shown that a Turing machine can model any stored-program computer and can represent any computable function or "realizable procedure." The nonfinite nature of the Turing machine is seen in the determinacy covering termination of computations.

Henceforth the reference computing device in this chapter is a Turing machine T and a tape t which contains an arbitrary finite string of symbols,

---

[6]The properties of Turing machine calculation are widely documented and discussed. Again, see Arbib (1980), Minsky (1967), Hopcroft and Ullman (1969), Kac and Ulam (1969), Hofstadter (1979), or any advanced computer science text. This section recapitulates standard results. Davis (1965) treats the broad range of undecidability problems.

2.2. PRELIMINARIES

some of which differ from the null symbol. T accepts t as input and, according to the programming of the finite device that controls T and according to the content and order of symbols on t, the machine will either halt on completing computations or it will compute indefinitely. (In the latter case the machine might have entered a loop, or perhaps gotten stuck in the decimal expansion of π, or perhaps be only one step away from completing a calculation.) As with finite automata, one is concerned with equivalent devices or the capacity to reproduce the behavior of a reference device. It is next shown that a universal simulating device exists, for example, that T is not unique.

2.2.4.2 A universal simulator

An intermediate-sized machine U is labeled a "universal simulator." U is a machine that will accept as input $d(T)$, a description of T. U is said to "simulate" T if for input $\{d(T), t\}$, U halts when T does or U computes indefinitely when T does. U is clearly constructible on one of several design principles. A brute-force design principle to build a machine $\bar{U}$ that will always work specifies for $\bar{U}$ a sector of blank finite-state memory M as large as the largest finite-control on a machine T. $\bar{U}$ then consists of $M+L$ where L is a load program that reads $d(T)$ into M and transfers logical control to M. Thus $\bar{U}$, given input $\{d(T), t\}$, reads $d(T)$ into M. Thereafter M becomes an exact duplicate of T and processes t exactly as does T. In more concrete terms, the existence in the economy of an element at the level of a Turing machine is no barrier to the analytical simulation of that economy.

2.2.4.3 A universal predictor

Given that T can be simulated, is it possible to devise UTM, a universal machine that will predict the behavior of T? Also it is important to know whether T will halt for input t. We know that UTM can contain a substructure equivalent to U permitting UTM to input and process $d(T)$. The issue is whether there can be additional circuitry or finesses in programming to permit UTM to compute as follows: Load UTM with the tape $\{d(T), t\}$: if T halts with t, UTM will compute a "yes" and halt; if T does not halt, UTM will compute a "no" and halt. The design intention, thus, is to build UTM so that it will always terminate calculations after determining the behavior of T. UTM is therefore a richer machine than U, which simply replicates T. It is clear that UTM is needed if one is to deal sensibly with systems containing T.

2.2.4.4 The halting problem

In computer science the problem of the constructibility of UTM is called the "halting problem" to which the following theorem applies.

Theorem 2.1 *UTM is unconstructible!*

Proof. The theorem is proved by demonstrating that its existence forces a logical contradiction. Assume that UTM exists and augment the basic machine with two accessory units, C and E. The unit C is an accessory "front end" that simply duplicates a tape input. Thus the machine C+UTM accepts the tape $\{d(T)\}$ as input and computes as would UTM with input tape $\{d(T), d(T)\}$. Next add an accessory "rear-end unit" E. E is an exit routine with the following properties: if UTM computes a "no," E causes a halt; if UTM computes a "yes," E causes the machine to loop indefinitely. Call the augmented machine UTM* = C+UTM+E. Now suppose T was given as input data the tape $d(T)$—there is no deception here; $d(T)$ is simply a string drawn from the same symbol list used for t. T will either halt or compute indefinitely on this input. If T halts, UTM will compute a "yes" and UTM* will go into a loop. If T does not halt UTM will compute a "no" and UTM* will halt. Suppose we feed UTM a tape containing $d($UTM*$)$, a self-description; what will be the outcome? From the preceding constructions we have:

—UTM* with input $d($UTM*$)$ halts when UTM* with input $d($UTM*$)$ does not halt

or

—UTM* with input $d($UTM*$)$ does not halt when UTM* with input $d($UTM*$)$ halts.

A clear contradiction which can only derive from the assertion that UTM was constructible, since there are no problems with the steps that gave us the simulator U, the copier C, and the exit routine E (the control for each of these components is individually finite, and their composition is easily sequenced and also finite).

Two important corollaries follow directly.

Corollary 2.2 *The extent to which a finite device can "satisfactorily" approximate a universal simulator U is itself an undecidable matter. It can be seen that whatever is the criterion for "satisfactory approximation," the automaton which predicts whether the criterion is met must be a UTM.*

Corollary 2.3 *Undecidability problems in one model can not be elided by specifying a second "simulating" model. On similar logic it is easily shown that the device which verifies the simulation is a UTM.*

2.3. UNDECIDABILITY

The impact of these corollaries (and many equivalent statements) is that the form in which undecidability is exhibited may be transformed (e.g., from systems undecidability to uncertainty concerning the goodness of an approximation) but it cannot be escaped.

2.2.4.5 Comments

The halting-problem, UTM impossibility, theorem is a specialized variant of the Gödel theorem. In Gödel terms the result is interpreted as meaning that a system rich enough to perform universal computation (the hypothetical UTM encompasses the rich machines, T and/or U) and rich enough to contain itself (e.g., the description $\{d(\text{UTM}^*)\}$ contains propositions which can be clearly specified (e.g., the assertion of the UTM's functions) but which are nonetheless undecidable (as shown by the impossibility of building the general UTM).

Note that the Gödel interpretation permits some predictability of Turing machine behaviors. It is possible, reasonable, and realistic to design a machine that will predict the behavior of some Turing machines on some data. The questions of interest to economic theory are: (1) What types of model are free of undecidability problems? (2) What types of propositions in what types of economic model are proven to generate undecidability problems? (3) Of what theoretical or practical significance are undecidability problems where they arise?

On the first question it is clear that where data sets and functions are strongly constrained it is possible to predict definitively the evasion of undecidability problems. Such is the case for linear equation systems and any number of activity-analysis forms. The only problem that can arise is that of finite-calculation of inordinate length. The second question, and the third, are of course the issues in this chapter.

2.3 Undecidability in generalized formations

This section shows that a model economy built up of individually identified finite-automaton components can be composed into a finite formation—again all problems of mismatch and communication are eliminated *arguendo* by the effective-structure convention. This model does not appear to pose special computational problems. However, the model is shown to be inconsistent with an assumption that one or more actors are capable of decision or forecasting rationality. In particular, the model can be no more than the finite surrogate for a richer system or generalized formation in which one or more elements must have capacities at least at the level of a Turing machine. It is shown further that within this generalized structure, or adjacent to it, there must be decision or evaluative mechanisms at the level of a universal machine. Therefore, there must be at least one class of intrinsic undecidable determinations associated with an economy which is in all other respects well specified.

2.3.1 An economy with finite automaton components

We consider the following elements to constitute a finite economy:

E: *A set of enterprises.* An enterprise $e_j \in E$ is a finite automaton (or a sequential machine composed of automaton departments). We think of e_j as processing price-symbol inputs into symbols representing: (a) orders for resources to alter its internal state, and (b) product outputs.

C: *A set of consumer units.* Each consumer unit is a finite automaton which processes price-type data into symbols representing: (a) labor availability and other factor rentals, (b) commodity orders. Again, there is no need to restrict quantity and type of data input although it is convenient to do so. It is also understood that income earned from factor rents conditions the unit's present state.

M: *A set of markets.* By convention, we label particular outputs with commodity designations, particular resources with factor designations, particular collections of enterprises with sectoral designations, particular people with class designations, and so on. Some of these designations constitute analytical categories (see subsequent discussion). Others identify economic goods and resources for which there are prices or price equivalents (such as imputed prices or shadow prices). Thus, for the jth identified economic good there is a market $m_j \in M$ which processes quantity-dimensioned symbols into price-dimensioned symbols. There is no harm at this time in specifying M also as a set of finite automata.

I: *The information set of descriptions of the economy.* An element $\mathbf{I}_t \in I$ is literally a vector of "statistics" dated as of the time t. The vector may be compiled from observables, for example, the price and quantity data; or, using some metaphysical process, $\mathbf{I}_t$ may include statistics computed from the internal states of participants in the economy. Statistics may be calculated at any level of aggregation for any analytical category. It is required only that the process of calculation itself forms a finite semigroup. Statistics, however, can also be referred to by outside analysts, philosophers and pundits who are at liberty to invent analytical categories for which statistics are computed free of cost. Statistics are also used by government as described next.

G: *A government.* The government collects a particular set of statistics $\mathbf{I}_t^g$ and effects a policy $\mathbf{g}(I_t^g)$ which consists of purchases, restrictions on price, taxes, transfers, and the like. We will examine the programmatic

2.3. UNDECIDABILITY

and welfare-theoretic structure of $\mathbf{g}(I_t^g)$ subsequently; for the moment we only require that the effects of $\mathbf{g}(I_t^g)$ be compatible with the behaviors of the automaton components of the system. This means, for example, that, if the government is making purchases, the impact on the market should not be other than that which could occur with increased consumer-unit purchases because of altered internal state (i.e., higher budgets) or altered price signals. Similarly the government's tax impact should be equivalent to an alteration of wage rates or prices as could occur through market reaction to some constellation of firm and consumer-unit behaviors. This restriction is here for convenience only; we simply place the government outside the system but limit its intervention in influencing system outcomes to those which seemingly are compatible with behaviors of an unregulated system.

T: *A set of timing conventions*. For the purpose of analysis it is necessary to require agreement on the length of the work day, accounting periods, times at which, ready or not, a decision must be made, and the like. It is assumed that agreement is reached on such conventions and that the timing of automata components is tied to this system of "clocks."

2.3.2 Structural properties of a finite economy

Referring to the scheme in Section 2.2.2 it is seen that the economy just described can be put into correspondence with a finite formation in which the element set E contains the automaton sets represented by firm, consumer, and markets (**E**, **C**, and **M**). The *ancillary set* A contains the government and perhaps the foreign sector and sources of external shocks. The structural framework for this model has as its graph the paths of interaction among participants. The automata sets of the framework handle all communication at the level required by theory. According to the effectiveness convention, all formations can be matched; while according to the substitution conventions the model can be broadened to cover larger numbers of participants or deepened to cover participants with compounded internal calculations. The set of "statistics" **I** is separated from the decision symbol sets of the finite calculating units.

2.3.3 Archival expansion: An economy with Turing machine components

Consider an enterprise $\mathbf{e}_j \in E$ which is constrained as before to generate finite sets of symbols corresponding to resource orders and product levels. Now give $\mathbf{e}_j$ access to a set of historical data $\mathbf{I}_j \subseteq \mathbf{I}$ and permit e_j to alter its responses at time t according to calculations made on $\mathbf{I}_j$. In effect $\mathbf{e}_j$ is permitted to project trends and condition its behavior in $(t+1)$

on a forecast of critical variables using historical state data running to time t. Assume that the firm's statisticians and econometricians produce "forecast" data sets $\mathbf{F}^k = \mathbf{f}_k(\mathbf{I}_j)$ where the $\mathbf{f}_k$ consists of a family of linear weighting schemes and the generation of the family can be represented as a procedure. Without further elaboration, it is clear that $\mathbf{I}_j$, the original archive of data, can be expanded indefinitely: for example, at any time $\mathbf{F}^k$ is finite computed to that date, but $\mathbf{F}$, the product set of $\mathbf{F}^k$, is not. In other words, the capacity to "project," as usually assumed for the firm engaged in rational decisions, is equivalent to an inherent capacity to expand archives and derived data to the limit of resources. The element is therefore put into correspondence with a Turing machine, and the formation describing the model economy becomes a generalized formation.

2.3.4 Conditional forecasting: Economies with universal machine components

Once one admits the possibility that an economic unit $\mathbf{e}_j$ is at the level of a Turing machine, it is inescapable that some other unit $\mathbf{e}_k$ will attempt the rational act of trying to forecast the behavior of $\mathbf{e}_j$ or of simulating an economy containing a replica of $\mathbf{e}_j$.

2.3.4.1 Universal forecasting

The appropriate format for such calculations is given by the universal forecaster, a Turing machine $\mathbf{U}_k$ with the capacity to accept as input a tape $\{d(\mathbf{T}_j), \mathbf{t}_j\}$ which contains $\mathbf{d}(\mathbf{T}_j)$, a description of Turing machine $\mathbf{T}_j$ and $\mathbf{t}_j$, representative data input to $\mathbf{T}_j$. $\mathbf{U}_k$ is said to forecast $\mathbf{T}_j$ if given input $\{d(\mathbf{T}_j), \mathbf{t}_j\}$, $\mathbf{U}_k$ produces output $\mathbf{O}_k(\mathbf{T}_j)$ when $\mathbf{T}_j$ produces $\mathbf{O}_j(\mathbf{T}_j)$ given input $\mathbf{t}_j$ and $\mathbf{O}_k(\mathbf{T}_j) = \mathbf{O}_j(\mathbf{T}_j)$. The output $\mathbf{O}_k(T_j)$ becomes part of the information set $\mathbf{I}_k$ on which $\mathbf{e}_k$ bases its determinations.

2.3.4.2 Rational forecasting

To recapitulate, the model economy is specified initially on the assumption of finite computing units. There are no problems with this construction; the economy reduces to a set of simultaneous equations in commodity-dimensioned data and these equations may or may not be solvable—a familiar topic for analysis. There is also no problem with conjectural variation in the original model, the finite computing automaton specified for unit $\mathbf{e}_j$ may have embedded within it a finite simulator of $\mathbf{e}_k$ without altering the logic of the structure in any fundamental way. Also, problems with stochastic data or system matching have been eliminated by assumption;

2.3. UNDECIDABILITY

while government at this part is given a purely passive role. In short, everything turns on the use made of archival data. If a unit is permitted to collate data on past states of the system and various subaggregates of the system, correlate these data sets with one another and parameters derived from previous correlations, and, finally, compute decisions based on these data, the unit has the structure of a Turing machine. Furthermore, on parallel reasoning, other units will react, implying that universal simulation must also exist within the economy. One way to eliminate these facts is to forbid an optimizing unit from using data which are available to it. This is the point at which the "decision-rationality" or "rational-forecasting" assumption bites.

To exclude rational feasible use of available data flies in the face of a major precept in economic theorizing, to include the assumption opens the door to undecidability problems. (The reader can anticipate that Theorem 2.1 will be applied to an economy in which the assumption gives rise to Turing machine components.) However, before investigating undecidability properties and the difference they might make, it is useful to examine the direct implications of the decision-rationality assumption and the possibility of its inoffensive evasion. On formal grounds we find that there is no simple escape. According to Corollary 2.2 it is improper to flatly assume that the calculations made by a component at the level of a Turing machine can be approximated by a finite structure. An alternative analytical strategy would involve metalogical constructions of the following sort: actors are not precluded from calculations at a Turing machine level; however, competitive conditions are such that every one is a price taker, expectations are homogeneous, and the only conceivable behaviors amount de facto to simple linear functions of market data from the preceding period. Under these conditions the ability to calculate on archives is a costly privilege that buys no benefits; it can therefore be excluded as an effective behavior. Not much can be said about this type of construction. Its verifiability would appear to require the ability to simulate deeply, thus bringing in either Theorem 2.1 or Corollary 2.3. Or the conditions can be taken on faith—a metaphysical escape from the metalogical. Otherwise, I see no evasions on this point that do not reduce to the given arguments.

2.3.5 Undecidability propositions

Given that ordinary calculation and decision-rationality assumptions imply the embedding within the economy of substructures at the level of the Turing machine or universal forecaster, the logical next step is to ask if putative UTM functions are anywhere implied by theory, and, if so, what determinations about the economy thereby rendered undecidable.

2.3.5.1 Microlevel nonconjectural calculations

The first case to consider is essentially an exercise that demonstrates that undecidability can exist without implying important welfare consequences. Internal to the individual firm there may be both Turing machine calculations over archival data and large-scale calculations on finite data which, for economic reasons, can be terminated before a global optimum is reached. In either instance the firm or an outside analyst could attempt to predict the extent to which actual calculations approximate optima. By construction this monitoring exercise requires a UTM, implying that general assertions as to whether internal calculations will be completed are untenable. But this, of course, is already well known in the many contexts where machine computation is used as a managerial tool. Firms do the best they can and on welfare grounds the pragmatic best, "the best results possible," must suffice. One can simply regret that the "best possible results" were not obtained and attempt to refine the decision and monitoring instruments to improve both the degree of approximation and estimates of the degree of approximation. Undecidability in this context appears to be an intrinsic property analogous to residual uncertainty or uncontrollable accounting errors and omissions.

2.3.5.2 Undecidability in conjectural forecasting

In the generalized-structure model of the economy given in Sections 2.3.3 and 2.3.4 universal forecasters $\mathbf{U}_k$ are embedded at one or more decision positions within the economy. These simulators compute variously: on data selections from $\mathbf{I}$ specific to unit $\mathbf{K}$, on simulations of unit j's data selections from $\mathbf{I}$ and calculations on these data, on simulations of unit j's simulations of unit k's calculations, on further rounds of recursive conjecture, on expanding archives of earlier analyses, and worse. These calculations are of course simulations at the level of U type automata. (They may or may not be economically justified in terms of net benefits for more complete use of available data.) Prediction of the outcome of such processes must be at the UTM level and this is so for inside participants (the decision units themselves) and for outside evaluators (e.g., a welfare economist). A listing of pertinent undecidable propositions is given in Table 2.1 along with sketch comments. Proof for each of the propositions is obtained by applying Theorem 2.1 and using Corollaries 2.2 and 2.3 to eliminate out-flanking of the theorem.

2.3.6 General comments

The structure of each proof is much the same. Each specifies a computer in the position of "seer" or predictor of systems outcomes. The propositions

2.3. UNDECIDABILITY

are statements about system outcomes taken from the seer's position while the proofs of undecidability translate into a denial of the existence of an infallible seer.

2.3.6.1 The firm

It is interesting to note that where the seer is an arm of a participant, the undecidability proof has no normative significance. The participant perforce must forecast and predict system outcomes even though a seer cannot guarantee the usefulness of the process in advance. Thus the customary disclaimer is formally based. Put another way; "not forecasting" consists in following some arbitrary rule. One cannot know in advance whether a systematic decision approach will improve on the rule and one does not know how much calculation in the seer's position is needed in order to substantiate that systematic decision making will produce a gain or not. It may be that the answer will be known after a microsecond of computation: it may be that one can never demonstrate the advantage of the systematic approach (the arbitrary rule might even be very close to correct for the circumstances). Obviously the prospect of undecidability should not be taken as an argument against using bigger and faster computers. The ability to complete more calculations during the decision interval means that some cases that formerly were on the verge of solution but were dumped in the undecidable category can be solved thus reducing the "residual" incompleteness of the systems. Finally, one notes that the participants always have some incentive to seek out intelligence on their competitors' decision processes. Once it is known that a counterpart operates a finite routine on a restricted data base, the behavior of that element can be calculated and the seer's function alters from UTM to U.

2.3.6.2 The government

Undecidability becomes an interesting system property where the seer is external to the system, either in the semiindependent position of predictor of policy effectiveness within the government or as a completely independent "welfare economist." When the seer sits within government, three different types of questions arise. First, for obvious political reasons, the inability to "give a definite answer one way or the other" on questions of policy prediction is a more significant admission than that of the private-enterprise seer also faced with undecidability. The second turns on the fact that the government seer also must act with regard to optimization over the augmented data set I. This adds one more level to calculations. For example a system outcome may turn out to be computable in the absence of government but now government contemplates intervention to approximate a state described in I; this can throw the calculation back to the seer for further computation as before; but it can also open up a new problem—that of adjusting welfare criteria to accommodate the realities of the set of attainable sets. This issue implies a different type of evaluation and is the subject of Section 2.4. The final question concerns the role of government as a coordinator of activities, for example, as the instrument or predictor of an indicative plan. Here there may be a route for partial evasion of undecidability problems. Indicative planning is usually thought of as an interactive systematically designed exchange of information aimed at reducing uncertainty about the prospective behavior of participants. The information-exchange process can be terminated at any stage at which pertinent commitments can be struck, penalties on noncompliance agreed to, the system, in effect, reduced to a linear finite form. From this point on, undecidability has no welfare significance since a bargained position has been reached. Of course, undecidability surrounds prior predictions of the commitment point.

2.3.6.3 The welfare theorist

With the seer in the position of welfare economist three points are suggested. First, there is no problem with regard to the technical "existence" of equilibrium. Equilibrium is a topological property—there is either a fixed point under some group of transformations or there is not and this fact may be ascertainable without calculating the transformations. Undecidability does enter on the issue of "attainability" of an existing fixed point since the dynamic process of search can be translated directly into a program of computation which need not be finite. There is no great surprise here—one has always known that a fixed point could be evaded by freakish or contrary behavior—the proof shows that it is not necessarily attainable with systematic behavior (or, more properly, the general question of attainability is undecidable).

The second point is that an additional disclaimer should be attached to general welfare conclusions predicated on the achievement of some approximation of competitive equilibrium since the degree of approximation is unascertainable. The third point is that in partial-equilibrium analysis one should suspect assumptions that substructures are adjusted to a general equilibrium position. "Homogeneous expectations" in the theory of finance is one such suspect convention as it implies the perfect simulation of deep and recursively conjectural calculations of a counterpart sector (firms vis-à-vis investors with regard to distinct capital-budgeting and valuation computations) (Albin, 1975). The feeling with regard to "rational-expectation" assumptions is similar.

2.3.6.4 Provisional conclusions

As suggested in the introduction there is an insubstantial and ephemeral quality to the Gödel theorem. This should have been brought home to the reader by the examples given thus far. Just what do these results mean? An analogy may help. In historical context, the Gödel result put to an end the Hilbert program of "arithmetizing" all of mathematics; that is, attempting to find a simple structure in primitive statements that would subsume all formal axiomatic systems or serve as their generator. The Gödel theorem showed the futility of that grand ambition but implied no inhibitions on the systematic development of individual mathematical fields. An economic system is shown on its own terms to be as rich as general mathematics and the analogy suggests the impossibility of proposing nonvacuous universal properties for its functions. The assertion of such properties is *Hubris*. To be sure, one can derive hypotheses on general system functions from analysis of partial or finite systems and it is not unreasonable to specify them as assumptions with a disclaimer attached. Typically, the degree of harm or benefit which accrues from analysis or action predicated on such assumptions is itself undecidable. The proof is left to the reader.

2.4 Social welfare evaluations

The analysis in Section 2.3.6 left off on one important question: the action of government where there is adequate knowledge of attainable system states but where a problem of accommodating the choice of states with welfare criteria remains. This is a higher-level question than those considered in Section 2.3 since recursive conjectures are *arguendo* assumed away and the attainability of a set of system states is not in doubt.

2.4.1 The decision setting

The elements in the social decision problem are stylized as a state set, a set of individual "opinions," a social-welfare operation whereby social rankings of states are computed from individual opinions, and a list of acceptability criteria.

2.4.1.1 States

A state st_j consists of a finite description of the economy and/or social environment. ST, the state set, is a finite set of such descriptions. ST may contain incomplete descriptions, omitted states, even descriptions of unfeasible states and utopias. For convenience, the status quo is distinguished as st_0. The intent, here, is to impose no restriction or calculating problem on determination of ST. *Arguendo*, state descriptions can be as detailed or simple as one pleases. $\text{ST}^m \subseteq \text{ST}$ is the state set agreed on as operating for the mth decision context.

2.4.1.2 Opinions

An opinion o_{ji} is the ith individual's opinion of the jth state; o_{ji}^k denotes an opinion formed under conditions of the kth state; o_{ji}^0 is an opinion formed under the status quo. An opinion may be in any format: a table of pairwise rankings of states; a complete cardinal utility index over states; incomplete rankings for some individuals, complete for others; fragmentary data on preferences, such as might be obtained from surveys; data for a few representative individuals; data for particular groups within the polity. The only restriction is that the set of opinions for the mth social determination be finite. This set is designated $O^m \subseteq O$, O being the set of opinions in all contexts.

2.4.1.3 Social welfare operations

The social welfare operation is broken down into two computable components: evaluation and ranking. *Evaluation* consists of a procedure whereby a numerical index wt_j is attached to the jth state. Specifically, an evaluation function $w^a(\text{ST}^m, O^m) \to wt_j$, for all $st_j \in \text{ST}^m$, is a computable routine; where $w^a()$ is the ath member of W^m, the class of evaluation routines designated as admissible in the mth context. *Ranking* consists of forming binary relationships r_{jk} over wt_j, wt_k, where $r_{jk} \equiv wt_j \cdot r \cdot wt_k$ connotes wt_j is in the relationship $\cdot r \cdot$ with respect to wt_k. R_a^m is the set $\{r_{jk}\}$ formed under the ath evaluation routine in the mth context.

In summary, the social welfare operation consists of forming a set of binary relationships in state space. These are obtained by computable steps. The calculations could cover all possible states but need not; they could be responsive to individual preferences but need not be; they could result in a strong ordering over states; but for trivial intermediate calculations R_a^m could end up as a contentless equivalence relationship over all states. The test comes when R_a^m is judged against criteria for acceptability or rankings as a basis for social action or choice.

2.4.1.4 Acceptability criteria

A ranking may or may not be politically acceptable. We consider the rankings R (either pairwise or entirely) in conjunction with one or more criteria $L^{()} \in L$. Among the classes of criteria are:

2.4. SOCIAL WELFARE EVALUATIONS

$L^O = L^O(R, O)$, which requires consistency between rankings and individual opinions. The Arrow axioms and system are an example.

$L^{st} = L^{st}(R, \text{ST})$, which requires consistency between rankings and some restriction based on parameters in ST, for example, rankings must be consistent with Pareto dominance on some simple characteristic.

$L^I = L^I(R, I)$, where I represents some set of ideological requirements.

$L^Q = L^Q(R, O)$, which establishes basic restrictions on the consistency of rankings; for example, strong ordering.

$L^k = L^k(R, O)$, which establishes a restriction on orderings according to opinions in states other than the status quo. The Kaldor-Hicks analysis, which considers pre- and postchange rankings would fit this category (Nath, 1969).

$L^y = L^y(R, Y)$, which covers some other restriction, reasonable or not.

This scheme generalizes the evaluation process. A social ordering is produced by computable routines in a format which permits computable comparisons with acceptability criteria. The criteria can be imposed with greater or lesser degrees of restrictions: thus in the class L^O is the full set of Arrow axioms L_F^O, but also a weaker version L_W^O, which, say, permits the dictatorial outcome. In the class L^I is L_F^I, a full set of market freedom requirements, but also L_W^I, a weakened requirement permitting price controls. A ranking may be unacceptable under L_F^O and L_F^I but acceptable under L_W^O and L_W^I, implying that acceptance of the ranking by implementing its state ordering connotes controls under actual or tacit dictatorship. Generalizing the notion, in each criterion class is a null or noneffective form so that any ranking can be acceptable ultimately; but ultimate acceptability means that some welfare or political tests are not satisfied. More to the point, there is assumed to be a prevailing, established, or traditional set of acceptability criteria which constitutes the framework of social and political action. The "political-process" has two aspects; the first involves the development of policies and/or programs to be consistent with the framework, the second involves modification of the framework to obtain a fit with feasible states presented as policies or programs. Thus, the political process constitutes a procedure which terminates when a fit of one sort or another is obtained between programs and criteria. The process must terminate since the system must be in some state, whether bliss, pragmatic compromise, lingering status quo, chaos prior to revolution, or dictatorship. In this respect the social welfare operations and evaluation procedures are seen as provisional calculations which describe the political implications of states under consideration or which predict the consequences of a political process.

2.4.2 The political process

We require a general metamodel of political processes. A policy proposal or, variously, a candidate, platform, slate, or government is considered. The proposal is described as a state st' in ST and the state is evaluated as in Section 2.4.1 according to the following stylized procedures.

2.4.2.1 Acceptable and provisionally acceptable proposals

A proposal st' can be consistent with the established restrictions in L, in which case: (a) it can be accepted for implementation; or (b) it can be provisionally accepted but steps are taken to find other acceptable proposals which produce a higher welfare evaluation; or (c) it can be treated as provisionally unacceptable.

2.4.2.2 Unacceptable proposals

A proposal st' appears as unacceptable (or provisionally unacceptable) because of inconsistency with established restrictions in L. The problem, then, is to offer new proposals which can satisfy L or otherwise alter the decision process. Recall that rankings of candidate proposals are generated via the function $W(O)$; thus abridging the selection of opinions might be one technique of developing acceptability. Similarly the list of states in S to be considered could be reduced (thus eliminating the "relevant alternative" that might disrupt rankings), the selection of functions from W might also be replaced or (with reluctance or not) the standards in L might be relaxed.

2.4.2.3 Computable routines for generalizing alternative proposals

We consider five steps which could be taken in light of the above. The symbol given first represents the title of a computable subroutine.

Step 1 (ρ) Continued search under a composition of W and L to improve the evaluation. That is, if proposal st_j emerges as acceptable under a ranking R_{ij}, the routine searches for other proposals st_k that satisfy the same criteria. ρ connotes the enumeration of acceptable states beyond simply finding the first.

Step 2 (Θ). Elimination of opinions from O and recalculating W on the basis of an "alternative constituency." Θ corresponds politically to eliminating and selecting the members of coalitions or determining constituencies to find a new group that counts.

2.4. SOCIAL WELFARE EVALUATIONS

Step 3 ($-\Sigma$). The operation of eliminating proposed states from those considered under W and recalculating rankings among the remaining states. The elimination of irrelevant (or relevant) alternatives can result in finding an acceptable proposal, albeit within a restricted subset of states $st' \in S$. On the same reasoning one could define $(+\Sigma_j)$ for the addition of a state to a restricted subset: that is, $(+\Sigma_j)$ adds states st_j to the set st'.

Step 4 (ϕ). The operation of selecting an alternative function W_ϕ, from W. The functions in W are finite and indexed. ϕ consists of selecting the index of an eligible function.

Step 5 (λ). The last resort: changing (relaxing) the restrictions in L. The restrictions are finite and indexed. Λ consists of selecting the index of the next restriction to be imposed.

2.4.3 The computability of a political program

2.4.3.1 Definitions

We define a program as a sequence of steps—for example, (ρ, ρ, Σ, Σ, ρ, ϕ), or (ρ,Σ,ρ, Σ). Such a program is, by previous definitions, a computable routine since all of the sets and operations involved are finite. A program consists of a computable operation on a selection from these elements; thus programs form a class of computable operations.

2.4.3.2 Labeling of programs

For convenience in what follows we number programs according to a specific convention (Gödel numbering). We arrange routines lexicographically: routines with one operation (ρ), (Θ), (Σ), (ϕ), (λ) are numbered respectively 1, 2, 3, 4, 5; the numbering continues with two-element programs, for example, (ρ,ρ), (ρ,Θ), (ρ,Σ),..., (λ,λ) become 6, 7, 8, ..., and so through 3, 4,...N-element programs. However, we distinguish as separate entities the category of one-element programs P^1, the category of two-element programs P^2,..., the category of N-element programs, and so forth. We note that the category of a program can always be discovered from its place in the numbering; for example, the program numbered 27 must be in the two-element category, that numbered 42 must be in the three-element category and so forth.[7]

A program is therefore given as a sequence of political operations or calculations that must eventually terminate. Note also that the operations cover most of what is considered apposite and relevant in choice theory.

---

[7]The lexicographic numbering could, of course, be altered to cover cases of specific selections: e.g., (Θ_j), (Σ_j), ($\Theta_j, \Theta_k, \Sigma_i$), and so forth.

Thus a sequence of Θ operations consists of a sequence of trial coalitions; a specific Θ sequence is one politician's program on how to form a constituency and by repeated operations of $+\Theta$ and $-\Theta$ all possible coalitions over the set of individuals can be formed. Similarly a sequence of Σ operations represents an attempt to order the choice among states so that an acceptable ranking can be found within a restricted list of alternatives, and a similar programmatic interpretation applies to the other operations.

The problem is to discover *where* the process will stop. A "pundit" is defined as a computer which can predict the Gödel number of the program which causes an acceptability match and a halt to the political process. Since the Gödel number uniquely identifies the operations and selections performed in the process, it uniquely defines the social welfare and political properties of a policy or programmatic solution. As one has been led to expect, the pundit computer is unconstructible.

Theorem 2.4 *The pundit computer is unconstructible: that is—the pundit problem is undecidable.*

A detailed proof for a simpler case is given in Albin (1975); its logic is similar to that of Theorem 2.1 and will be stated here. The proposed pundit computer P^* must be able to predict whether a halt will occur for input P^n, the Gödel number of the nth program. An inconsistency connoting undecidability occurs (as before) if the nth self description P^n is imbedded in any of the "ideal" data sets (e.g., S, O, or the descriptions of W, L) required by the program. A program to screen out these potentialities is similarly excluded. One is left with the routine exercise of trying out P^n and seeing if it works. There is no hope of a pundit machine that can generally anticipate the outcome of such exercises.

2.4.3.3 Interpretations

The unconstructibility of the pundit machine is a result in metaeconomics or metapolitics as the case may be. In metapolitics it offers an undecidability answer to a natural question—but one which, to my knowledge, is not asked within the discipline of politics itself. In metaeconomics the result is more interesting as it raises doubts which touch on practices within the discipline. According to the theorem, it is not unreasonable to check the consistency of a particular social ranking (derived with reference to individual preferences, or not) of states with a particular list of criteria (associated with individual preferences, or not). Two things are unreasonable, however: (a) within the discipline of economics, it is unreasonable to assume that a generalized political process leads to satisfaction of welfare criteria more restricted than the null restrictions in L; such blithe assumptions are

2.4. SOCIAL WELFARE EVALUATIONS

equivalent to assuming the constructibility of P^*; (b) within the metadiscipline of welfare economics, it is unreasonable to engage the problem of the social welfare function on other than an ad hoc basis. In other words, one act carried out by social welfare theorists as a class is the systematic amendment of the Arrow axioms (an element of L) and parallel restriction of the state set. This program can be put in one-to-one correspondence with the pundit program; therefore the general outcome is undecidable. The text specifies L and W so that they would subsume all standard operations and forms in welfare theory. In this subjective sense, the pundit theorem is comprehensive. Its strength is shown by the discussion and theorem following, which cover undecidability in a context where a local optimum is well specified.

2.4.4 Predictability of restricted programs

Now suppose that a proposal st passed the acceptability criteria at a level of restriction $\bar{L}$ corresponding to a particular set in $L^{()}$. Suppose also that there is foreknowledge that a local optimum $\bar{st}$ exists, that is, $\hat{w}(\bar{st}) \geq \hat{w}(st)$ or $\bar{st} \cdot r \cdot st_j$ for some evaluation function in W. The foreknowledge can even be so great as to include an upper bound for $\hat{w}_t$. The context for this situation could be an instance in which a pragmatic solution is reached but there is external evidence or belief that it can be improved upon.

2.4.4.1 A competition to improve welfare

Our concern is with a set of "candidate" programs $< P^G, q >_\pi$. π is an index denoting a specific program in the set. G connotes the lexicographic level of the Gödel number of a program, specified earlier. Thus P^1 connotes 1-instruction programs; P^2, 2-instruction programs, ..., P^N, N-instruction programs, etc. q is an upper limit on the number of steps the program can take (equivalent to a time bound for calculation). Define c_π as the number of "critical steps," taken by the πth program, where a critical step is understood to be, simply, a check as to whether an amendment of the original proposal could lead to an increment in welfare. Such an amendment could be the extension of the set of individuals for whom a proposal is favorable to cover one more person, or testing whether a unit tightening of criteria in L can be met. The πth candidate program contends against $< P^N, q >$ programs. A winning candidate $< P^N, q >_{\bar{\pi}}$ is the first valid entry (N-instruction program meeting the time bound) for which it can be shown that $C_{\bar{\pi}} \geq C_\pi$ for all other valid candidates of the form $< P^N, q >_\pi$.

Clearly the set of valid programs $\{< P^N, q >_\pi\}$ is finite since P^N and q are both finite, therefore $\pi \leq \bar{V}$, an arbitrary bound, and the set of entries $C_N = \{C_\pi | \pi \leq \bar{V} \text{ for some q}\}$ must be finite. $M(N) = max(C_N)$ is, accordingly, well defined, and the winning candidate $< P^n, q >_{\bar{\pi}}$ must have $c_{\bar{\pi}} = M(N)$. However, we have the following.

Theorem 2.5 *M(N) is uncomputable.*

A detailed proof is given in Appendix A.[8] The logic here is slightly different from that in Theorems 2.1 and 2.4 and is given in sketch form. To paraphrase the proof, we begin with the assertion in the economic domain that application of program subroutines as defined for Theorem 2.4 could lead to opportunities for welfare improvement—each opportunity labeled a critical step. It is shown that the actual number of improvements can not exceed the number of critical steps. Attention centers on predicting the number of critical steps a program of particular size and complexity might encounter. Prediction of the outcome of such a process is tantamount to possessing a function which gives the maximum of a set of function productions. A corresponding simple Turing machine is proposed for this function and, using only housekeeping-type routines, it is shown that this machine leads to a numerical contradiction. Working backward along the chain of contradictions, the invalid construction was the initial stipulation of being able to pick out the best way to improve on the initial position via restricted finite programs. In metaeconomic terms the preselection of the best finite optimizing strategy starting from an acceptable social welfare suboptimum cannot be determined.

2.5 Conclusions

Each of the three theorems given here has essentially the same structure and teaches the same lesson: that a system can be composed of finite elements and can feature well-specified operations; yet propositions pertaining to some important aspect of the system could end up formally undecidable. In certain respects the results are surprising, particularly if one is inclined to think about an economy in terms of the many models deriving from the physical sciences. There, a system is either solvable or it is not and unsolvability is usually attributable to obvious causes which can be discovered in the geometry of the model. The calculations concerning these features are essentially extrinsic to the subject matter of the theory itself.

The metamathematical approach is different in that it presupposes calculation as an intrinsic part of the system. On these grounds, economic systems which feature internal calculation are intrinsically rich and it should come as no surprise that there are unknowable aspects in a system which is complicated enough to include its analysis.

---

[8]Theorem 2.5 is a variant of the "Busy Beaver Club" problem (see Thatcher, 1970).

Table 2.1
Undecidable propositions in the generalized-formation structural model

Case	Context Type of calculation (1)	T equivalent (2)	U equivalent (3)	UTM equivalent (undecidable proposition) (4)	Comments/welfare connotations (5)
A	*Firm* Local optimization	Family of models (e.g., various OR models) operating on data archives.	Simulator gives equilibrium of firm for each model in (2).	"Consultant" on best modeling strategy. (Attainability of "best" local position cannot be determined a priori.)	Undecidability is of negligible practical importance in this case. "Best approximation" or "bounded-rationality" solutions are accepted as facts of life and are accounted for in welfare theory. Note that practical problems of computational complexity in algorithms (e.g., NP complexity) may be of dominating concern.
B	*Firm* Forecasting[1]	Forecasting model operating on data archive.	Forecasting model specifying conditional behaviors of units forecasting as in B(2). "Forecasting-rationality" assumption applies.	"Consultant"'s evaluation of system forecasting procedures. (A general procedure to anticipate conjectural variations in behavior is unattainable.) (An evaluation device to determine the "best" forecasting model is unconstructible.)	Undecidability is a significant system property; however, one which in practice may be swamped by stochastic uncertainty—to a degree unknown. (See table footnote on p. 102.) Outcomes in systems containing self-referential conjectural behaviors are subject to "residual uncertainty." This does not eliminate the incentive to improve private forecasts: however, "forecasting rationality" implies indeterminacy in an otherwise finite (linear) system.

Table 2.1 (continued)

Case	Context Type of calculation (1)	T equivalent (2)	U equivalent (3)	UTM equivalent (undecidable proposition) (4)	Comments/welfare connotations (5)
C	*Government* Forecasting as a basis for policy	Control model (can be assumed to be algorithmic) operates on system states to produce "policy influenced" states. Data archive as in B(2) plus additional set of "statistics" (see text) applying to criterion functions.	Simulation of system states under different policy regimes in C(2) by simulating Turing machine accepting parameters of control model as data.	"Economists" formulating theory of optimal macrodynamic policy. (A general procedure to determine the best global control model is unconstructible.) (The optimal complexity—e.g., depth of intervention—of a control procedure or model is indeterminate.)	Again, undecidability should not inhibit attempts to find better control models. It simply urges caution in extending claims for their generality. Note that undecidability appears to be a property of the thought structure presumed for "rational expectations." Would not recognition of the presence of such an intrinsic limit to calculation create dominating system uncertainty that would invalidate the approach?
D	*Firm* Forecasting where government policy is an element of the system	Models as in B(2) but where system states connoting government intervention are data. Archives as in B(2) along with proxies for government statistics.	Simulation as in B(3) plus an additional level of C(2) functions.	"Economist" as in C(4). (Undecidability as in C(4) is unaffected by deeper recursiveness—more precisely, the degree to which undecidability is relieved by additional recursiveness is undecidable.)	Same as C(5).
	Deeper recursive structures—e.g., government forecasting, firm forecasting government	Models one level deeper.	Further depth.		

Table 2.1 (continued)

Case	Context: Type of calculation (1)	T equivalent (2)	U equivalent (3)	UTM equivalent (undecidable proposition) (4)	Comments/welfare connotations (5)
E_1	*Firm* Capital budgeting	Capital budgeting model incorporating a rationing criterion (e.g., cost of capital) based on capital market behavior (stock valuation).	Imbedded simulation of investor model $E_1(2)$ using archive of capital market data to isolate valuation criteria.	"Financial theorist"'s capital market model. (The extent to which the system conforms to the assumption of "homogeneous expectations" can not be determined.)	If there is residual uncertainty concerning the homogeneity of expectations, then rational actors (firms or investors) must correct their anticipations to take account of discrepancies. There must then be undecidability with respect to a theory of the "goodness" of corrections and for recursive corrections. This argument would seem to undercut the usefulness of the assumption.
E_2	*Investor* Portfolio selection based on security analysis	Valuation and/or portfolio-selection models incorporating predictions of firm performance using behavioral models incorporating a rationing criterion.	Imbedded simulation of firm $E_2(2)$ using archive of firm data to isolate behavioral criteria.		
E_3	*Capital market* Capital allocation process	Above models.	Composition of $E_1(3)$ and $E_2(3)$.	"Welfare theorist"'s analysis of market-controlled dynamic investment path based on $E_3(3)$. (A program to determine whether the economy is on a discrepancy-free path—above—is unconstructible.)	Even without bringing in undecidability, dynamic efficiency is difficult to defend as a welfare property except in extremely artificial models. Undecidability is one more straw on an already backbreaking load.

Table 2.1 (continued)

Case	Context Type of calculation (1)	T equivalent (2)	U equivalent (3)	UTM equivalent (undecidable proposition) (4)	Comments/welfare connotations (5)
F	*External welfare theorist* General-equilibrium calculations	Sets of actors and archives as in text. Specific model of behavior.	Simulation of F(2) for a class of models with respect to attainability of equilibrium.	Welfare economics as a program. (Although individual model configurations may demonstrate attainable equilibria, a program to refine and evaluate attainability criteria is unconstructible.)	"Attainability" has always been distinguished from "existence" as a stronger condition. The result applies to a program of research activity aimed at refining conditions for attainability over broad classes of models. Results holding for one model configuration do not necessarily go through if the model is augmented with additional recursiveness or expanded archives.

[1] "Forecasting" should be interpreted here as "projecting via simulation" in a deterministic model. The deterministic model may be specified with parameters that derive from econometric analyses, but stochastic uncertainty is not at issue here. Undecidability is a property of the formal system—that the system can only be described with stochastic uncertainty is an additional concern. Needless to say, there is no formally decidable way to discriminate between the two types of indeterminacy. In short, the usage here isolates the simulation or system-projecting aspect of forecasting from estimation properties.

Appendix: Proof of Theorem 2.5

$M(N)$ as defined in the text is to be put into correspondence with a Turing machine which computes a monotonic function $M'(N)$, for example, $N_1 < N_2 \Rightarrow M'(N_1) < M'(N_2)$. This machine also contains a stereotyped K_0-step subroutine that must result in one critical step being taken.

The critical step corresponds to the simplest test routine in the instruction set for P^c. It follows therefore that $M'(N_1) < M'(N_2 + K_0)$ and also $N_1 < N_2 + K_0$ (this must be so since the default case $N_2 + K_0 < N_1 \Rightarrow M'(N_2 + K_0) \leq M'(N_1)$, which would contradict the original assumption, $N_1 < N_2$ used to define monotonicity).

Given $N_1 < N_2 + K_0$ it must be that

$$M'(N_1) \leq M'(N_2) \Rightarrow N_1 \leq N_2 + (K_0 - 1) \tag{2.1}$$

Now assume M' is computable via a K_1-step program, P'_m and consider a composite program $n_2 P'_m P'_m$ which (starts with blank tape and writes the number N_2) $\rightarrow$ (computes $M'(N_2)$) $\rightarrow$ (computes $M'(M'(N_2)))$. It is known that the program n_2 must have at least $2N_2 + 2$ instructions (one instruction to start; N_2 mark tape instructions, alternating with N_2 advance-tape instructions; and a final instruction to transfer control). By assumption, P'_m has K_1 instructions: therefore the composite program has at least $2N_2 + 2K_1$ instructions (the composition of programs allows us to drop the first instruction in P'_m initially and for the replication). Thus $M'(M'(N_2))$ can be no larger than the number of instructions needed for its inscription, for example, $2N_2 + 2K_1$, and, since the maximum for $(2N_2 + 2K_1)$ is $M'(2N_2 + 2K_1)$, we have

$$M'(M'(N_2)) \leq M'(2N_2 + 2K_1)$$

and by inequality (2.1) above,

$$M'(N_2) \leq 2N_2 + (2K_1 + K_0 - 1) \tag{2.2}$$

To obtain a contradiction we need to show

$$2N_2 + (2K_1 + K_0 - 1) > M'(N_2) \tag{2.3}$$

This is done through the auxiliary routine bSQ, which when started with a blank tape prints B^2 marks. b has $2B+2$ instructions and SQ is arbitrarily assigned K_3 instructions. Therefore, on the logic used for the function N_2 the following inequality must hold

$$B^2 \leq M'(2B + K_3 + 1)$$

(this time there was only one sequencing so only one instruction was lost in the composition). However, we know that there must be some B large enough so that an arbitrary linear function in B is exceeded by B^2. Therefore, for some value B_0,

$$2B_0 + (K_3 + 1) + (2K_1 + K_0 - 1) \leq B_0^2 \leq M'(2B_0 + (K_3 + 1)) \quad (2.4)$$

Now assign to N_2 the value $2B_0 + K_3 + 1$. Substituting in (2.4) gives

$$N_2 + (2K_1 + K_0 - 1) < M'(N_2)$$

which directly contradicts (2.3) and, thus, demonstrates the theorem.

Chapter 3

Microeconomic Foundations of Cyclical Irregularities or "Chaos"

3.1 Introduction

Phenomena described variously as pseudorandom, irregularly cyclical, or chaotic can appear in comparatively simple aggregate models.[1] This chapter takes a microeconomic perspective and examines conditions in the small which appear to underlie irregular behavior in the large. A useful point of departure is a nonlinear version of the familiar neoclassical aggregate growth model (Day, 1982a) which exhibits both conventional and irregular dynamics. A parallel microeconomic analysis will tell us more about why the chaotic anomaly occurs in this and similar formats; it will also give us a better fix on the likely frequency of chaotic phenomena and insights into their informational properties. In addition, the microeconomic approach yields the unexpected dividend of a rigorous and easily applied classification scheme for dynamic systems and the data produced by them. We will

---

[1] Papers looking explicitly at the chaos phenomenon are cited in Benhabib and Day (1981) and Day (1982a, 1982b). A wide literature encounters other nontraditional dynamic phenomena including strange attractors, limit cycles, bifurcations of various types, catastrophes, and general pseudorandomness. Many of these nonlinear dynamic effects overlap chaos or coinhabit the same model types. See Semmler (1986) for a review from the perspective of limit cycles and Simon (1984) for methodological justification of microeconomic approaches to complex dynamic processes. In Samuelson's classification scheme for nonlinear systems (1947, ch. X, fig. 6) the chaos potentiality is recorded as a case of "neutral oscillation." To the extent that nomenclature matters, we will find that this descriptive is apt.

see that a deterministic microeconomy which supports chaotic macrodynamics is capable of generating two simpler types of behavior: uniformity over time and regular periodicity. This we should expect. A greater surprise, however, is the finding that the same economy can also produce a type of behavior that is qualitatively richer than chaos and far more interesting in its economic implications. The last phenomenon can manifest itself in aggregate data compiled from the micromodel as an apparent profound structural or regime change. It turns out that only seemingly minor alterations in the parameters of a model microeconomy account for which of these four qualitative macrobehaviors will appear. Each poses quite different policy and informational problems; so it is particularly useful to view the chaos case within this larger framework.

After the background discussion of the general research problem in Section 3.2, we turn in Section 3.3 to a microeconomic model that illuminates the source of the chaos outcome and also expedites the general classification of dynamic behaviors. Section 3.4 explores implications and alternate interpretations; while Section 3.5 considers additional applications and lines for further research.

3.2 The research problem

Models very close to the neoclassical growth schema can generate "irregular growth cycles," described as "wandering," "chaotic" patterns "not unlike those observed in reality" (Day, 1982a). The patterns are produced by deterministic difference-equation models which differ in a few not-unrealistic specifications from models which many have come to associate with regular dynamic behavior. This line of analysis which draws on the recent mathematical discipline of chaos theory (Smale, 1967; Li and Yorke, 1975) demonstrates: (1) that quite simple model structures can produce complex behaviors such as those commonly associated with reactions to sporadic massive shocks; (2) that the same deterministic model can exhibit stable monotonic growth, regular cycles or chaos; and (3) that the phenomena in question obtain in "wide classes of difference equations."

The informational implications of phenomena of this sort can be quite unsettling. How useful can inferences deriving from a model be if ostensibly minor alterations in its specification lead to dramatic changes in system performance and behavior? Less clear are matters of applicability, appropriateness, and causation: Are the phenomena more or less significant than "true" random shocks or structural changes? Does the problem lie in the choice of the aggregate difference-equation format as an approximating scheme?[2] What are the micro-foundations of the phenomena? What is

---

[2]It should also be noted that the irregular consequences of nonlinear models hardly

3.2. THE RESEARCH PROBLEM

the expected frequency of their occurrence? What other important model forms produce them? Do they play any natural, constructive, or intuitive role in theory? What expedients or informational strategies are available to rational agents or policy makers who must face chaos (or worse)?

3.2.1 The meaning of "chaos" in dynamic systems

Irregular growth might appear to be a natural phenomenon—another "stylized fact" of a dynamic economy. Unfortunately, the chaos theory explanation of what is happening requires a level of abstraction several steps removed from natural economic behavior: ". . . [the] process . . . [is] somewhat like shuffling cards, so that the 'passage of time' through the nonlinear dynamic equation acts more or less like a random number generator!" (Day, 1982a). In effect, where reasonable economic assumptions do not exclude certain mathematical conditions (Smale, 1967; Li and Yorke, 1975), the solution interval of the system ". . . contains more and more 'wrinkles' . . . " that permit the generation of cycles of every order and no set periodicity. (Or see May, 1975, 461-463.) However, although the processes that build on the wrinkles are recondite, the wrinkles themselves may arise for mundane reasons.

A nonlinear neoclassical model of accumulation

Consider the following difference-equation variant of the Solovian neoclassical growth model:

$$K^{t+1} = K^t + \Delta K = K^t + s \cdot F(K^t, L^t) \cdot B(k^t)$$

where K is a measure of capital stock, L is the labor supply, and $F(\cdot)$: $Y = F(K, L)$ is a neoclassical production function with the usual properties for Y equal to net aggregate output after making good depreciation. The capital/labor ratio is given by k, and assume for the moment that the expression $B(k^t)$ is equal to unity. With s defined as the saving ratio and with the original Solovian assumptions, the equation describes the capital formation of the economy.

Next, perform the conventional substitution of $f(k)L$ for $F(k,1)L = F(K,L)$ and divide both sides of the equation by $L \cdot (1+\lambda)$, where λ is the

---

come as a surprise to those experienced with work in the medium or familiar with the vast literature on nonlinear dynamic systems. In addition, many of us have inadvertently encountered the phenomenon on the blackboard when attempting to reproduce the cobweb theorem with curvilinear demand and supply functions. Chaos theory codifies such phenomena for a class of common difference and differential equation systems.

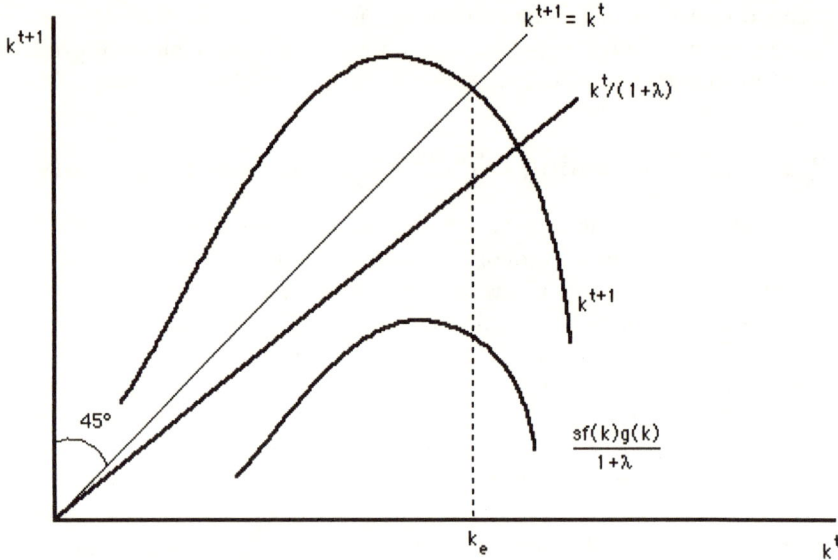

Figure 3.1: "Chaotic" equilibrium.

natural growth rate.[3] Now (with the + superscript denoting the succeeding period) we have a difference equation in the capital/output ratio:

$$k^+ = \frac{k + s \cdot f(k)B(k)}{1 + \lambda}$$

---

[3] The reader will note that I depart at several points from Day's notations and constructions. Day presents an equation for "k^{t+1}" (his equation 1 and particularizations in his equations 9 and 18) which is actually the standard equation for Δk (Solow, 1956; Wan, 1971)—in other words, he omits the $k/(1+\lambda)$ term on the right-hand side. His construction is defensible—e.g., for an economy in which the only capital good is inventory or where the time period is extremely long—but quite awkward. His geometric argument is consistent with the presentation here and his description of underlying behaviors is entirely valid; the problem is that exposition of economic interpretations becomes extremely cumbersome if one has to keep track of this nonstandard interpretation on top of the standard one. For this reason I have: (1) used the + superscript which signals the reader to choose the standard k^{t+1} interpretation given here or to translate Δk according to context; (2) used the expression $B(k)$ for a general "separable" nonlinearity. There is a loss of specificity here. I do not derive critical parameters for macrofunctions since no specific functional forms are given. However, this is a relatively unimportant matter since our concern is with microeconomic emulation of broad categories of behavior. The gain in comprehensibility should be more than offsetting and, of course, the model could be precisely respecified with the functional forms proposed by Day.

3.2. THE RESEARCH PROBLEM

The chaos nonlinearity

Now consider the effect of nonlinearities entered through the $B(k)$ term. Suppose that $B(k)$ is a separable factor and that $g = B(k)$ is a declining function with range $0 < g \leq 1$. We consider the two cases of "production effects" and "saving effects." For the first, assume that microeconomic ex ante production decisions are based, as before, on $f(k)$, but that there are "productivity inhibiting effects" (Day, 1982a, 409) which cause productivity to fall dramatically at high levels of k. These effects are captured by $B(k)$ so that realized income is given by $[f(k) \cdot B(k)]$. If we assume again the constant saving ratio s, capital accumulation now drops off dramatically, as shown in Fig. 3.1. The value k^e connoting the k/k^+ equilibrium is found in the precipice zone and ordinary graphic experimentation shows that trajectories starting near k^e will neither approach k^e uniformly nor cycle regularly around the equilibrium point. The "hump" and precipitous dropoff drawn here correspond to the chaos potentially shown in May (1975).

For the "saving effect" consider the possibility of a variable saving ratio which depends upon k—acting, for example, as a proxy for wealth. For convenience write $s(k) = s[g(k)]$, where $g(\cdot)$ has qualitative properties identical to those of $B()$. The resultant behavior is identical to that shown in Fig. 3.1. An exemplar economic analysis would combine the two cases; but since each has equivalent qualitative implications, Fig. 3.1 suffices to show the more general result as well.[4]

What causes the drop off in $B(k)$ or in a qualitatively equivalent nonlinear form? Day suggests several plausible technical conditions and economic behaviors which individually (or in various combinations) can generate the chaos result within an equation for the aggregate behavior of the system. (1) Within the technology there can be "pollution effect[s]" wherein productivity drops precipitously as capital becomes increasingly concentrated. (2) A saving ratio which depends upon both wealth (i.e., the capital/labor ratio) and a system-determined real interest rate can vary critically at high capital intensities. (3) Agents' "precautionary" reactions—either conventional economic reactions to adjustment costs (Lucas, 1967) or institutional conditions amounting to attempts at retarding the rate of change in either technique or way of life—can result in variable inhibitions on capital accumulation in the context of a real or presumed maximum in the system's potential growth rate.

---

[4]It is interesting to note that Solow covers the general case in his original article (1956, eq. 6c and accompanying text). However, he is careful to graph a particular outcome (his fig. 8) in which the dropoff in accumulation is not rapid enough to throw the system into unstable or chaotic behavior.

3.2.2 Nonlinearities and underlying microeconomic interactions

Several of the mechanisms which have been suggested to account for the hump and precipice (Day, 1982a, 1982b) constitute a conflation or aggregation of microeconomic interaction effects resembling externalities. These effects may be conveniently approximated by nonlinear aggregate expressions; however, if special problems arise out of the specification, it makes some sense to examine the implied microstructure.

Pollution effects

Consider first the erosion of productivity due to pollution and congestion at high levels of capital intensity. This type of phenomenon can be represented in the ex ante composite aggregate production function by the term $g(\cdot) = [g(k^m - k)] = (k^m - k)^\mu$, where k^m is a "saturation" level of k. With appropriate choice of the parameter, μ, the externality term has negligible effect until k^m is closely approached. The chaos phenomenon occurs if, after taking into account saving behavior, the ordinary equilibrium of the system falls into a specific part of the zone strongly influenced by the externality. This scheme is unexceptional for nonhuman biological population aggregates as where the second term represents the mortality consequences of epidemic disease in conditions of overcrowding. It sits less well as a component of an economic accumulation model since it connotes global myopia as to the consequences of overinvestment and instant amnesia as regards effects encountered shortly before. For an economy, it seems more appropriate to model both pollution and congestion effects at the scale of the interaction neighborhood in which threshold phenomena impact on decision-making units.

Behavioral growth restraints

A similar nonlinearity in the aggregate function attaches to "conservative" retardation of the accumulation impulse because of "purely psychological reasons," "adjustment costs," and/or "a tactic for avoiding the uncertainties inherent in a changing way of life" (Day, 1979, 1982a, 411). This type of phenomenon also begs exploration at the micro level, since each of these behaviors suggests an individual agent's response to information about qualities of the overall system.

This decision setting seems particularly to call for explicitly microeconomic treatment of search and the costs of information acquisition. On standard utility and search-cost assumptions (and also on bounded-rationality reasoning) the efficient way for the decision maker to obtain such environmental information in comprehensible form frequently involves focusing

3.2. THE RESEARCH PROBLEM

the search on sample neighborhoods of familiar contact: the immediate locale, industry, suppliers, and customers. If a number of counterpart agents in one or more of these neighborhoods exceed a threshold activity level the decision maker will have variously: (1) immediate information on the "rate of change in the technique of production"; (2) direct evidence on costs of adjustment within his/her line of business; and (3) staring-one-in-the-face evidence of a changing way of life. The decision maker adjusts capital accumulation according to preferences, the strength of the evidence, and costs of adjustment. The aggregate nonlinear form can capture the direction of the presumed adjustments, but its built-in wrinkles may not represent the true adjustment dynamics.

Microeconomic assumptions

A microeconomic model that captures the settings of the pollution externality effect and the local-experience/informational model and that isolates the interactive aspects of the nonlinearity is presented in Section 3.3. To expedite comparisons with the composite aggregate accumulation function, the model includes the following assumptions.

(1) Individual agents operate with $f^*(k)$, a scaled down analog of the aggregate production function $f(k)$. Each agent satisfies the standard neoclassical behavioral assumptions in arriving at the enterprise accumulation decision $k_i^+ = f^*(k^i)$ with no evidence of pollution or interaction effects (henceforth described simply as "interaction effects").

(2) With such evidence, the agent can hold to plan k_i^+ or expand (contract) the rate of accumulation according to favorable (unfavorable) response to the interactive influence.

(3) The interaction effect is separable for each decision unit and is representable as a factor $[1 + k^* g^*(A_i)]$. k^* is an arbitrary fixed percentage increment to k_i and A_i is the number of agents in a neighborhood of decision unit i who take "characteristic actions" which are noted by agent i as new information.

(4) The "characteristic actions" are defined as rates of capital accumulation above or below normal, that is, the rate defined by $f(\cdot)$ alone.

(5) The function $g^*(\cdot)$ can take on values $(-1, 0, +1)$ corresponding to (below-normal, normal, above-normal) accumulation response.[5] The value of $g^*(\cdot)$ is determined by rules which cover reactions to all possible configurations of neighbor actions and which admit response according to several

---

[5]There is no loss of generality in this and previous integer formulations; the model can easily be amended to handle a continuum of characteristic actions and responses to them. As we will see, the integer formulation expedites comparisons with the nonlinear aggregate formulation and simplifies the classification process.

criteria (e.g., "pollution" or "rate of change") separately or in combination.[6] This description of "interaction" is minimally restrictive.

(6) $g^*(0) \to 0$. This condition ensures that if all agents pursue the "normal plan" at an equilibrium level of k the equilibrium will not be disturbed unless there is a shock from outside the system.

In a nutshell, this microeconomic scheme handles interactions explicitly by defining interaction neighborhoods for all agents in the system and treating pollution externalities and all other deviations from "normal" accumulation behavior as information which can be sensed by the agent locally. In the dynamics of the system, the agent's own action subsequently becomes information in the neighborhoods of other agents.

Properties of the aggregated microsystem

Now, let us consider the aggregate behavior of a system of N agents where the accumulation activity of the ith agent is given by

$$\Delta K_i = s[f^*(k_i)] \cdot [1 + k^* g^*(A_i)]$$

Denoting aggregate measures compiled from microeconomic data by, respectively, K^a and K^{a+} for present and future time, we have by virtue of the separability assumption and with the substitution back of Y for aggregate income:

$$K^{a+} = K^a + \Delta K = K^a + [sY/N] \cdot \Sigma[1 + k^* g^*(A_i)]$$

which reduces to

$$K^{a+} = K^a + sY(1 + n^+/N)$$

where n^+ is the algebraic sum of agent responses to local information collected in the earlier time period. Dividing through by $L(1+\lambda)$ and substituting appropriately for Y/L we obtain:

---

[6] In computer simulations $g^*(\cdot)$ is given by (anglicized BASIC) rules of the following sorts: "IF 3 OR 4 OR 5 AGENTS IN YOUR NEIGHBORHOOD SIGNAL ABOVE-AVERAGE ACCUMULATION THEN $g^*(\cdot) \to 1$; ELSE IF 4 OR 5 AGENTS IN YOUR NEIGHBORHOOD SIGNAL BELOW-AVERAGE ACCUMULATION THEN $g^*(\cdot) \to -1$; ELSE $g^*(\cdot) \to 0$." or, "IF THE ALGEBRAIC SUM OF CHARACTERISTIC ACTIONS IN YOUR NEIGHBORHOOD IS 2 OR 3 THEN $g^*(\cdot) \to \ldots$ ELSE . . . ."

3.2. THE RESEARCH PROBLEM

$$k^{a+} = \frac{k + s[f(k^a)] \cdot [1 + k^*(n^+/N)]}{1 + \lambda}$$

Given that n^+ will be a positive function of k, the second term in brackets can closely mimic the nonlinear term in the general form of the chaos model. The term remains close to unity for low values of k; it need not stray from unity with the system at rest.[7] For appropriately scaled k^* the bracketed term gives the percentage deviation from the uncomplicated path associated with the linear model.[8]

This, then, is the true starting point of the essay. We have examined the general shape of a naive microeconomic model that explicitly specifies interactions which are the implicit cause of nonlinearities that can trigger chaos in aggregate models. It remains to examine the model in detail and chart its dynamic behavior.[9]

---

[7] Day's side comment that round-off errors in digital computation are sufficient to "cause rapid divergence of a computed model solution from its 'true' path" is not incorrect but turns out to be a red herring. As we shall see, "cyclical irregularity" and associated prediction problems can occur in binary models which track binary phenomena with perfect accuracy.

[8] If $k^* = 1$, the nonlinear term is a dimensionless percentage weight. In another interesting variation, k^* can be specified as a (positive) function of k; this version tracks Day's interest-rate model quite closely but offers nothing beyond our model in its qualitative behavior. The reader familiar with historic capital controversies will appreciate that I have avoided Day's interest-rate case and associated interpretations. The hump and precipice region implies interest-rate and profit-rate variations that connote notorious valuation problems. In the same vein, it will be noted that the conclusions of the chapter do not rely on suspect properties of the aggregate production function.

[9] A full mathematical treatment of the comparative properties of the macro- and micromodels is beyond the scope of the present chapter. The following points should be noted, however. (1) The qualitative complexity of models is what determines their potential for producing phenomena such as chaos. (2) There are a number of different approaches to complexity analysis including recursive function theory, several branches of computation theory, meta-mathematics (after Gödel), and mathematical linguistics. (3) The approaches are broadly equivalent and lead to a common hierarchic ordering of complexity levels, the Chomsky ordering (Chomsky, 1963; Hopcroft and Ullman, 1979; Albin, 1983; Wolfram, 1984a); nonetheless, they offer differential advantages in handling models of different specification types—and greater or less discriminatory power according to context. (4) The aggregate model (Day) and the microeconomic model to be detailed here are of different specification types. They both are capable of generating uniformity, ordinary periodicity, and chaos (corresponding to the first three Chomsky levels) according to particular parameter settings but they are not isomorphic nor is there an obvious correspondence between the relevant parameters in one model and those in the other. (5) Despite these differences of type, it is particularly advantageous to carry out economic analysis at the microlevel. The microeconomic model is inherently richer in the Chomsky sense, and we will see that the sorts of economic behavior which must be assumed in order to generate chaos nonlinearities in the aggregate system are fully consistent with deeper dynamic and informational phenomena. In other words, the process of aggregation suppresses important detail and consequences. In addition, the

3.3 A model of microeconomic interaction

The dynamics of the interactive microeconomy are best exhibited through systematic simulation.[10] In order to spotlight behavioral equivalents of the chaos nonlinearity, we rely on the separability assumption and concentrate on the time path of the vector of individual-agent capital-accumulation responses

$$\gamma^* = [1 + k^* g^*(A_i)]$$

The right-hand side here is equal to the second term in brackets of the preceding equation. Assuming for convenience that $k^* = 1$, we form the term $\gamma = \gamma^* - 1 = g^*(A_i)$ and the corresponding aggregate term $r = n^+/N$. (Again note that current values are not specially marked but that values for the following period are assigned the + superscript.) With these simplifications in place, the key features of the model which are subject to experimental variation and analysis are interaction neighborhoods and interaction conventions. Their specification is reviewed in terms of underlying economic assumptions and conditions of information propagation and search.

3.3.1 Specification of interaction neighborhoods

Our model economy consists of 100 agents/firms. Each reacts to the behaviors in the immediate past of its neighbors to set the value of a decision variable c. In some versions of the model the neighborhood will be specified so as to represent physical proximity—as where pollution effects are considered. In others, "economic distance" is proxied. In these cases the economic unit is the firm and by convention the economy is arranged into twenty industries of five firms each. Firms react to previous-period actions by other firms according to a two-level adjacency scheme which names: (1) the firms within firm i's own industry to which firm i reacts, and (2) other industries containing specified firms to which firm i reacts. The second level of adjacency reflects underlying structural conditions such as input-output chains in production or the existence of markets which serve as common sources

---

microeconomic model displays its dynamics as information propagation and response to information by the individual agent. This is a more congenial framework in which to study and understand the chaos phenomenon than that offered by the aggregate model. In the latter, the explanation must be sought in calculating processes which are external to the agent and which must be described in essentially unnatural terms—e.g., the card shuffling and wrinkle metaphors.

[10] As we will discover in Section 3.4, systems which are capable of dynamic behavior at or above the level of chaos can only be fully investigated through simulation or its equivalent.

3.3. MICROECONOMIC INTERACTION

of information for several industries. Given the obvious hopelessness of attempting to cover comprehensively the combinatorial possibilities in this situation, we seek restrictions, simplifications, and canonical forms.[11]

Near-neighbor restrictions

In the model simulated here an agent/firm reacts to no more than six entities including self—four or five being the usual case. In the simplest model structure agents/firms are arranged along a line segment according to index ($i = 1, ..., 100$) and each firm has the identical adjacency pattern or neighborhood index set. For example, the index set $\{i - 2, i - 1, i + 1, i + 2\}$ applied to firm i defines as neighbors the two firms to the left and the two firms to the right of firm i for all i. For this homogeneous-agent case, industry designations are nominal only. In cases where industry membership matters, a double indexing scheme is used to identify firms which react only to industry members and firms (leaders) which react both to firms within the industry and to information from other industries.

Directions of information flow

Consider the indices $i = 1, ..., 100$ for firms and $j = 1, ..., 20$ for industries to run according to a structural sequence corresponding to raw-materials processing → semifinished product → intermediate goods → final products—for example, firms in industries 1–5 are in the "basic extractive industries." The sequence can be either linear or it can be specified to reflect more realistic diagonal input-output structures—as where firms in the "intermediate-goods industries" have adjacency relationships with firms in the industry ("competitors"), in the successor industry ("customers"), and to near and remote predecessor industries ("suppliers"). Interindustry information flow can be either unidirectional following the input-output structure or it can be bidirectional—according to behavioral assumptions discussed in the following paragraph. The line segment for the 100 firms is bordered by firms

---

[11] The reader may find it useful to preview some results from this and later sections. It turns out that an outcome resembling chaos is obtained in the very simplest form of the model. Since this format appears to be quite artificial and "noneconomic," the result naturally comes under some suspicion. The suspicion, however, is mistaken; adding realistic complications to the model does not change its qualitative behavior—in fact, it seems to increase the likelihood of chaos-type dynamics. Similarly, I have restricted simulations to dichotomous and trichotomous values of g—or γ. This was done so as to obtain visual confirmation of the classificatory results—literally in black and white (and gray). The results go through for ordinary counting numbers or the continuum but are correspondingly "harder to see" in the absence of full-spectrum graphic displays. In brief, results bearing on the qualitative behavior of the model are not artifacts of simplifying assumptions.

in dummy industry 0 and dummy industry 21 which supply boundary conditions to the model. In the simulations here these firms all engage in "normal" capital accumulation; so this information input from the outside slightly damps the response of the system as a whole.[12]

3.3.2 Specification of interaction conventions

Interaction conventions are incorporated jointly in the neighborhood index set (Section 3.3.1) and a decision rule for the firm given by $g^*(\cdot), \gamma = g^*(A_i)$. As with the previous construct, γ can assume the values $(1, -1, 0)$ denoting, respectively above-normal accumulation, below-normal accumulation, accumulation within normal bounds. We also consider a dichotomous model where γ denotes {raises accumulation by more than a threshold amount, does not raise accumulation by more than a threshold amount}. The function $g^*(\cdot)$ can have as its argument A_i either the exact distribution of neighbor responses in the preceding period, for example, $A_i = \{2$ above normal, 1 below normal, 1 normal$\}$ or their algebraic sum, as where each "below normal" cancels out an "above normal"—resulting in $A_i = 1$ in the preceding case. As noted earlier, different forms of $g^*(\cdot)$ correspond to different rules for setting γ according to the information content of A.[13] Some characteristic types of interaction that are captured in variations of the model specification are briefly described here.

Homogeneity: Symmetrical interactive influence

Here each firm has the identical neighborhood index set so that "industry" is no longer a meaningful behavioral category. In the primary interpretation, adjacency connotes physical proximity—as where the firms are strung out along a valley in which smog can accumulate locally—and

---

[12] A plausible alternative model topology is the "wrap-around" or toroidal structure in which industry 20 has industry 1 as its right-hand neighbor thus completing the "circular flow." I prefer the present model topology because of the damping feature which strengthens any finding of chaos in its presence and because one should not specify the circular-flow feedback in comparisons with Day's first-order system. In any case, comparisons with findings in the large literature which specifies the toroidal topology (Wolfram, 1984c) indicate that our qualitative results bearing on the chaos potentiality are not significantly affected by the choice of model topology. The reader should also note that the present scheme has advantages in representing an open economy in other contexts—as where exogenous raw-material price increases are input to a similarly structured model through dummy industry 0 and one can chart the potential persistence of "structural" inflation propagated through the interindustry and firm adjacency relationships.

[13] The interaction convention was kept constant for all firms in each simulation run; but, since I had no prior view on which conventions were most meaningful, individual simulation experiments were conducted for all integer decision rules of the general type described. Day's text refers to general tendencies and gives no clue as to the appropriate behavior of the individual agent.

3.3. MICROECONOMIC INTERACTION

the interactions connote adjustments to the pollution externality.[14] In an "information-flow" interpretation, accumulation data are received from both supplier and customer firms and are responded to like price shocks in competitive models—albeit the linear succession of firms is contrived.

Heterogeneity: Follow-the-leader/input-influence

The neighborhood index set of the leader (or leaders) in each industry designates firms in the predecessor industry as adjacent. The index sets of the remaining firms in the industry designate only firms in the industry as neighbors. Here, information on levels of accumulation is transmitted through the markup on inputs and is reacted to within the industry as in oligopoly-pricing models.

Heterogeneity: Follow-the-leader/output-influence

The case is identical to that preceding except that information on levels of accumulation is transmitted from client firms as in accelerator models.

Heterogeneity: leadership/rivalrous-consonance

The neighborhood index sets of industry leaders include firms in both predecessor and successor industries (and may also include firms in a parallel input- output stage). The index sets for the remaining firms are as in the preceding examples. The alignment of an industry to neighboring industries is in accord with the rivalrous consonance model (Kuenne, 1984).

3.3.3 Simulation of firm behavior

Figures 3.2–3.6 give representative results for simulations according to the model specifications described already. The model is started in the "normal" state corresponding to $k^+ = k$ equilibrium in the neoclassical system and then shocked by an initial (probabilistic) distribution of above- and below-normal accumulation of actions of individual firms/agents. Successor values of γ are computer generated; thus, each individual panel is a picture of a time series of γ responses for 100 firms arrayed as columns and for 80 rows of model generations (arbitrary cutoff). Black dots are interpreted as increases above normal accumulation, gray as decreases in the trichotomous model. White denotes "no significant increase" in the

---

[14]For similar modeling of pollution-like effects on a two-dimensional surface, see Schelling (1978) and Albin (1975).

dichotomous models and "no significant increase or decrease" in the trichotomous models. The legends give the parameters of model type for each simulation. The reader may think of this format as a stylized picture of a collection of related time series, such as those residing in a segment of a conventional computer data bank.

3.3.4 Classification of simulated time series

After scanning the figures to make our wallpaper selections, we should conclude that the results pictured here fall into four qualitative types or categories. These types also prove to be robust in the sense that the same model parameters (governing information channels and behavioral rules) always produce data output in the same qualitative category for any distribution of starting values. Type 1 (Fig. 3.2a) is the simplest case: after some early mixed results the economy settles down to a uniform state—perpetual exuberance, pessimism, or normality according to context. Type 2 (Figs. 3.2b, 3.2e, and 3.2g) is also quite simple. The model settles down to some combination of cyclicality across firms and/or with time. Given that it is valid to associate these types with macrodynamic uniformity and regular periodicity, we should focus our attention on the two apparently richer types of outcomes.

Chaos in the small

Figures 3.2c, 3.3a, 3.3b, and 3.5 illustrate type 3 data records, an intrinsically more interesting case which, for the moment, is taken provisionally as the equivalent of chaos. The equivalence is clearest for the "homogeneous

Figure 3.2: Representative data structures for two-state models. All histories are generated from the same initial (equiprobable) distribution of states. Line-segment topology is employed. Figures 3.2a–d show complexity types 1–4, respectively, for "homogeneous" firms and the neighborhood set (-2, -1,1, 2), which excludes "self" and is not complex enough to support universal computation. The rules are "raise k_i above k^e if, in the preceding period: (3.2a) 3 firms in the neighborhood raised k"; (3.2b) 1, 2, or 3 firms raised k"; (3.2c) 1 firm raised k"; (3.2d) 2 or 4 firms raised k." Type 1 outcomes are not given hereafter. Fig. 3.2e shows a type 2 outcome with strong transients (for the rule, "if 2 or 3 firms raise k"). Figure 3.2f shows a "more-disordered" type 3 case (for the rule, "if 1 or 3 firms raise k"). Figures 3.2g and 3.2h give simulated data for a nonhomogeneous model with industry structure and weak price leadership. The rules are: 3.2g "if 1 or 2 firms raise k"; 3.2h "if 2 or 4 firms raise k."

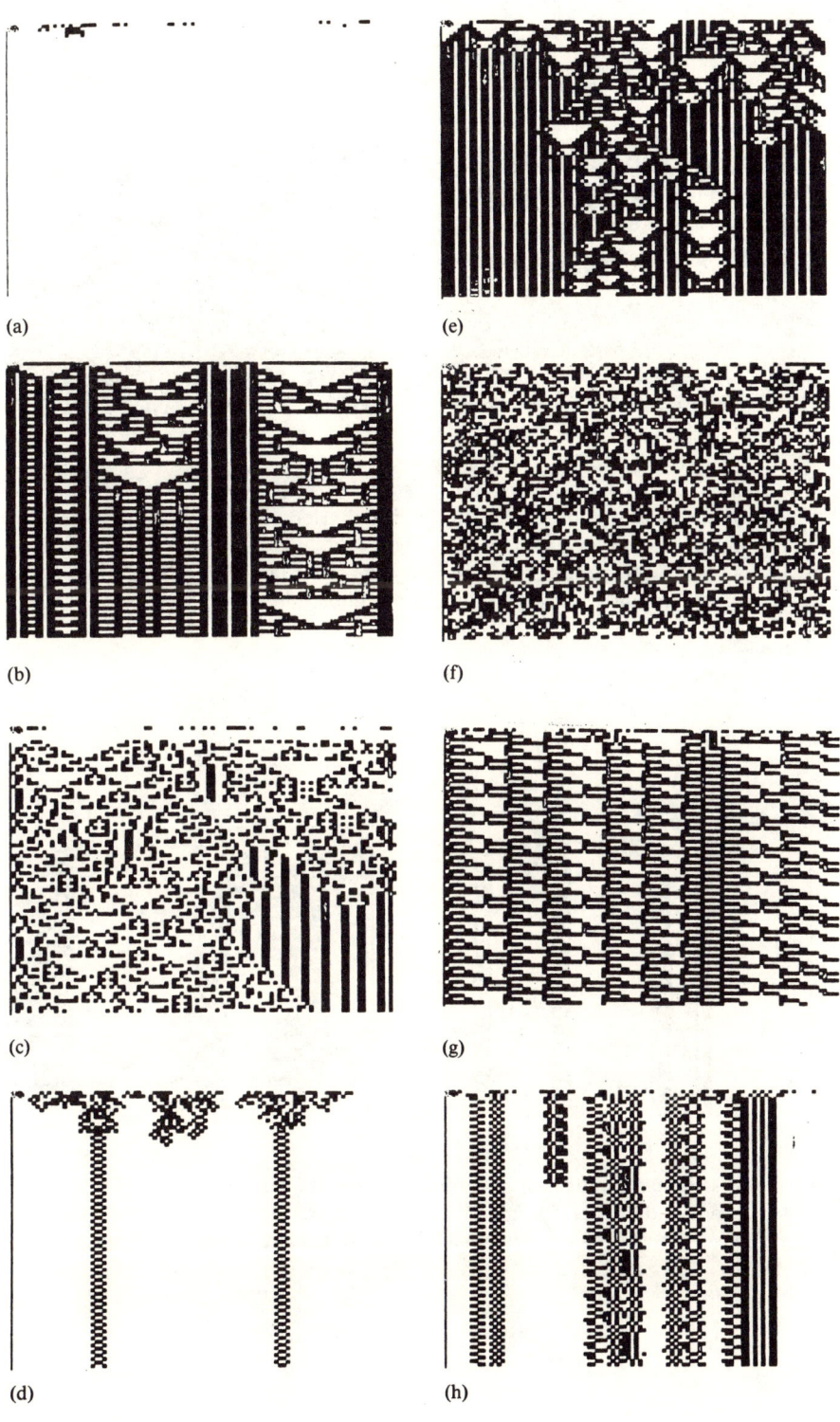

Figure 3.3: Type 3 outcomes for two-state models with industry structure (four-firm neighborhood excluding self). Initial distribution of states given with probability of "k increase" (black)= 0.5.) Fig. 3.3a. One strong leader and one weak leader, "supplier influence." 1- or 3-neighbor rule. Fig. 3.3b. Rivalrous consonance with one leading firm, 1- or 3-neighbor rule.

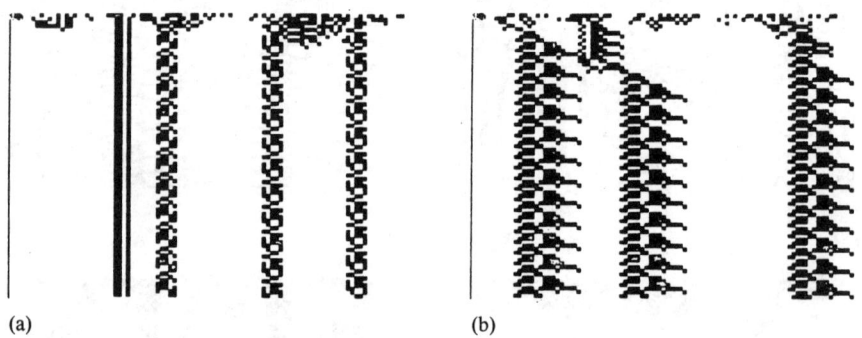

Figure 3.4: Type 4 outcomes for two-state models (same initial distribution of states as in Fig. 3.3, 2- or 4-neighbor rule). Fig. 3.4a. One weak leader, rivalrous consonance. Fig. 3.4b. One strong and one weak leader, "supplier influence."

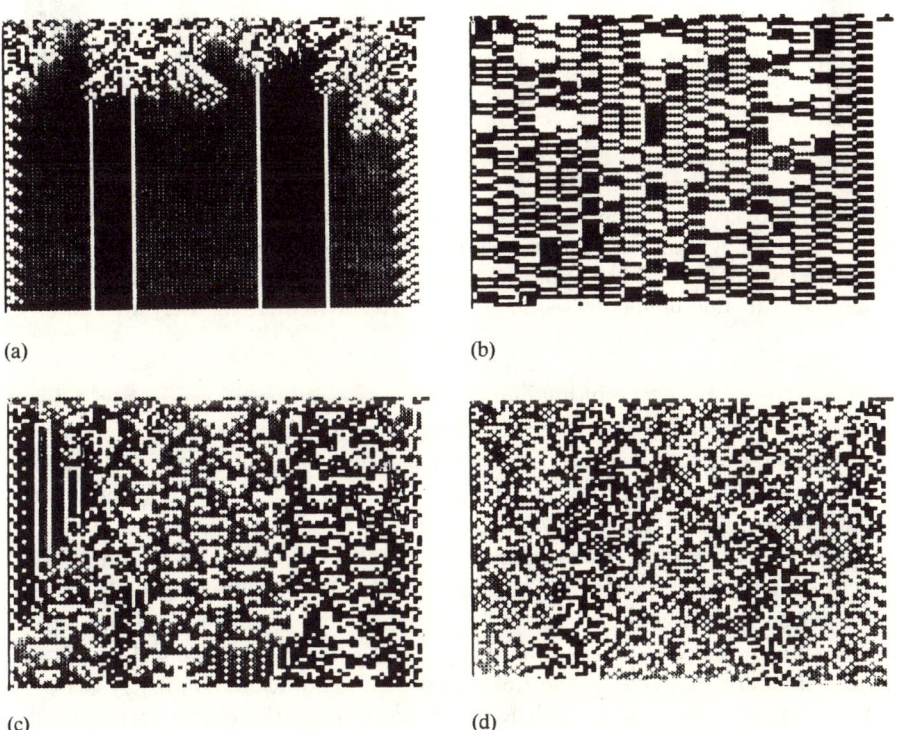

Figure 3.5: Type 3 outcomes for three-state models (initial distribution of states given with probability of "k decrease" (gray)= 0.5 and probability of "k increase" (black)= 0.28). Fig. 3.5a. Homogeneous firms. 1- or 3- or 4-neighbor rule. Note that this case is judged to be at a bifurcation borderline with type 4. Fig. 3.5b. Same rule but for nonhomogeneous firms—rivalrous consonance with 1 leading firm. Fig. 3.5c. Same rule but strong price leadership. Fig. 3.5d. Homogeneous firms. 1- or 3-neighbor rule. Note the tendency for "sectors" to form endogenously in all these cases.

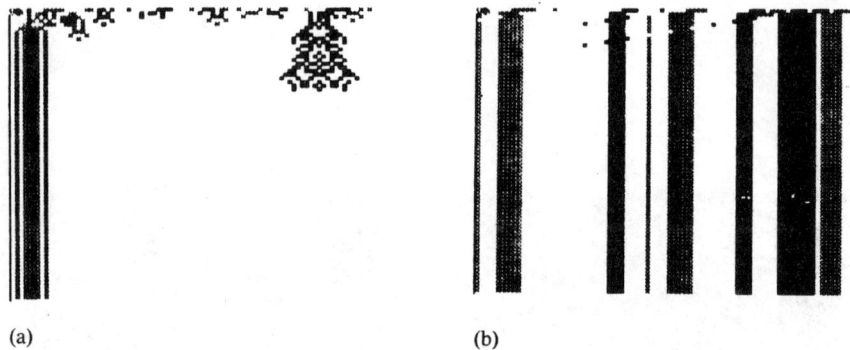

(a) (b)

Figure 3.6: Type 4 outcomes for three-state models (same initial distribution of states as in Fig. 3.5; transitions given by 2- or 4- or 5-neighbor rule). Fig. 3.6a. Homogeneous firms. Fig. 3.6b. Nonhomogeneous firms. Note in Figs. 3.5 and 3.6 the reduction in apparent system complexity with more industry structure.

firms" cases. Here, the individual data points seem pseudorandomly[15] distributed and with apparently stable density. This suggests that averages calculated on cross sections of the data will approach limiting values. This impression is supported by the "irregular cyclicality" seen in representative time-series plots of Γ, their aggregate (Fig. 3.7 and compare Day, 1982a). However, one also sees that some of the records contain the regularity of repeated triangular forms. In a related context (Wolfram, 1983b), this regularity is described as "fractal" (Mandelbrot, 1982) or "self-similar," carrying the suggestion that there is some structure in the underlying process that traces itself in the data record. In addition, "industry structure" appears to exhibit itself as local patterns in the data—"structured pseudorandomness"—a matter to which we will return.

If we limit ourselves to the figures and look at the data records through the eyes of a forecaster, we might venture with some confidence an ability to predict system outcomes locally and near term part of the time (e.g., successor values within a newly emerging block triangle) and global limiting densities most of the time. However, unless there were a way to collapse the code producing the pseudorandom outcomes, there would seem to be

---

[15]The data from these particular simulations have not been formally tested for "randomness"; however, other data from an identical model have been exhaustively screened and pass many tests as stochastic variates. The tests which are not passed relate to the obvious negative autocorrelation of the spiky generated time series—a sign-reversal test is simplest to apply. It should be noted that the simple aggregate nonlinear chaos model will always fail this type of test—although in different ways corresponding to the several chaos phases (May, 1975) which I have ignored to this point for expositional convenience.

3.3. MICROECONOMIC INTERACTION

no alternative to full system emulation if it were necessary to project exact individual responses well into the future.[16] Of course, for the previous cases we would only have to see a few lines of model-generated data to be quite confident of our ability to forecast with quite simple means the model's exact output any years into the future. It should be noted, however, that for both the micro- and aggregate chaos cases we might place some confidence in practical forecasting strategies that build on observable properties of model-generated data: sign reversals, absence of drift, local patterns. This is less than perfect certainty but more than one expects when projecting in a "true" stochastic regime.

More than chaotic

Now consider Figs. 3.2d, 3.2e, 3.4a, 3.4b 3.6a, and 3.6b. Some of the partial forms illustrated appear to have type 2 structure, others seem to have intrinsic richness beyond the "chaotic regularity" of type 3. These records are assigned to a special class, type 4. When the type 4 patterns appeared in a different context (Wolfram, 1983b), it was asserted that the data-generating system behaved, in effect, as a full-scale computer whose behavior could not be tracked or projected except by a computing device of equal complexity. If this is in fact the case, our hypothetical forecaster faces some formidable problems beyond those offered by the type 3 chaotic outcomes. In terms of our model, the figures might be interpreted to show that constellations of firms can persistently oppose the accumulation tendencies of the global system—behavior which seems intrinsically human in comparison to the irregular but nonetheless restricted responses of the chaos/type 3 case.[17] Postponing detailed consideration of type 4 until Section 3.4, I note only that there exist good reasons to associate the category with rich recursive functional forms and ample grounds to label the dynamics it produces as "rich."

---

[16] It turns out that the code is unbreakable and there is no short cut to the computations needed to project the data record for the full system. This condition, "computation-irreducibility," is discussed in Section 3.4. Note, however, that where the system is constrained—as here by the restriction to 100 firms—a given cross section of data must eventually recur and all successor terms will be registered in the data record to that point. In our model, a recurrence must register within 2^{100} iterations—or for the general binary case, within 2^n iterations for n agents in the cross section.

[17] One can observe a wider range of type 4 behaviors than those illustrated in Figs. 3.1–3.6. To establish comparability, all of these figures were generated from the same starting value (pseudorandomly selected). Other starting values in the type 4 models would produce patterns in the data that would be interpreted as fast and slow information channels (in a system with a one-period lag), merging industries, and spinoffs. In time-series plots these would be interpreted by an econometrician as "changes in regime."

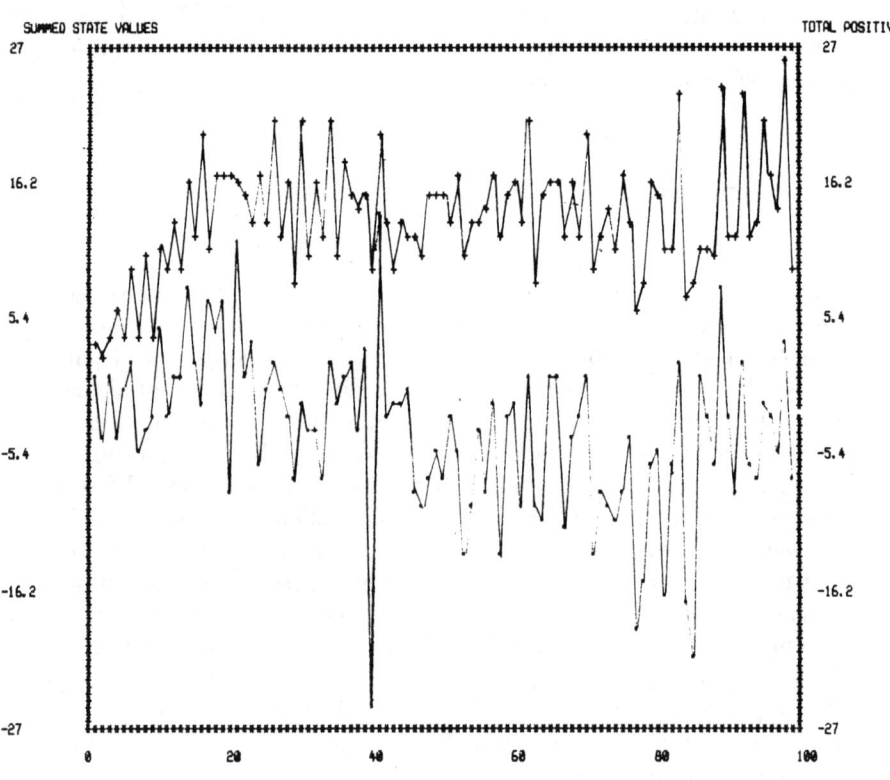

Figure 3.7: Growth of type 3 system. Right scale ("+" symbol) gives the trajectory of the percent of firms who "increase accumulation" in a "moderately disordered" type 3 model. Left scale ("·" symbol) gives the trajectory of the algebraic sum of $-1, 0, +1$ responses for the same model.

3.3. MICROECONOMIC INTERACTION

3.3.5 Preliminary indications

In starting out to emulate the chaos result in a microeconomic setting, we have ended up some distance from where the path might ordinarily be expected to lead. It is clear that a full exploration of the mathematical properties of the microeconomic model is needed before we can come to definite conclusions about the significance of the phenomena here encountered. This will be attempted in Section 3.4. Nevertheless, some provisional conclusions can be offered and questions more sharply drawn just on the basis of the simulation outcomes.

(1) As regards growth- and capital-theoretic properties, neither the aggregate nonlinear model nor the microeconomic homogeneous-interaction model produces a degree of pseudorandomness that offers much of a challenge. Samuelson's original term "neutral oscillation" (see note 1) is certainly as descriptive as "chaos" for the data generated in the pseudorandom cases and is far more apt in its economic connotations. Although "irregular growth" deserves to be recorded as a "stylized fact" of dynamic systems, spiky oscillations with frequent reversals and no drift do not correspond closely enough to irregular reality to command instant attention. The k/k^+ equilibrium defined by the underlying Solovian model might perhaps be relabeled as the origin in a phase space containing a "strange attractor," but otherwise the substantive properties of the model should hold here if they are also robust in a model subject to ordinary stochastic shocks.

(2) Turning to informational properties, matters become more interesting, since we are obliged to consider both predictability of the system as it stands and adaptive reactions by system actors. (For convenience in exposition I will henceforth refer to the original aggregate nonlinear model as MAC, to MAC in the chaos zone as MAC^C, and to hypothetical adaptively modified forms of MAC as MAC'; as noted earlier, MAC is most appropriately applied to nonsentient actors. The interactive microeconomic model will be referred to as MIC with data type and variants given by superscripts, that is, MIC^3 is a system producing the type 3 pseudorandom outcome, $MIC^{3.h}$ is, for example, a homogeneous variant.) The information properties of MAC^C are such that an observer could: a predict outcomes that fall within the range of the system's oscillations with high likelihood; (b) improve these predictions by using projection strategies that take account of sign reversals; and (c) adjust projection strategies to chaos phase according to calculations on the model's basic parameters. Although it is perfectly correct that accurate tracking of MAC^C requires full simulation, the expedients described make projecting data for MAC^C roughly comparable with projecting for MAC around ordinary stable equilibria.

(3) If somewhat effective projection strategies for MAC^C exist, then one must contemplate the possibility of adaptive behavior on the part of

126   CHAPTER 3. FOUNDATIONS OF "CHAOS"

intelligent system actors. The problem setting is virtually identical to that surrounding the cobweb theorem (Muth, 1961). Similarly, one should contemplate control potentialities. These matters need not be pursued here, beyond noting that because of these behavioral omissions MAC^C is incompletely specified as regards agent rationality, whereas the ordinary stable neoclassical model imbedded in MAC is not.

(4) $MIC^{3.h}$ the homogeneous-agent interactive microeconomic model which emulates chaos has essentially the same economic and informational content as MAC^C. That is, it produces neutral oscillations in its aggregates for which there can be derived projection strategies. These are imperfect but presumably of some practical use—as are the possibilities of accurate local projection of successor terms. In summary, MAC^C and $MIC^{3.h}$ can be interpreted as "clean" models with neutral oscillations. However, ordinary requirements for economic rationality beg their modification into "dirty" models where accretions of statistical projection tools or expectational assumptions reduce the amount of residual uncertainty—if derivations from the k/k^+ equilibrium can be interpreted in this way.

(5) The first important difference between MAC and MIC as economic models appears on this matter of specifying behavioral modifications. For MAC^C such modifications could initially take the form of additional or more complicated nonlinearities—in effect, adding twists and kinks to the k/k^+ phase diagram.[18] Ignoring for reasons of space the tactic of specifying higher-order dynamics, a more sophisticated modification would involve moving in the direction of specifying additional levels of recursion—as where MAC' consists of functions over $\{k, k^+\}$. In essence, my contention is that once chaos is introduced into the system, open-ended respecification of the basis model either in the direction of richer interaction or richer functional forms must follow.

(6) In MIC, however, richness and many lines of adaptation are already built into the model. For a given neighborhood of interaction, the model sequence $\{MIC^1 - MIC^4\}$ represents the qualitative dynamic sequence {limit point, limit cycle, chaos, rich dynamics}. Which type is triggered depends on the iteration rule. But the rule, as the model was specified, is a direct representation of how information is processed by the agent. Furthermore, neighborhood variations within MIC^3 model types, for example, representing different input-output sequences, leadership patterns, and the like, have been shown to lead to different degrees of local predictability amounting to reduced chaos. In short, instruments for adaptive or policy

---

[18]Many such modifications could be given microeconomic justification, e.g., as secondary thresholds implied by scenarios such as: "pressure on productivity increases as congestion builds with higher k but then relaxes at still higher levels of k when the situation becomes so hopeless that people work with energy born of despair." In other words, for every nonlinearity there is a story to tell.

control inhere to the specification (see Albin, 1989).

My original contention was that, once one appealed to inherently interactive processes to warrant a nonlinear specification, one was obliged by theoretical proprieties to examine the implied microeconomic substructure.[19] A second contention is that once such a nonlinear model generates chaotic behavior in the context of potentially reactive human behavior the obligation becomes absolute. This point is presented formally in the discussion that follows.

3.4 Interpretations

A full interpretation of the behaviors exhibited by MIC requires examination of the mathematical underpinnings of the model. I present an overview of formal properties in Sections 3.4.1 and 3.4.2 with some side commentary. Re-examination of economic implications follows in Section 3.4.3.

3.4.1 The background model

Properties of a model virtually identical to the homogeneous form of MIC have been extensively studied in other contexts by Wolfram (1983b, 1984a, 1984b, 1986) and other researchers and research groups (Packard, 1983, 1984; Martin, Odlyzko, and Wolfram, 1984). The visual likenesses between Wolfram's simulated data and those here (Figs. 3.2–3.6) are very much to the point. I report on mathematical properties which are relevant to our inquiry. Most are proven formally but a number constitute conjectures which have received strong support in simulation studies. The basic modeling format is called a one-dimensional cellular automaton (one-dimensional CA) or "line automaton." It has received attention only comparatively recently. The two-dimensional form invented by von Neumann (1966) has been extensively studied in a variety of contexts (Aladyev, 1974; Wainwright, 1971–73) including economics (Albin, 1975; Albin and Hormozi, 1983). General results for N dimensions—which, of course, include the one-dimensional form—have also been compiled (Smith, 1971); but the power of the one-dimensional format was not generally recognized until Wolfram's figures were published and widely disseminated (Wolfram, 1984c; Dewdney, 1985).

---

[19]It remains to be seen whether MIC is or can be developed into a comprehensive model of interaction (the provisional answer is affirmative) and whether MIC is practical to use in applied research (no answer is available).

The Wolfram scheme

The one-dimensional CA is defined on a partition of a line into indexed "sites" (firms, agents, activities, in economic versions). Each site (cell) is occupied by an automaton (abstract decision-making device) which can assume k states (behavior categories). Infinite line and finite line-segment versions exist; our attention is on models developed on bounded line segments; these have essentially the same properties as the finite Wolfram model built on a circle (wrap-around topology).

Each site automaton c_i has an index set S_i which defines the "neighborhood" of other sites associated with cell i. The range parameter r defines the furthest extent of the neighborhood—for example, for the automaton which references its two left and two right immediate neighbors, $r = 2$. All sites are synchronized to a clock which operates in discrete time steps. A function f_i gives s_i, the state of the ith site automaton at time t as a function of states of automata in S in some predecessor period.

The Wolfram models: (1) operate with a one-period lag; (2) are homogeneous, meaning that f_i and S_i are identical for all c_i except for a small set where the circle is closed; (3) restrict f to "totalistic" functions—rules of the form $s_{it} = f[\Sigma s(i+j)(t-1)]$, where the summation over j runs from $-r$ to r; (4) require that if all elements of $S_i(t-1)$ have zero value, $s_{it} = 0$; and (5) require that all rules be symmetrical. The homogeneous case of MIC is of this type; see Wolfram (1984c) and Dewdney (1985) for intuitive descriptions and further examples. Extensive sample studies support the conjecture that the qualitative behavior of the Wolfram models cover all one-dimensional CA—including the inhomogeneous varieties introduced here. The Wolfram format offers many convenient advantages for theorem-proving and computer experimentation; so this conjecture is relied on widely.

Taxonomy of model types

The four qualitative types described in Section 3.2 were originally labeled by Wolfram. The identification of types 1 and 2 with limit points and limit cycles in general dynamic models is obvious. The association of type 3 with chaos and strange attractors involves: a standard statistical analyses of model-generated data; (b) theoretical and quantitative analysis of "entropic" properties; and (c) analyses of linguistic properties. The last two lines of inquiry are particularly instructive for their informational implications.

3.4. INTERPRETATIONS

Entropy

A particular pattern of site states appears as a dot pattern in the printout. A composite of such patterns is described as "maximally disordered (chaotic)" if at the limit all printable patterns of all feasible lengths can appear and each pattern of a particular length is equiprobable. Computable entropy measures quantify this notion (Wolfram, 1983b). Certain type 3 one-dimensional CA appear to be maximally chaotic but those in which "standard patterns" such as block triangles appear have reduced entropy.

This is a powerful and suggestive line of analysis. The tying of degrees of chaos through an entropy measure to pattern-generating totalistic rules represents in the economic model and interpretation the linking of dynamic behavior to organizational and decision principles underlying the search for information—for such are the characteristics which underlie the specification of MIC. Although MIC is too crudely drawn to warrant detailed inferences from specific decision practices, it is reasonable to compare entropic properties of variants of MIC^h with inhomogeneous versions incorporating similar totalistic rules. On preliminary indications, if within-industry behaviors matter, entropy falls. MAC provides no comparable lines of analysis to link dynamics to microeconomic decisions.

System complexity

If one again takes the perspective that the one-dimensional CA produces dot patterns and symbol strings, it is natural to treat the model as a linguistic form. The questions one then asks are: (a) How sophisticated a grammar or language structure is needed to process predecessor patterns (strings) into successor patterns (strings)? (b) How powerful a computer is needed to "parse" these strings and derive the underlying rule or a satisfactory proxy for it? The answers to these questions clearly bear on the informational resources required to explain and replicate the trajectories of a dynamic system.

Following Wolfram's (1983b) analysis one sees that type 1 models associate with a "regular language" of simple unlinked constructions and a computer with no memory. In effect, a simple operation on an ordinary hand calculator suffices to project the model at its limit point. For type 2, the limit-cycle case, a "context-free" language (e.g., an interpreted computer language which is implemented one instruction at a time) suffices to generate the data and a machine with finite memory organized in sequenced stacks to hold the repetitive patterns can be used to project all model trajectories. type 3 associates with a "context-sensitive" language (e.g., a computer language in which the "meaning" and implementation of an instruction vary according to the sequence of predecessor actions). The associated machine must have expandable memory (at least up to the point that a pattern recurs in a finite model).

In terms of our concerns with MAC^C and MIC^3 these last requirements begin to clarify the resource requirements for projections or analysis of a potentially chaotic system. In the worst case of maximum disorder there is no alternative but brute force simulation on a machine which is scaled to the size of the system. But is the worst case all that bad? After all, grinding out all the terms for MAC^C, although not so handy as projecting a limit point, is really not enormously burdensome. A further conjecture for economic nonlinear systems based on Wolfram's "computation-irreducibility" hypothesis for type 3 and type 4 structures suggests otherwise.

Type 4 structures

Before we can examine this conjecture, it is necessary to examine the extremely irregular type 4 result. It has been proven for a number of one-dimensional CA that particular patterns produced by type 4 systems correspond to the architectural elements of a general-purpose computer (Turing machine) which has the capacity to emulate computers of any design and engage in the process of computing general recursive functions. (See Wolfram, 1984b, 1984c, for examples of some of these "component designs.") The associated language, "general" or "unrestricted," is mutable and associative in the way human languages are. In effect, particular configurations of patterns operate—autonomously, as it were—to take data out of the system and calculate on them. There is no attractor for trajectories and the only way to learn the final outcomes (if any) of such processes is to follow them step by step on a computing device of comparable scale. In fact, the problem of predicting outcomes is assuredly Gödelian (Minsky, 1967; Albin, 1982a).

It is commonplace to liken the workings of a price system to a giant computer which assists in the attainment of system limit points or limit sets. It is quite another matter to contemplate the possibility that agents in the system will interact in an ordinary fashion with the result that they wire themselves together as components of a computer that calculates to no set purpose and may in fact induce the system to draw away from presumed equilibria. This is an implication of MIC^4. Against this implication we have the fact that the behavior in question involves a mechanical response to a search problem—but yet it is not at all clear that we want to inject more intelligence into the individual site (Albin, 1982a). In the case of type 3 trajectories, the induced oscillatory patterns are of a type that prompts search for prediction strategies—either by agents or policy makers in a system regulatory role. The type 4 patterns, being more irregular and localized, do not seem to command a demand for system adjustment.

3.4. INTERPRETATIONS

3.4.2 The computation irreducibility hypothesis

Working from the computational requirements for projecting types 3 and 4, Wolfram (1985) has proposed that where there is a distinct microstructure to a (physical) system with interactions at or above the complexity of a line automaton there may be no theoretical shortcuts to full computer simulation for trajectories of the system in the small—excepting established limit points (type 1) or limit cycles (type 2) and the possible existence of projection strategies that preserve some computational resources in the face of chaotic disorder (type 3). This proposition casts considerable suspicion on aggregate theoretical forms that encounter the critical dynamic behaviors unless these forms incorporate computational resources equivalent in scale and power to those required for microemulation. The proposition gains in interest with the information that types 3 and 4 are common in occurrence within the one-dimensional CA framework—observed, respectively, 53% and 6% of the time in the $k=2, r=2$ model and with greater frequency in more complex versions (Wolfram, 1983b).

3.4.3 Reexamination of economic implications

Obviously, results for an abstract physical system should not pass automatically into the economic and social domains; but in this instance the computational and informational foundations for the irreducibility proposition and the overall Wolfram scheme command attention. The economy is quintessentially a body of institutions that process data, compute, and decide. The proposition would appear to be germane for theoretical formulations which bear on informational properties and specify aggregate proxies for this behavior.

The necessity for disaggregation

The original well-behaved Solow model does not appear to be touched by the Wolfram proposition; but some investigation is needed to show why it is probably exempt and the nonlinear form eligible. Essentially, my argument rests on: (1) the assumed separability of linear and nonlinear (microeconomic search) components in both the aggregate and disaggregate versions; and (2) assumptions on search costs and behavior which govern the enabling or disabling of the nonlinear (search) components. A simple and convenient set of assumptions on the economies of search includes: (2a) The agent or firm receives data on own product and factor prices for no incremental cost above the ordinary outlays of doing business and there is no cost to storing such data for some finite number of time periods. (2b) Acquiring current information on the economic condition or investment behavior of firms or agents in the immediate economic or geographic neighborhood requires some outlay or effort that amounts to an incremental step in cost. (2c) Acquiring current data on system aggregates and conducting scientific forecasts and projections entail still higher incremental outlay. (2d) Firms underwrite higher search costs only if plans based on a cheaper search strategy go awry; in addition, no change in search strategy is undertaken unless some feasible outcome of that search entails a change in firm profit-seeking behavior.

It is also convenient and inoffensive to assume: (3) All channels for information acquisition are open and available at all times without cost to the agent. Costs are incurred only when the agent uses the system. One can think of this scheme as a complete socially provided information network. "Hookup" to the network is free; but there are charges for "local message units" and higher charges for "out of area" contacts and special services. The network is the economic counterpart to the information paths or (circuit diagram) of MIC. It is available for immediate use when conditions warrant. The scheme also represents the implicit logic of MAC in Day's version.

For well-behaved growth equilibria in the aggregate Solow model (and many other formulations), own prices and factor costs (determined in an accompanying general-equilibrium framework) suffice to define each agent's operating plan at the microlevel. Since either the plan is fulfilled or convergence to the plan can be determined from data in the finite memory store, there is no need for costlier information, and none is sought: the nonlinearity in MAC and the search mechanism in MIC remain disabled. The finite memory suffices even if the system were to encounter some special configuration of parameters generating regular periodicity in the Solow model (or limit cycles in other forms). In short, the information-search component of MIC is never activated; and, since the remaining component of the model receives only price data which is, in all practical cases, of lower dimensionality than firm-status data, the Wolfram computation-irreducibility proposition does not apply.

It does apply, however, at the level of MAC^C/MIC^3. One could tell two types of story here—with the potential of quite a few plot embellishments. One begins with the MAC version: as capital deepens beyond some critical level, some combination of pollution effects, tightened financial markets, and future shock result in actual or anticipated nonfulfillment of agent plans. This is sensed with only the small amount of price-type data at hand. At this point there are two ways to finish the story.

In the long version the search mechanism is triggered for economic reasons and the system turns into MlC. The decision function determines whether the system goes into well-behaved MIC^1 or MlC^2—in which case the story ends—or whether the plot embellishments of MIC^3 or MIC^4

3.4. INTERPRETATIONS

emerge. In both the MIC^3 and MIC^4 subplots there are further possibilities of system agents moving to higher levels of economic search involving deeper forecasting and projection. In all of these plot embellishments we are brought into the domain of the Wolfram computation-irreducibility proposition and the following critical analysis applies: (a) At worst the system requires computer emulation at a level of detail that represents individual agents. (b) Depending upon the "inherent degree of disorder" or upon entropy decrease due to industry structure, local institutions, and so on, there may be some reduction in the resource requirements for system emulation. (c) In the same vein, less costly predictions of limiting densities (with residual pseudorandom uncertainty) may be of some use for policy purposes. (d) Simulation costs may go up if system recursiveness increases because agents use deeper projection strategies at the second step of information costs. (e) Full-scale emulation is required if the system turns out to be MIC^4. In many instances the system will quickly converge to limiting values, resulting in no great prediction problems. In others it will take an irregular path which can only be tracked step by step from initial conditions.

Without knowledge of the decision functions embedded in MlC, there is no way to select among these versions and embellishments and determine a priori which story is most representative of an actual economy. My instinctive guess is that a tale that blends outcomes (b), (c), and (e) may come closest to verisimilitude for actual economic systems.[20] In particular, properties under (b) suggest that the system may be represented quite well by a relatively small number of subaggregates—which number may be estimable from (neg)entropic properties of actual firm-level data in a manner complementary to ongoing econometric research on large systems. The blend of versions gives the system spice and a bit of human, as opposed to pseudorandom, unpredictability.

Now for the short version. Begin with MAC. Stipulate a nonlinearity that gives oscillations. Assume that the nonlinear specification approximates the underlying search, decision, and accumulation processes. Simulate the system with MAC^C, as required. Note that the story ends differently for small variations in parameters and initial conditions, but that grinding out a few hundred terms with MAC^C is a far less demanding use of computational resources than simulating any version of MIC. The story is finished.

No it isn't. Can the search mechanism be assumed away without, in effect, assuming away all microeconomic foundations? If not, can a simple macro approximating function be demonstrated to be equivalent to the

---

[20]Inhomogeneous forms which blend interaction "sectors" of different behavioral types are consistent with the general CA framework. It exceeds the scope of the chapter to go beyond a mere mention of the potentiality.

search model without reproducing the search model itself? Will not an embellished macrosystem that fully emulates the micromodel via additional nonlinear components, higher-order terms, and possibly a degree of recursion end up as large in the computational sense as the underlying micro model? It would appear that the computation irreducibility problem is not easily evaded, and so we are led to the following conclusion.

Conclusion. In a system which specifies rational agents and search processes which are not prohibitively costly, a nonlinear economic model that presents the chaos potentiality in the aggregate can only be projected by a simulation scheme with the intrinsic complexity of the underlying microeconomic search mechanism.

The extent of bounds to rationality

The use of totalistic rules to represent decision functions within MIC was originally justified as a bounded-rationality expedient permitting the agent to organize common local data with implications bearing on several attribute dimensions (i.e., pollution effects and future shocks are both signaled by accumulation rates within the neighborhood; so the agent may have to have multiple criteria for reaction). Although the bounded-rationality interpretation is very much in the spirit of the CA scheme, it should be noted that MIC with totalistic rules models decision functions of considerable generality and a case can be made for their informational efficiency and compatibility with approaches such as rational expectations (Muth, 1961).

To begin with, it should be clear that the notion of cost steps corresponding to the distinction between price-type data deriving from ordinary business, on the one hand, and information relating to the condition of the system, on the other, derives directly from the original Hurwicz (1969) framework. Similarly, the assumptions that information costs vary directly with economic distance and that a neighborhood of suppliers, customers, and competitors (or physical neighbors) provides the most comprehensible status information at lowest incremental cost are conventional, if not classical.

Given that the information technology is appropriate to the problem,[21] attention focuses on the decision function. The "totalistic" rule is a nonstandard function wherein the agent's decision depends upon units of status information given as the distribution of integer status values in the predefined neighborhood. The critical point, however, is that this distribution

---

[21]The use of integer and step formulations is a convenience that does not affect the qualitative results, i.e., cost functions derived from a CA model can be smoothed to any limit of discrimination by expanding the number of site values and redefining functions accordingly. This would be costly but uninformative on qualitative behaviors.

3.5. EXTENSIONS AND APPLICATIONS

constitutes the full information available at the given level of search and must be the argument of the decision function of a hypothetical rational agent. Linear first-order functions, meeting ordinary tests for decision rationality, will therefore be closely approximated by particular members of the set of totalistic rules utilized here. It goes beyond the scope of this chapter to consider relationships between general decision criteria and the rule structure of *MIC* in any greater detail.[22] It suffices that the results discussed here are seen as compatible with decision rationality in the generally accepted sense and are not artifacts of an arbitrary simulation framework.

Institutions and information

One of the more interesting provisional results in this chapter concerns the effect of simulated industry structure and "noncompetitive" behaviors on the information properties of data generated by the system. That institutional characteristics should be evidenced as counterentropic should come as no surprise. Interest should stem from the possibility of developing a rigorous approach to disaggregation in empirical work based on this effect. Although the analysis here also points toward the appropriateness of greater disaggregation on institutional lines in dynamic theory, it does not really present guidelines for conducting such analysis except with the simulation framework.

3.5 Extensions and applications

If this chapter has been at all successful it will have attracted attention to an extremely promising modeling framework as well as providing answers and interpretations bearing on the chaos potentiality in macrodynamics. Rather than recapitulate results on the latter issue, I will conclude by suggesting some promising extensions of the methodology.

To my mind the most striking aspect of the general simulation scheme is the suggestive correspondence between the printout format and that of typical economic data structures, for example, the data bank consisting of time series of variables which are related in cross section. Examples of such data banks include the familiar sources of financial information for firms arranged by industry. In a successor paper I will report on empirical observations that are, in effect, visual sightings of the characteristic signatures of line automata.

---

[22] In a successor paper I will examine variable weighting of the neighbors—the totalistic rules give each neighbor equal weight in the distribution—and functions which use additional historic data, i.e., higher-order schemes.

If neighborhood-type relationships of the sort discussed here are indeed characteristic of actual economic data, the problems of optimal inference and efficient projection from microeconomic time series require some rethinking. We economists are prone to think of our data as divided into stochastic and systematic components, with the latter solvable given enough observations to bring our inferential apparatus to bear. If the systematic component in actual data is subject in some degree to computation-irreducible processes, more observations may yield no additional information and statistical criteria fall in their efficiency.

The specification of industrial-leadership and rivalrous-consonance forms in the models of Section 3.3 should suggest applications of the CA scheme to industry structure questions. Suppose we relabel the variables in the model to represent price changes or changes in markup and subject the system to initial shocks resembling the OPEC actions of the 1970s. How would type 4 patterns of persistence in pricing be interpreted? Would there be any basis for resurrecting "institutional" or "structural" models of inflationary dynamics?

Acknowledgments

The author gratefully acknowledges the suggestions and helpful comments of Christophe Deissenberg, Duncan Foley, Mark Glick, Farrokh Hormozi, Janos Kornai, Robert Kuenne, Norman Packard, and Stephen Wolfram.

Chapter 4

Qualitative Effects of Monetary Policy in "Rich" Dynamic Systems

4.1 Introduction

It is widely presumed that monetary policy has informational effects on business expectations as well as allocative effects. The former influence may affect system dynamics particularly, in already volatile settings. This chapter reports on ongoing computer experiments aimed at isolating the qualitative informational effects of procyclical (accommodative) and countercyclical monetary interventions. The modeling approach is described first and is followed by an explanation of the associated schema for complexity classification of dynamic systems. The next section contains the specification of monetary controls. The results and interpretations are then presented. The analysis shows that intervention according to conventional rules can: (a) alter the intrinsic dynamics of the system, for example, from periodic to aperiodic (chaotic) or the reverse; (b) delay natural equilibrium seeking tendencies; (c) worsen the tradeoff between approximating an aggregate target and reducing fluctuations around the target; (d) worsen the trade-off between approximating an aggregate target and achieving "selective" objectives. A "countercyclical" rule is not necessarily superior to an "accommodative" rule under these conditions nor does "finer tuning" necessarily lead to finer results. Although the models specify only myopic expectations and intervention rules, the analysis generates a strong presumptive case with respect to higher-order specifications as well.

4.2 The experimental setting

The experimental setting is a computer model simulating variations in the investment of individual firms who draw information on the likely path of the system from observation of the actions of their economic neighbors. The system's dynamic behavior in the absence of policy intervention is examined first. Detailed properties of the system are given in Albin (1987, Chapter 3 in this volume); its salient characteristics are summarized here.[1]

1. The economy consists of N firms organized in M industries. It is convenient to operate with 100 firms in 5-firm industries.

2. Each firm sets a *three-option investment plan* contingent on expectational information as to whether the business climate will be unfavorable, normal, or favorable. Normal is the firm investment level that aggregates to the level of capital formation which supports a balanced growth path in the sense of Solow (1956) and as translated to a nonlinear system by Day (1982a). The unfavorable and favorable climates can be thought of as worst-case and best-case scenarios.

3. The data needed to *calculate* the three separate plan options are assumed to be price-dimensioned and obtainable by the firm without additional cost in the ordinary course of doing business. These data and the mechanics of calculating optimal plans are of standard type and are not considered here.

4. The strategic information needed to *choose* the appropriate plan option is costly and available only with some delay. The firm is assumed to base its strategic decision on "leading indicators" drawn from observation of the immediate past actions of its "economic neighbors." This is the most timely and least costly source of strategic information.

5. The "economic neighborhood" can overlap the industry but is not identical to it. Neighborhood relationships represent variously intraindustry relationships among competitors, supplier-customer relationships, and/or interindustry input-output relationships.

6. The neighborhood is specified as an index set. Thus the index set $(-2, -1, 1, 2)$ defines for firm J the neighbors $(J-2, J-1, J+1, J+2)$. If all firms have the same index set, the system is *homogeneous* and the industry distinction is purely nominal.

7. If the neighborhood set varies according to the firm's position within its industry, the system is *heterogeneous*. Typically, one can designate one or two firms as "leaders" who draw information from outside the industry,

---

[1] The underlying mathematical structure of the model is that of a one-dimensional cellular automaton. Wolfram (1986) is the primary source of foundation papers and detailed bibliography concerning this form. Also see Albin (1975) for a general discussion of cellular automata models in economics.

4.2. THE EXPERIMENTAL SETTING

while the remaining firms react to the leaders and within-industry competitors. Heterogeneous models can capture a variety of oligopolistic behaviors and "consonant rivalry" (Kuenne, 1979).

8. The firm selects a negative, zero, or positive increment — designated -1, 0, +1 — to its normal investment level. The selection is made according to an algorithmic rule for reacting to the investment actions of its neighbors as observed in the immediately preceding period. The rule is a model parameter which is varied experimentally. Since there is only a relatively small number of observable actions within the neighborhood, it is feasible to simulate all possible integer rules, thus generating the full strategy set of the firm (which set includes both meaningful and nonsensical behaviors).

9. In the simulations described here the rules are restricted to functions of the algebraic sum of neighbor actions. In anglicized BASIC, a rule takes a form like: IF THE NET TOTAL OF NEIGHBOR ACTIONS IN THE PREVIOUS PERIOD IS 3 OR 4 THEN SELECT +1 (a positive investment increment) ELSE IF THE NET TOTAL OF ACTIONS IS -3 OR -4 THEN SELECT -1 (a negative increment) ELSE SELECT 0 (normal investment).

10. Firms are arrayed on a line segment and the leftmost and rightmost industries are treated as experimental boundaries. In the cases reported here, the boundary industries are constrained to *normal* investment at all times.

11. For convenience, firms are assumed to be approximately equal in size. In addition, the investment increment can be assumed to be of constant dollar amount for all firms. Thus SUM, the algebraic sum of firms' actions can be construed as either an "index of business sentiment" or, with a scale transformation, as a measure of "excess aggregate investment."

12. The system is started by distributing an initial pattern of nonzero shocks to firms selected probabilistically. Thereafter, the system evolves deterministically. The distribution of shocks is varied experimentally.

Figure 4.2 gives representative outputs for a homogeneous, 100-firm model in which the neighborhood and pattern of initial shocks are fixed, and the rule is varied experimentally. Firms are arrayed horizontally. Above normal, normal, and below normal investment levels are displayed as black, white, and gray, respectively; and each line of patterns represents a time step of the system. To help in identifying characteristic patterns, Fig. 4.1 gives outputs for a simpler two-state model (above normal = black; normal or below normal = white). The displays can be thought of as low-detail snapshots of the contents of a data bank giving values of a firm-level variable. The organizing principle is that found in many standard data sets: firm records organized according to industry, and industry records according to product or process adjacency (as in SIC codes). Looking ahead to Fig. 4.3, the conventional plots to the right of the snapshots give the time series of SUM around the base line of zero excess aggregate investment.

4.3 Complexity classification of dynamic behaviors

Four distinct types of dynamic behavior appear in the figures (indicated by numerals and notes). It has been determined that the same rule will consistently produce the same qualitative behavior for all nontrivial initial configurations. Each distinctive visual presentation, or *characteristic signature*, has been shown (Wolfram, 1983a; Albin, 1987) to correspond to a qualitative level of computational complexity that embraces dynamic properties, statistical characteristics of generated data, and linguistic properties. The latter are critical since they determine the scale of data and computational resources needed to comprehend a system and project its future path.

4.3.1 Qualitative types of dynamic behavior

Properties of four behavior types are given in summary form.

1. Uniform stable behavior. All sites (firms) quickly assume a common value indicated by a uniform black, white, or gray field.

Dynamics: The system represents a stable equilibrium with all trajectories of summed site values attracted to a single limit point.

Computational complexity: After transients die out, the system can be replicated or projected using only a simple calculator or a computer without memory.

Linguistic category: Patterns of white, gray, and black dots representing site values can be thought of as strings of symbols which can be processed according to linguistic rules. The manner in which various initial strings are processed into uniform data is characteristic of a (Chomsky) regular language.

2. Simple stability or periodicity. Particular sites or local groups of sites take on constant or simply periodic values. This behavior is observable as horizontal or vertical banding of greater or lesser complication.

Dynamics: The system is described as stable periodic. Summed site values form limit cycles. A system evolving from a finite configuration of nonquiescent sites remains finite.

CRITERIA

Type 1

Type 2

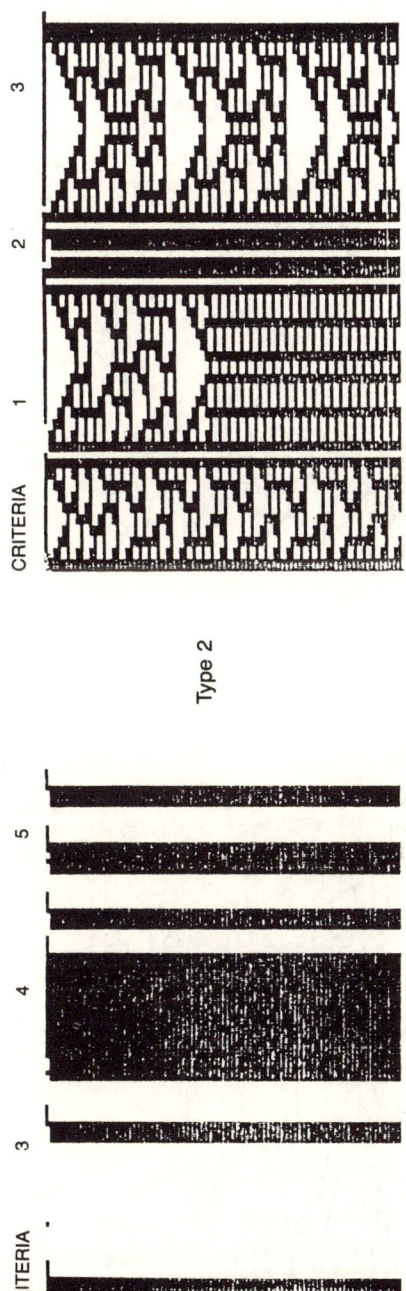

Figure 4.1: The four qualitative types in two-state models.

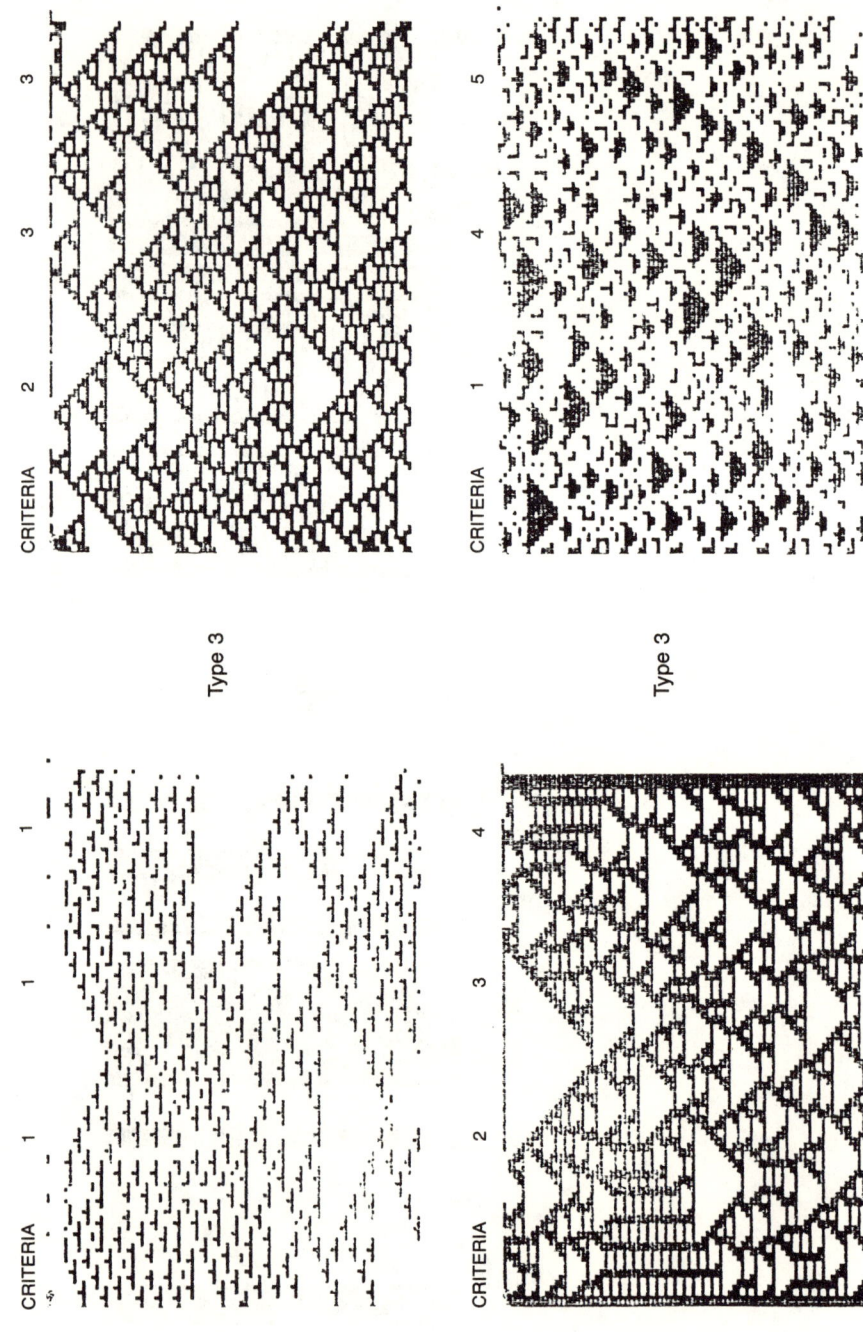

Type 3

Type 3

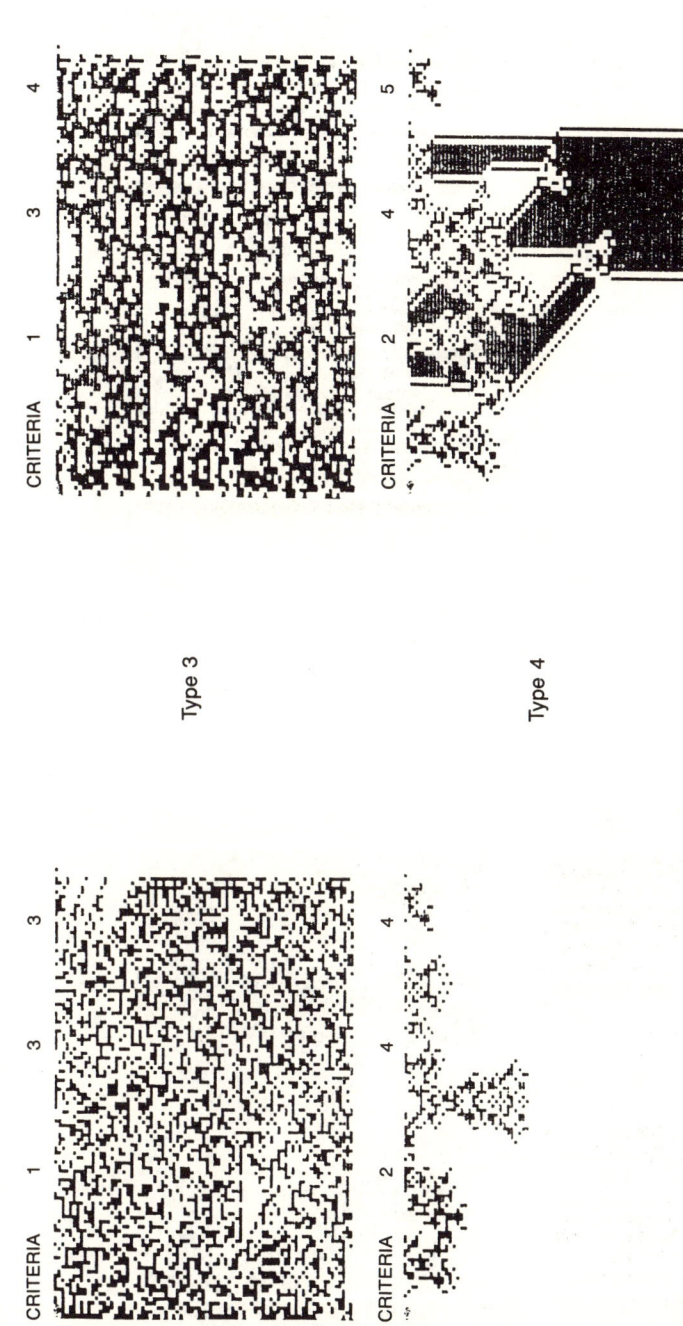

Type 3

Type 4

Notes: In each panel values for 100 sites (firms) are printed horizontally for 80 vertical time steps. Plotted sums are not given in these panels—but see Fig. 4.3. The "criteria" are rule parameters: thus "CRITERIA 1 4 5" represents the rule "print as black if 1 or 4 or 5 of your neighbors printed black in the previous time step." All cases are generated for an identical pattern of starting values which was initially produced randomly.

Note that the case on the right for type 2 is "transitional." It yields complicated cycles with periodicities that vary with the initial pattern—thus, it does not emulate a limit cycle in the strictest sense. In other topologies this rule generally produces aperiodic output. Incidentally, this rule, "print black if 1 or 2 or 3 neighbors previously printed black," is a quite plausible formulation in expectational models.

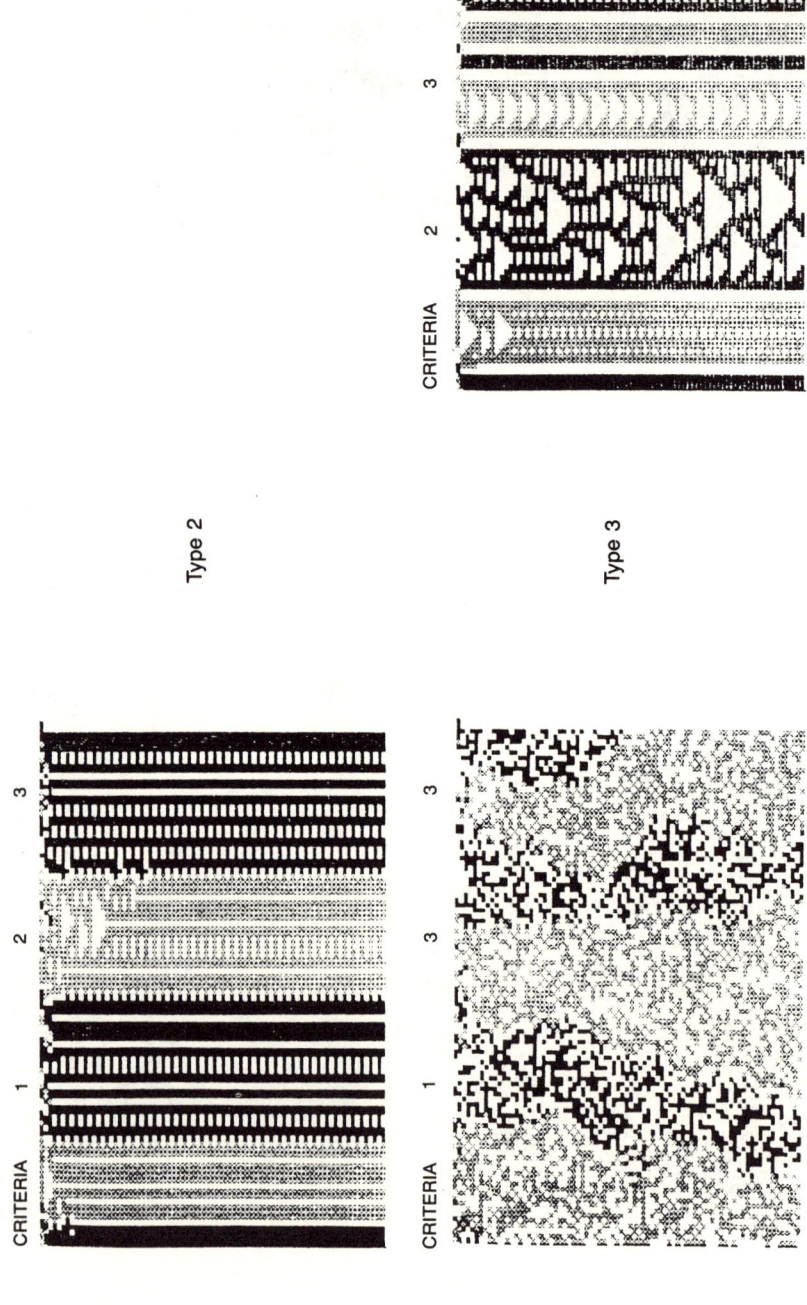

Figure 4.2: The four qualitative types in three-state models.

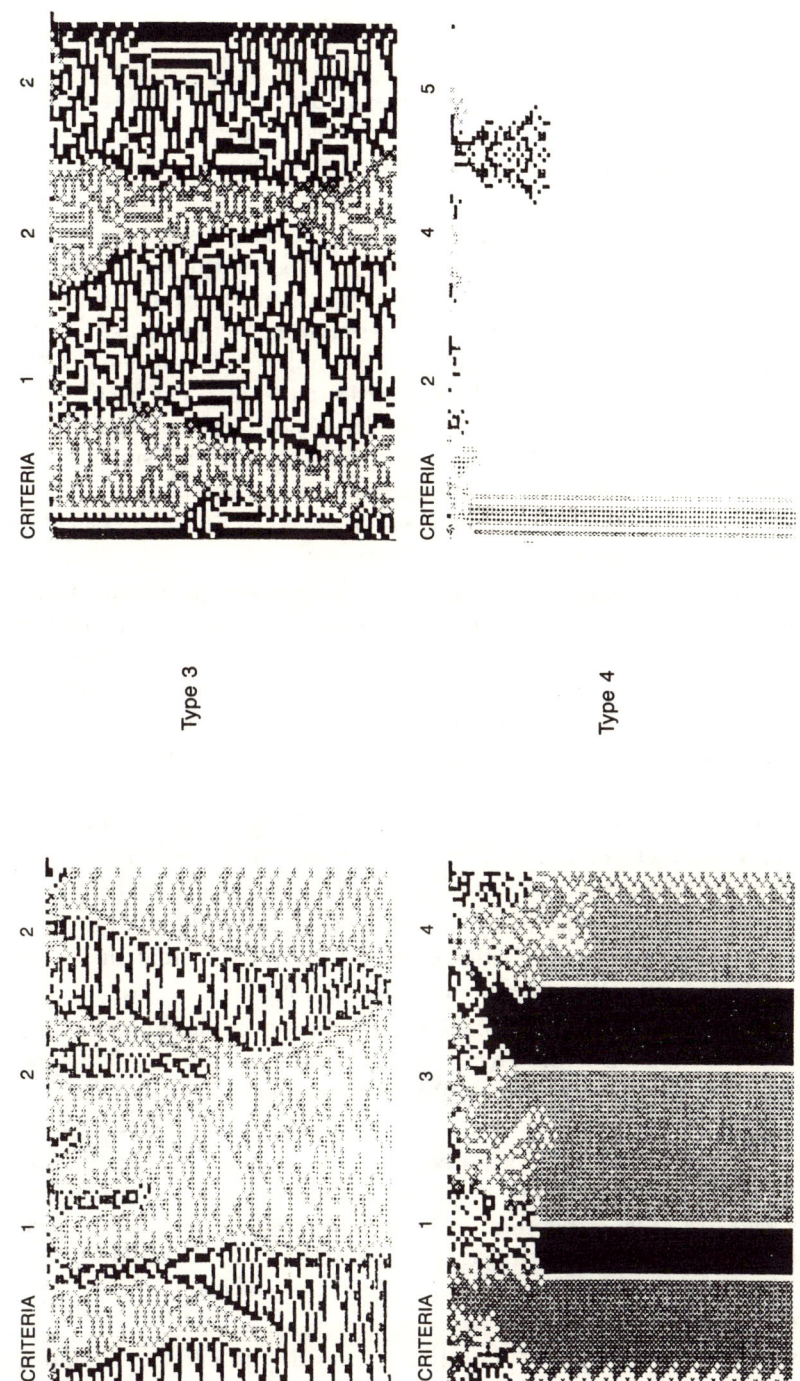

Notes: Type 1 cases (all black, white, or gray) are not shown. The case in row 1 is type 2. The case on the right in row 2 is transitional as noted in Fig. 4.1. The other type 3 cases display "pseudosectors" of like activity. The case to the left in row 4 is transitional in the line-segment topology: it displays long transients with type 4 properties.

Computational complexity: The system can be simulated on a finite memory device.

Linguistic category: The processing of symbols representing site values constitutes a context-free language—for example, a given string of local site values regardless of where it is situated in the snapshot diagram always produces the same future strings.

3. Aperiodic behavior. In one manifestation, the characteristic signature appears "noisy" with no apparent regularities. Closer inspection confirms the appearance of a wide variety of dot patterns in strings of arbitrary length. In the technical literature, this presentation has prompted rigorous description via ergodic theory (Are all possible strings encountered?) and entropic measurement (Do all possible dot patterns occur with equal frequency? Is the system maximally disordered?). In another manifestation, the characteristic signature displays recurrent patterns, such as the self-similar "blocking triangles," and a reduced set of dot patterns. This presentation is confirmed by entropic measurements and prompts calculation of fractal dimensions.

Dynamics: The system is aperiodic and time irreversible. Summed values suggest chaotic trajectories around strange attractors. An unbounded system expands into vacant sites, and "pseudosectors" with one value predominant in multistate systems may appear and persist. As noted, strings of site values may exhibit statistical regularities; these properties are unique to each generating rule (firm strategy) and are insensitive to the initial pattern of shocks.

Computational complexity: The memory requirements for a simulating device grow without restriction. These requirements are "irreducible," also meaning that there is no "analytical" shortcut to full system emulation.

Linguistic category: The evolution of the system is "context-sensitive," meaning that a given string of site values may produce different successor strings at different locations in the snapshot diagram.

4. Irregular and persistent behavior. The characteristic signature consists of several irregular forms which interact in unexpected ways. Different initial patterns may produce dramatically different snapshot diagrams.

Dynamics: Depending on the initial pattern of shocks, this type of irregular system may grow, cycle, contract, or die out. Intricate local structures may persist, die out, or propagate leading to intricate interactions with other local structures, and "time irreversible" systems suggest historical development. Few statistical regularities can be detected in time series of system aggregates; these may exhibit shifts which mimic structural changes.

Computational complexity: Local structures act, in effect, as components of a universal computer. The system is computation irreducible; fur-

4.3. COMPLEXITY CLASSIFICATION

thermore, limiting system behavior and statistical properties for arbitrary input are effectively unpredictable.

Linguistic category: The "human unpredictability" of the system is captured by the Chomsky category of "unrestricted language"—formally corresponding to the arbitrarily large simulation device required to emulate the system.

4.3.2 Projective properties

For the economist, an intuitive understanding of the classification system can be gained by asking how a forecaster for a firm might decode a time series of local observations to derive a closed-form representation or to project the system and thus improve upon the current myopic rule for forming expectations. For example, there would be little problem in handling the type 1 uniform equilibrium. It is clear that one need only observe a few time slices to confirm uniformity and that this information would suffice to project the system arbitrarily far into the future. In terms of computational resources, one would need only a pocket calculator (without memory) to multiply the equilibrium value by t and so effect a growth extrapolation t years into the future.

For the type 2 periodic system, a time slice of observed data thick enough to contain the full record of a cycle would suffice for projections. These data would fit within a finite memory device. Thus, for a cycle of period p, in order to project the system to period t arbitrarily far in the future, one needs only the capacity to calculate a modular division of (t/p) and look up the corresponding value in the memory device. Perhaps, one might wish to observe more cycles to confirm the dynamics, but the principle is clear: there exists an observation of finite length on the past behavior of a determinate system that tells all that is necessary to project the future behavior of the system with simple means.

This commonly held presumption on resource bounds for observation and extrapolation no longer holds for the third and fourth types of systems. Put one way, in order to predict the tth state of the system, the entire record to $t-1$ is needed; put another way, there is no bounded store of data which tells all that is necessary to know about the system; put still another way, the marginal value of an additional observation does not decline. The computer needed to represent such systems must have memory that grows in size with the length of the projection; furthermore, the computer needed for the type 4 system must be without any effective restriction on its logic. The distinction between type 2 and type 3 systems is particularly important for the theory of economic expectations. In a type 2 system, an economic agent needs only to observe a full cycle of data within a restricted band of adjacent sites. Once a particular pattern of site values recurs, the whole future history of that local band can be extrapolated. In a type 3 system, the recurrence of a particular local pattern is of limited use in forming projections. The further future in the local band varies according to "context," the values at distant sites. The data and computational resources needed to project the "context-sensitive" case are far greater than those needed for the "context-free" setting and greatly exceed those generally assumed for practical expectations formation. The "context-free/sensitive" designations allude to an isomorphic system for classifying linguistic complexities—the Chomsky ordering.

4.3.3 Modeling considerations

The four qualitative categories exhaust the dynamic potentialities for reciprocally interactive systems. The characteristic signatures appear in systems with more states (color printing is required), narrower or broader neighborhoods of interaction, higher-order lags, mixtures of rules and neighborhood boundaries, and additional dimensions (Smith, 1971; Albin, 1975; Wolfram, 1986). This particular modeling scheme was chosen for a number of reasons. The three-state plan specification corresponds quite closely to the familiar (worst-case, normal, best-case) scenario format for expectational data and is convenient for black and white printing. The five-firm neighborhood is suggestive of an industry size in which strategic interaction is likely. Finally, the model is small enough so that all strategic rules (of the integer type specified) can be investigated. This is probably the simplest model that is "recognizably economic" in its information cost assumptions, consistent with a general equilibrium growth framework, and capable of generating the full range of dynamics. The model was stripped of obscuring detail, hence the austere assumptions. Note, finally, that this type of system is characterized by "complexity trade-off," wherein a particular level of dynamic richness can be obtained in narrow-neighborhood models with many states or in broad-neighborhood models with fewer states. Thus, the dynamic behaviors of a fully elaborated model can be no richer than those exhibited here.

4.3.4 Dynamics and expectations

Limit-point, and limit-cycle trajectories are, of course, quite familiar in the literature pertaining to monetary dynamics. The strange-attractor (chaos) case is of comparatively recent interest—mostly following work by Day (1982a)—but is produced with some awkwardness and considerable obscurity by curvature tricks in nonlinear systems. The extremely rich irregular

4.4. POLICY INTERVENTIONS

dynamics of the fourth type are not considered in the literature at all, although a natural consequence of a market economy acting as a mesh of interconnected computers. How important are the rich cases? In models of appropriate scale—2 to 5 expectational states, 3- to 7-firm neighborhoods—the extremely rich type 4 cases are almost as likely to occur as limit-point equilibria (for approximately 6%–10% of the rules in a given model). The limit cycle appears somewhat more frequently (generally, between 10% and 20% of the time), while the varieties of chaos are the most likely to occur and increase in frequency as model size grows.

Are there a priori grounds founded in economic theory for anticipating one or another type of dynamic behavior to prevail? I think not. A case can be made for just about any one of the rules as a strategy for reacting to specific expectational data. So long as there are advantages (timeliness, reliability, availability) to be gained from drawing on low-cost local data channels and direct observation, these sources will be used. The assumption made in each simulation that all firms in the economy adhere to the same rule is, however, patently implausible. It is employed in the spirit of experimentation. I conjecture that in an actual market economy only a fraction of firms are situated in industries where there is play for reciprocal interactions. Furthermore, such industries may differ as to the prevailing rule, and rules may alter over time either spontaneously or in an evolutionary way. Thus, the actual system might be viewed as a photo mosaic made up of several snapshots with accordingly complex composite dynamics.

4.3.5 Industry structure

According to the preceding conjecture, there may be zones of differing intrinsic dynamic behavior within the economy. Furthermore, tendencies for self-organization into expanding or contracting "pseudosectors" have already been seen within several snapshots. What about industry structure per se? Included in the policy simulations to come are heterogeneous specifications which assume the strategic leadership of key firms, along with restrictions on channels whereby firms within an industry draw information on conditions outside the industry. Briefly, the four complexity types reappear. However, sectors of like behavior persist longer, and frequently the system is easier to stabilize in the manner to be next described.

4.4 Policy interventions

Active stabilization policy, in general and in the context of our model, involves attempts to achieve one or more of the following objectives:

1) centering the trend of the economy on a target path (taken here to mean the line of zero excess aggregate investment);

2) reducing the amplitude of fluctuations in key aggregates (thus reducing the real burdens of excess-capacity and tight-capacity production;

3) reducing sectoral imbalance within the aggregate (zero excess aggregate investment achieved with a sectoral boom and offset by depression in other sectors is likely to reduce the potential growth rate of the system);

4) reducing within-sector variability (thus reducing excess startup and shut-down burdens at the level of the firm or industry).

One might think of these objectives as priority ordered. In practice, though, loss functions might be such that the system is better off sacrificing a primary objective, for example, straying somewhat from the target path may yield better results than centering on the path at the cost of wider fluctuations. In brief, the objectives may also be viewed as ends whose attainment can involve trade-offs because of system interdependencies. In addition, two ancillary outcomes of intervention which might be viewed as policy significant under certain circumstances will be considered. The circumstances are where authorities cooperate and the actions of one authority may facilitate the operations of another. These outcomes are:

5) transforming the qualitative dynamics of the system; and

6) selective simplification of dynamics.

The notion here is that if monetary intervention can turn a chaotic economy into a periodic one or reduce the complication of preexisting periodicity, the tasks of another policy agency may thereby be made easier—or, perhaps, the economy becomes less sensitive to shocks which otherwise might have to be sterilized.

In modeling policy interventions, an "external entity," for example, the monetary authority, is specified as the shared neighbor of all firms in the system. This entity transmits a common signal to each neighborhood, in effect, through the agency of the banking system. Firms interpret this signal as an expectational datum. Recall that firms prepare three-contingency investment plans that incorporate assumptions regarding long-term real interest rates and monetary conditions. Thus, capital-allocative effects are already built into the plans. The choice of plan option in the short run rests on a reading of the local and aggregate business climate. The current monetary signal is viewed as an early warning indicator to be included with observations of the immediate past actions of the firm's economic neighbors.

There is, to be sure, a degree of artificiality in this attempt to isolate the cyclical and expectational from the capital-theoretic—no provision is made for plan revision based on realized experience. The scheme does,

4.4. POLICY INTERVENTIONS

however, have the virtue of simplicity and captures salient aspects of the signaling function.

The authority bases its signal (policy) on observation of the immediate past value of excess aggregate investment. It follows either a myopic countercylical rule (tightening credit in response to excess investment) or a procyclical rule. In different experiments, the policies are applied with greater or lesser sensitivity to the margin of excess (coarse or fine tuning).

4.4.1 Simulating monetary interventions

The computations are performed as follows:

1. A 100-firm economy is simulated; first, for a homogeneous model and a selection of rules, then for several different heterogeneous models and the same rules.

2. The economy is allowed to run without intervention for 20 periods in order to display its basic dynamics and characteristic signature. A control regime is instituted in period 21 and then "inverted" in period 41.

3. The control is based on SUM, the algebraic sum of $(-1, 0, +1)$ actions of all firms. Thus, SUM can range (for a 100-firm economy) from -100, connoting total slump, to $+100$, connoting exuberant boom. SUM $= 0$ can result either from all firms uniformly investing at the normal level or from above-normal outcomes offsetting below-normal outcomes. In the present implementation of the system, the authority does not differentiate between these cases (which surely matter in a real economy) nor are there real output effects from persistent over- or underinvestment.

4. SUM is plotted to the right of the characteristic diagram. The dashed line indicates zero net aggregate investment.

5. The monetary control MON can be set at $(-1, 0, +1)$ according to experimental rules. The current value of MON is plotted as a dot, blank, or black square, respectively, just to the left of the rule line at the right of the diagram.

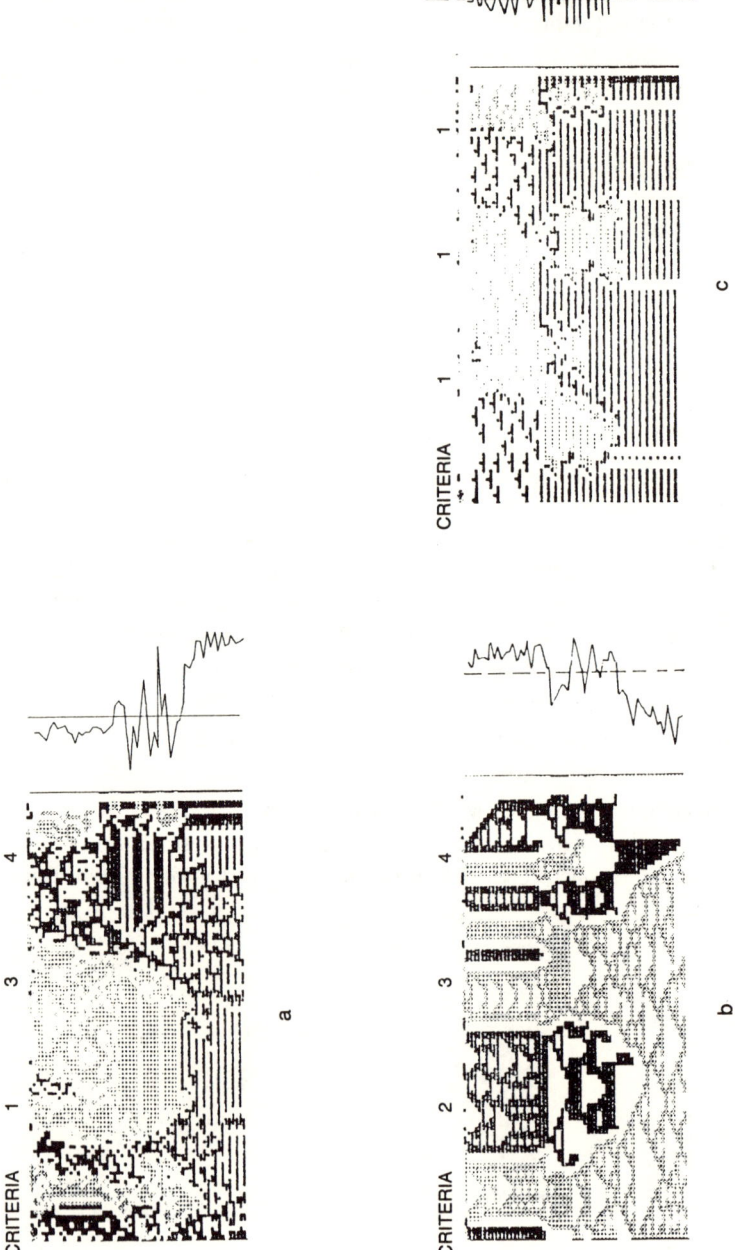

Figure 4.3: Qualitative effects of "monetary" interventions working through cellular automata expectational models.

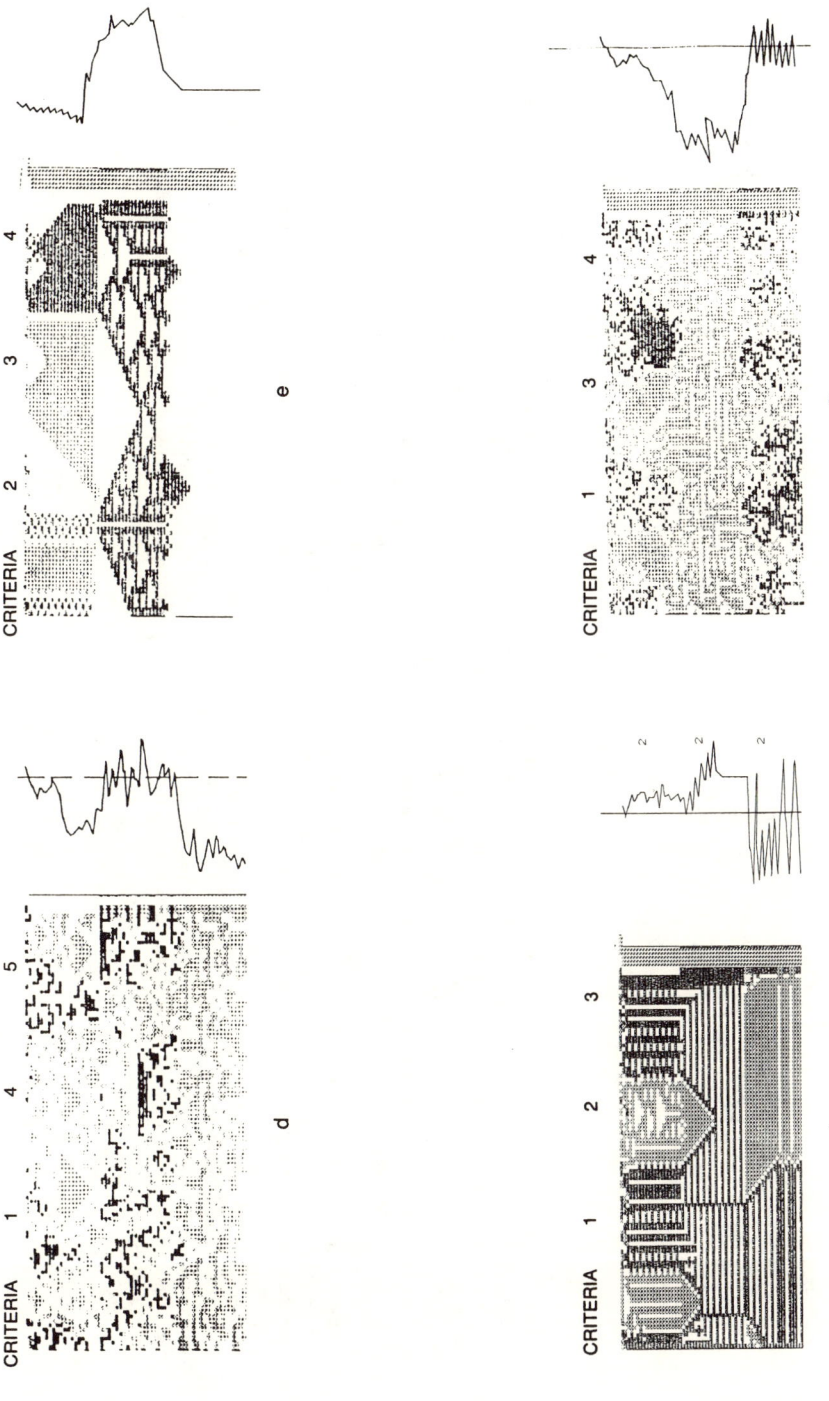

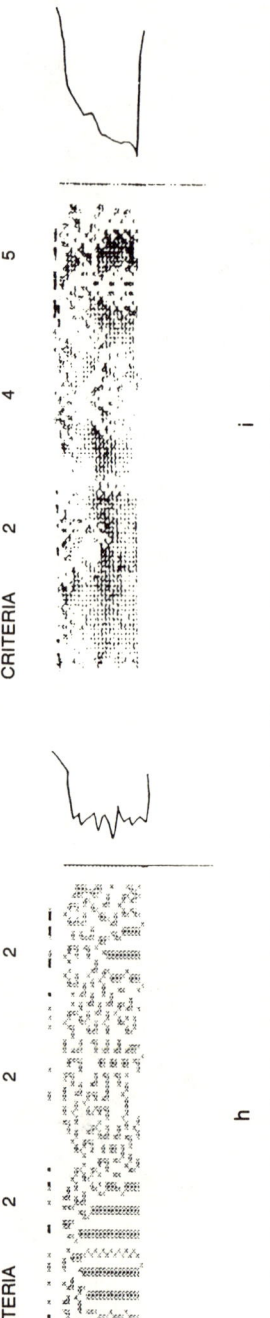

Notes: The plot to the right of each panel gives the time path of "aggregate investment" with the "target" or "0" level representing the volume of investment consonant with a Solow growth path. In panels 4.3a–g, the system develops without intervention for 20 periods. In 4.3a–d, a "countercyclical" policy is instituted in period 21 and an "accomodative" policy in period 41. In 4.3e–g, the sequence of regimes is reversed (but for models in which the firm's own state is not an argument of its expectation function). In both regimes, an intervention is triggered if actual investment differs from target investment by more than 4 percent.

In 4.3a, an initially chaotic regime is "centered" on target by the intervention but at a cost of wider fluctuations. In 4.3b, a periodic economy becomes aperiodic with wider fluctuations, but again, improved centering. In 4.3c, fluctuations widen, centering deteriorates, and the economy becomes pronouncedly cyclical. 4.3d comes close to being a success for "stabilization": a chaotic system increases measured entropy, corrects a tendency toward depressed output, centers on target but with a relatively high fluctuation range. In each of 4.3a–d, the later shift to "accomodative" policy results in greater homogeneity and often a shift to or back to aperiodicity. Cases 4.3e–g also show dramatic shifts in qualitative type, for example, type 2 to type 3 in case 4.3e and shifts between different periodic subtypes in 4.3f.

Panels 4.3h and i show what happens when a "countercyclical" regime is instituted immediately after the initial shock—leaving no time for the standard behavior to develop. In 4.3h, a rule which ordinarily results in type 1 equilibrium leads to complex persistent forms which mix features of other models. In 4.3i, a type 4 system displays a number of unusual forms not otherwise observed. It appears that the imposition of a global control can lead to any of the twelve possible transitions between Chomsky-Wolfram types and to many subtypes as well.

4.4.2 Properties of the system and experimental protocols

MON is treated by each firm as the equivalent of a unit of expectational information received from firms in its neighborhood. Thus, if a firm would expand investment if three of its neighbors signaled positively in the preceding period, it will now expand investment if MON = 1 and two firms signaled positively.

In the first group of experiments, an "accommodative" rule is applied in period 21: if SUM > 0, SUM = 0, SUM < 0, then MON = $-1, 0, +1$, respectively. The rule is inverted in period 41 to become "countercyclical." In a second grouping of experiments, MON = 0 only if SUM deviates from 0 by more than 5 in absolute value. In the third and fourth groups of experiments, the countercyclical rule is applied first with different degrees of fineness.[2] In a final group of experiments, interventions are initiated in period 1 for models whose inherent dynamics are of type 1 or 4.

4.5 Results and preliminary interpretations

At this pilot stage of the research, visual classification of model dynamics and verbal descriptions should suffice. We see from inspection of the pattern changes in Fig. 4.3 instances in which the monetary intervention leads to increases in dynamic complexity (e.g., from limit cycles to chaos [4.3e]) and decreases in complexity (e.g., from chaos to simple limit cycles [4.3f]). In fact, all possible transitions between the four complexity types have been generated by the imposition of a stabilization rule or its inversion. Careful inspection also suggests that interventions can also lead to higher or lower "complication" within a dynamic complexity classification (e.g., shortening or lengthening of cycle periods, more or less chaotic disorder). This casual observation is supported by calculations of system entropies but further experimentation is needed on this point. One tentative conclusion is offered, however. On the record of several hundred experiments covering a wide variety of firm decision rules and authority stabilization protocols, interventions are highly likely to affect the qualitative dynamic properties of the system. Such effects change the statistical properties of the system, often in ways that would encumber firm or industry forecasters or other policy makers.

---

[2]These rules are quite naive. In future work, I will experiment with higher-order autoregressive schemes and built-in artificial intelligence geared to devising the best adaptive rule.

4.5.1 Incomplete stabilization

But what of conventional stabilization? The moment of intervention is easily detected in the time-series graph of SUM to the right of each characteristic diagram. A typical sort of result is that illustrated in 4.3a and 4.3b where the economy is better centered but at the trade-off cost of wider fluctuations in the aggregate. In many other instances, the trade-off cost of wide fluctuations within the aggregate is encountered. The outcome in 4.3c, worse centering and dramatically wider oscillation, occurs infrequently but is a thought-provoking illustration of the dangers in fine tuning. A few of these dangers are exemplified in 4.3h and 4.3i, which illustrate systems that are stable in isolation but not if "stabilized" from outside. Actually, the result in 4.3d, escape from a low fluctuation "recession" to a fluctuating centered economy, is as near to a stabilization success as any observed. It is a rarity in economies whose basic dynamics are of type 3. Accommodative policy (Figs. 4.3e, f, g) tends to drive the system off center, as one might expect; but it also tends to eliminate fluctuations within the aggregate, thus making a later countercylical intervention more effective.

4.5.2 Economic implications

Results at this point must be judged as preliminary and conjectural; nonetheless, a few themes emerge from the analysis.

1. A monetary instrument based on a macroeconomic criterion, when mixed with micro or local "leading indicators," can alter the qualitative dynamics of an expectations-driven economy.

2. The alterations may increase or decrease the complexity and complication of system dynamics. System behavior appears to depend more on the way firms use expectational information than on the procyclical or countercylical intent of the intervention.

3. Preliminary procyclical interventions may be needed to stabilize a system; countercyclical interventions may increase aggregate or within-system disorder. Interventions may also work in the manner usually ascribed to them—but do so rarely. What happens depends primarily on firm-level expectational procedures.

4. The coarseness or fineness of filter rules for intervention matters—usually, but not necessarily in the manner expected.

In brief: monetary intervention does alter the dynamics of systems whose dynamics are already rich, but it does not do so in a way that suggests definitive rules for policy. Although the models here abstract from realism to a considerable degree, the results support the view that the expectational effects of monetary interventions are uncertain and potentially perverse.

Chapter 5

Decentralized, Dispersed Exchange without an Auctioneer: A Simulation Study

5.1 Introduction

We present the results of a simulation of exchange among geographically dispersed agents who face real costs of communication.[1] Exchange is entirely decentralized: it is initiated by individual agents who broadcast costly messages indicating their interest in trade; it is accomplished by bilateral bargaining between pairs of agents; agents use the information gained from previous probes, searches, and attempts at local trade to calculate their communication and search strategies for succeeding rounds.

Simulation study reveals several interesting features of this type of exchange. First, with regard to welfare effects, the decentralized mechanism can achieve a substantial improvement in the allocation of resources and the average welfare of agents as compared to a randomized initial endowment. But the process entails a sequence of trades at disequilibrium prices. Because of this, agents who begin with endowments of equal value end up with substantially unequal wealth after the exchange process. The inequality of utility among agents is reduced by exchange, but the wealth effect distinguishes the outcome of the process from a Walrasian equilibrium.

---
[1]This chapter was written by Peter S. Albin and Duncan K. Foley.

Second, system outcomes are highly sensitive to costs of information and communication. The magnitude of the improvement in allocative efficiency depends critically on the cost of broadcasting willingness to trade — advertising, as it were. A moderate degree of rationality in advertising strategies reduces but does not entirely eliminate excessive advertising, both in fruitless repetition of advertising when no trade is in fact possible, and in carrying on advertising past the point at which it is yielding individual or social gains in trade that exceed its cost. This possible excess advertising is seen as a tolerable burden for such an economy, since our results suggest that the communication and calculation demands of systems with realistically large numbers of participants can be handled by processes that are essentially local and by agents whose perspective is myopic.

Third, the geographic dispersal of agents leads to some detectable neighborhood effects in prices at the end of the exchange process, despite the effectiveness of the process in equalizing bid and asked prices locally. These neighborhood effects decline markedly as the cost of advertising falls.

Section 5.2 outlines the model and its setup for simulation. Section 5.3 describes the strategies we posit for the individual agent and discusses degrees of rationality in this setting. Section 5.4 describes the results of simulations. Section 5.5 reports results concerned with information costs. Section 5.6 reviews some related literature, draws conclusions, and suggests extensions.

5.2 A model of dispersed exchange

We simulate an economy with 100 agents and two goods. "Agents" are the bounded-rationality proxies of "players" whose rationality, in principle, is unrestricted. The agents execute a trading strategy according to an algorithm that determines their actions on the basis of the local data generated by the rules of interaction of the economy. We assume that the higher order players have selected the agents and their algorithms, so that the outcome can be evaluated in terms of the utility functions of the players.

The players all have the same symmetric Cobb-Douglas utility functions over the final holdings of the two goods. Economic interaction begins when equal amounts of the two goods are distributed randomly as endowments to the agents, under the experimental condition that the sum of each agent's endowments of the two goods is 100 and that the aggregate endowment of the two goods is $10,000 = 100 \times 100$.[2] With this condition the Walrasian equilibrium of this economy would establish a price of unity between the two goods; each agent would consume equal amounts of the two goods; and

---

[2]This restriction is achieved by matching pairs of agents in assigning endowments.

5.2. A MODEL OF DISPERSED EXCHANGE

the consumption levels of agents would be the same. Notice that at the Walrasian equilibrium price the value of the agents' endowments (which we will call wealth) are all equal. We summarize these assumptions as restrictions (5.1) and (5.2):

$$u^i = x_1^i x_2^i, i = 1, ..., 100 \qquad (5.1)$$

$$w_1^i + w_2^i = 100, i = 1, ...100 \qquad (5.2)$$

Here u is utility, x_j^i is the ith agent's holding of the jth good ($j = 1, 2$), and w_j^i is the ith agent's endowment of the jth good. If an agent holds (x_1, x_2), his marginal rate of substitution of good 2 for good 1 is $y = x_2/x_1$. This is the amount of the second good the agent would pay for one unit of the first good, the agent's bid price as a Buyer and asked price as a Seller.

5.2.1 Endowments and utilities

Following the random distribution of the endowments, the initial marginal rate of substitution of an agent is

$$y = \frac{x_2}{x_1} = \frac{100 - x_1}{x_1} = \frac{100}{x_1} - 1 \qquad (5.3)$$

If x_1 is uniformly distributed on $[0, 100]$, and x_2 is also uniformly distributed on $[0, 100]$ under the constraint that their sum equals 100, the cumulative distribution of y will be (for arbitrary t):

$$F_y(t) = Prob\{y \leq t\} = Prob\{\frac{100}{x_1} - 1 \leq t\} = \frac{t}{1+t}, t > 0 \qquad (5.4)$$

This distribution has an infinite mean.

5.2.2 Advertising neighborhoods, information costs, and trade protocol: The rules of the game

We assume that the 100 agents are arrayed in a circle and we refer to the r close neighbors on either side of an agent as the agent's neighborhood. Neighborhood size is a parameter of the simulation model.

In order to focus on the informational costs of exchange, we posit the following arrangement for trade. At the beginning of each round of trading each agent can broadcast a signal to neighboring agents, indicating a willingness to Buy or to Sell the first good for the second. The broadcasting of this signal is costly; the cost can be paid in either good, and is proportional to the size of the neighborhood and a parameter called advertising cost. We assume that agents pay the cost in terms of the good they have most of at the beginning of the round. After this spell of advertising, an agent who advertises meets each neighbor who has broadcast the complementary signal (Buyers meet Sellers). In the version of the model considered here, they reveal their current marginal rates of substitution to each other (and record this information).[3] If these marginal rates of substitution permit a trade in the advertised direction (i.e., the Buyer's bid price is higher than the Seller's asked price), an exchange will be made at a compromise price which is the geometric average of the bid and asked price,[4] and in which the sum of the amounts exchanged equals a parameter called the trade step.[5] In the simulation these trades are sequential. The computer starts each round with a particular agent. The choice of initial agent was rotated around the circle in some simulations, but this had no effect on the qualitative properties of the results, so we report simulations in which the starting point is always the same. The agent is paired with each neighbor in order to see if the pair is a candidate for trade and if a trade can be effected. After all neighbors of the initial agent have been encountered, the program moves on to the next agent. Each trade is made on the basis of the agents' current holdings, including changes that may have taken place earlier in the same round of trading as a result of trades with other agents.[6] When the program finishes with the last agent, a new round starts. Trading ceases when no agent advertises.

Notice that this trading protocol has several distinctive features. An agent who does not advertise does not receive advertising. An agent can advertise only on one side of the market in each round. Agents pay an advertising cost that is proportional to the number of recipients of their message, but must broadcast to all the agents in their parametrically given

---

[3] The question of whether it might not be rational for players to reveal their marginal rates of substitution truthfully is considered in section 5.3.

[4] The choice of the geometric average is suggested by the form of the utility function and tends to protect agents who are outliers in endowment proportions from trading at very unfavorable prices.

[5] Other models employing the setting of neighborhood markets might further restrict the amount of information that is disclosed at this stage of the process. The crudest models would limit agent information to nonprice data on the pattern of signals within the neighborhood and knowledge of whether trades were accomplished. An intermediate model form would permit disclosure of marginal rate of substitution data only if a trade is actually accomplished—in effect, the agent would have to infer the trading partner's marginal rate of substitution by reasoning backward from the observed price of a completed exchange. The present model is designed to probe how close to exchange efficiency algorithmic rationality and local information exchange can take agents when they have no prior knowledge of the equilibrium price or other global conditions.

[6] The starting point and exact pattern of matches have little effect on the outcome, because the trade step is small.

neighborhood. Agents who are initially potential trading partners may fail to trade because they both advertise on the same side of the market or because they advertise on the wrong side of the market, or because one fails to advertise at all, or because earlier trades have eliminated possible gains to trade between them. The price at which a trade takes place represents a splitting of the difference of gains from trade at the moment the agents meet, but does not allow for any negotiation. The same pair of agents may meet twice in a round, and may trade at different prices on these two occasions because in the intervening time one or both of them made another trade. Finally, the size of each trade is constrained; this eliminates one economic variable from the model. The convention means that agents cannot exploit what they might interpret as especially favorable prices by making large purchases. On the other hand, once a pair of agents has discovered the possibility of mutually beneficial trade, it can continue to trade on succeeding rounds.

The exchange process in this setting is transitory. It starts with the distribution of dissimilar endowments, and continues until no agent advertises.

5.3 Strategies of agents

In this model an agent can be represented by an algorithm operating within strict bounds on computational resources. We comment on the rationale for this construction before describing the algorithm we have implemented.

5.3.1 Boundedly rational agents of fully rational players

The rules of economic interaction just described define an n-person, iterated game with restricted information. Rational players can be thought of as selecting boundedly rational agents. These agents consist of a mapping from information sets to actions (advertising to buy or sell good 1 or refusing to advertise). The players are fully rational and capable of calculating the expected utility payoffs from selecting a particular agent. The general problem of analyzing the outcome of such a game poses formidable problems. One might start, for example, by investigating the set of Nash equilibria for this game (which is nonempty since the best response to the situation where no other agent ever advertises is never to advertise). The complex dynamic structure of this game makes enumeration, let alone systematic examination of possible Nash equilibria a daunting task.

We have chosen instead to suggest a candidate algorithm requiring limited computational resources that has desirable properties. We cannot demonstrate that this candidate algorithm constitutes a best response when all the other players have chosen it for themselves. Our results show that it has desirable systemic properties. Other programs obeying the same resource limitations might well do better in either of these respects.

5.3.2 Truthful disclosure

Trading in small amounts at a compromise price is effective in this model because we assume that agents will truthfully disclose their bid prices. This is a strong assumption for which there is, as usual, no compelling behavioral justification. The assumption that trading proceeds in small steps makes truthful revelation at least plausible. The gain from misrepresenting one's marginal rate of substitution in any given encounter is small, since the amount of goods to be exchanged is small. A player who misrepresents his current marginal rate of substitution may make a small immediate gain in the price at which a small amount of goods is traded, but faces incalculable and potentially large losses over the whole process of trading. For example, misrepresentation may lead a neighbor to cease advertising and trading even when mutually beneficial trades are possible. Where the gain from misrepresentation is small and the potential losses hard to calculate but possibly large, it does not seem implausible to assume truthful revelation.

5.3.3 The agent's computational capacity

Given the rules of interaction, an agent is programmed to choose whether to advertise, and what to advertise, in each round. We limit the agent to memory capacity sufficient to store the following information: (1) the agent's own current holdings of the two goods, (2) the advertising cost and neighborhood size parameter which determine the cost of advertising, (3) a record of whether the agent has ever met the neighbor, (4) a record of marginal rates of substitution of neighbors on the occasion of their last meeting (if such a meeting has taken place), and (5) parameters of an estimated distribution of the two goods among the agents. Agents do not have a record of what trades took place in the last period.

The distinctiveness of our model rests largely on the fourth component, the formation by agents on behalf of players of estimates of the initial distribution of the endowment, or, equivalently, of the Walrasian equilibrium price. No player in fact knows this distribution, but players are able to program their agents to develop estimates on the basis of their local data.

Even when an agent has information about a neighbor's marginal rate of substitution, trade between them is impossible without advertising. We refer to neighbors about whom an agent has information as acquaintances

5.3. STRATEGIES OF AGENTS

and other neighbors as strangers. This information allows the agent to estimate possible trades with acquaintances on the opposite side of the market, and to estimate possible utility gain from each such trade. The agent does not know the aggregate endowment in the economy, nor the Walrasian equilibrium price.[7]

5.3.4 The candidate algorithm

In each round, the agent estimates the expected net utility gain from advertising on either side of the market. If the maximum of these estimates is positive, the agent chooses the maximizing message (either Buy or Sell). If both are negative, the agent chooses not to advertise, and does not participate in trade.

5.3.5 The expected gain from signaling

The process of estimating the gain from an advertising message can be thought of in two parts, one concerning acquaintances, the other concerning strangers. First, the agent can calculate the gain from trade with any acquaintance conditional on the neighbor's advertising on the opposite side of the market. This gain may be zero (if the agent is considering a Buy message, and estimates that the acquaintance's bid price will be higher than the agent's own).

Second, the agent must estimate the gains from trading with strangers in the neighborhood. In estimating the gains of trade with strangers, provisional estimates of the stranger's marginal rate of substitution are required. The agent assumes, in effect, that the ratio of the total supply of good 2 to the total supply of good 1 is an unknown parameter z, and that the goods have been distributed so that each agent's wealth at the Walrasian price (which the agent assumes will be z) is equal, and that the distribution of good 1 is uniform. Under these assumptions the agent will—by Bayesian reasoning parallel to (5.6)—estimate that the cumulative distribution of marginal rates of substitution is[8]

$$F_{y|z}(t) = \frac{t}{z+t} \qquad (5.5)$$

---

[7]It is on this important point that our "search technology" differs from that in Peter Diamond (1984) and in many successor works to Edmund S. Phelps (1970). While our model shares with this literature a process of pairwise decentralized trading (thereby dispensing with the fiction of the Walrasian auctioneer), the literature assumes that the Walrasian price is known to all. See also Steven Salop and Joseph Stiglitz (1982).

[8]This is the only use the agents are assumed to make of these assumptions about the form of the distribution of marginal rates of substitution. These assumptions could represent the historical memory of the form taken by endowments in the past.

We assume that the agent estimates z by taking the average of known marginal rates of substitution (mrs) including the agent's own, y. When considering a Buy message, the agent assumes that the stranger, if a Seller, will have an mrs equal to the median of the agents whose mrs are lower than y in the distribution resulting from (5.5). When considering a Sell message the stranger, if a Buyer, is assumed to have an mrs equal to the median of the agents whose mrs are higher than y in the distribution resulting from (5.5). For a Buy, the estimated stranger's mrs is $yz/(2z+y)$, where y is the agent's own mrs. For a Sell the estimated stranger's mrs is $(2y+z)$. This method was chosen in order to avoid more complicated calculations (such as taking an expectation over the distribution). It turns out that the stranger rule rarely plays much role in the simulations, after the initial iterations because agents rapidly meet their neighbors.[9]

5.3.6 Estimating the likelihood of neighbor actions

The agent's calculation of expected gains from advertising is completed by estimating the probability that each neighbor will bid Buy or Sell, or refuse to advertise at all. We assume that the agent maintains a Markov model for estimating the probability that an agent who did not advertise in the last period will begin to advertise (Buy and Sell being equally likely choices in this situation), and that an agent who did advertise in the last period will either choose the same message or switch. These probabilities may sum to less than one, the residual being the estimated probability that an agent who advertised last period will not advertise this period at all. Every time any of these behaviors is observed, the agent updates this model by multiplying the current estimate of the probability by a parameter, the probability weight, and adding 1 minus this probability weight to the estimate. Thus if p_{sw} is the current estimate of the probability that an advertiser will switch bids, δ is the probability weight, and the agent observes a neighbor actually switching, we have:

$$p_{sw}^{new} = \delta p_{sw} + (1 - \delta) \tag{5.6}$$

This method adapts expectations to the actual frequency of observed changes. Notice that restrictions on computational capacity prevent the agent from keeping a separate model for each neighbor; instead in our algorithm observations on all of them are pooled and the same probability model is applied to each. Agents following this algorithm avoid the difficulties of trying to anticipate the actual decisions of individual neighbors.

---

[9]The stranger rule does play a role in one type of overtrading (continued futile bidding) that appears in some of the simulations, as we will discuss in the next section.

Such calculations would require the agent to estimate each neighbor's information set. However, such sets would include the marginal rates of substitution of agents outside the original agent's neighborhood. Furthermore, by extension fully rational agents would also attempt to infer neighbors' information sets so augmented: the train of inferences would grow to intractability. Our construction avoids this problem.[10]

5.3.7 Simulation procedures

The simulation model is initialized with players conveying arbitrary estimates of these transition probabilities to their agents. We assume that players have rather optimistic estimates of the probability that their neighbors (none of whom advertised in the last period) will switch and choose to advertise, an assumption that is sufficient to ensure some initial advertising and trading.[11] After trading starts the probability estimates of agents quickly converge to the actually observed averages (since in the simulations $\delta = .9$).

Each simulation begins with a random distribution of endowment according to the restrictions described in Section 5.2. The neighborhood size, advertising cost, probability weight, and trade step are given parameters. Each agent calculates the next period's advertising choice according to the principles assumed, and the round of trading takes place according to the trading protocol described in Section 5.2. Agents then begin a new round with new probability estimates (incorporating their observations of behavior in the last round), possibly new information about their neighbors' bid and asked prices, and a new own endowment and new own bid and asked prices as a result of paying advertising costs and trading in the last round. The statistical module of the program accumulates a considerable bank of information about the round of trading, including the number of messages broadcast, the number of trades, utilities, wealths, and probability estimates. The information collected by this module is, of course, not available to the agents.

---

[10]The agents' calculating procedure can be interpreted as a "bounded-rationality" rule (Simon, 1978), which turns out to perform well on efficiency grounds. We suggest—and discuss further in Section 5—an alternative interpretation based on the costs of computational "intelligence" as a component of information cost.

[11]In effect, the changed endowment triggers a thought process of the following sort. "My endowment has been changed. I don't know if I am the only one for whom this has occurred, nor do I know if the proportions in my new endowment are typical. I am going to assume that others have received new endowments according to some unknown distribution, and that the others are as unsure of the situation as I am. I optimistically assume that the distribution is sufficiently varied that it will be to my interest to test the market. If I am right, and others do likewise, our probes will disclose profitable exchange opportunities."

5.3.8 The coefficient of resource utilization

We are particularly interested in the efficiency of this system. One way to measure the progress of the system of traders toward equalization of their marginal rates of substitution is to calculate the coefficient of resource utilization (CRU) (Debreu, 1951). For a particular allocation, this coefficient is the minimum fraction of the original resources of the economy that could be allocated so as to give every consumer the same utility level as in the current allocation. For the model we are studying the coefficient of resource utilization for an allocation $\{x_1^i, x_2^i\}$ given a total resource availability of $\{w_1, w_2\}$ is

$$r = \frac{\sum_{i=1}^{n}(x_1^i x_2^i)^{1/2}}{w_1^{1/2} w_2^{1/2}}$$

5.4 Simulation results

Figures 5.1 and 5.2 show record computer screens reporting respectively the initial position and final outcome of a simulation. Table 5.1 gives step-by-step accounts of the same simulation.

5.4.1 Reporting format

The window in the upper portion of each figure is a cumulative record of the advertising by the agents. For example, each site in Fig. 5.2 moving across the window corresponds to the action taken by one agent; gray indicates no advertising, black, Sell, and white, Buy. Successive rounds of trading are recorded moving down the window. Thus the state of the market in one round can be recovered by reading across a row, and the history of each agent by reading down a column.

The window at the bottom of the figure plots the logarithm of the agents' marginal rates of substitutions. Fig. 5.1 shows the random distribution at the beginning of trading, and Fig. 5.2 the smoother distribution that results after several rounds of trading.

Table 5.1 shows the results of the same simulation as recorded by the accounting part of the program. Reading across, we have the trial number, the number of traders who increased utility on that trial, the number who bid, the number of trades, the coefficient of resource utilization, the proportion of good 1 remaining after the trial, the mean and standard deviation of the logarithm of the marginal rates of substitution after the trial, the mean and standard deviation of utilities after the trial, and the mean and standard deviation of wealth, defined as the value of the agents' current

5.4. SIMULATION RESULTS

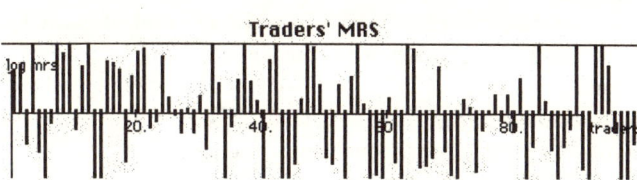

Figure 5.1: The initial state of a simulation with neighborhood size 2 and advertising cost 0.1.

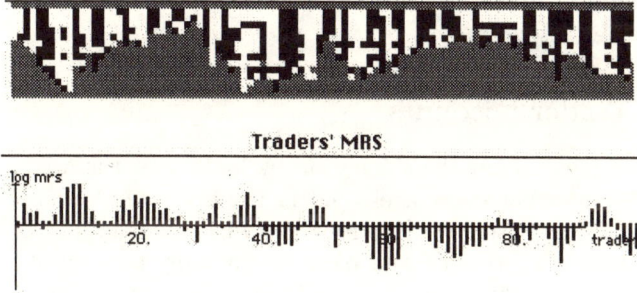

Figure 5.2: The final state of a simulation with neighborhood size 2 and advertising cost 0.1.

holdings at the Walrasian equilibrium prices (in this case, the sum of the endowments, since the Walrasian equilibrium relative price is unity).

5.4.2 Illustrative results

This simulation, which sets neighborhood radius at 2 (so that each neighborhood includes five traders), and advertising cost at .1, so that it costs .4 units of goods to send an advertising message to the neighborhood, illustrates some of the general features of this simulation system. In Fig. 5.1, which shows the initial round of trading, we can see the original highly irregular distribution of the log of marginal rates of substitution as a result of the random distribution of the endowment. The coefficient of resource utilization begins at .7812. No agent bid in the last period, and there was no trading. Fig. 5.2 shows the fourteenth and last round of trading in the same simulation. The logs of the marginal rates of substitution have converged to a considerable degree, though the waves in the bottom panel indicate substantial neighborhood effects on price. The coefficient of resource utilization has risen to .9454, while the amount of good 1 remaining has fallen to .9692. In other words, the agents have expended a bit over 3% of their endowment in advertising costs, and have reached utility levels that could be achieved with a bit less than 95% of the original endowment if there were some costless way of redistributing the goods.[12]

The pattern of bidding shown in the top left window of Fig. 5.2 indicates the complicated interaction of buying and selling bids produced by the simple decision rules in the model. There was a very small amount of overtrading at the end of the simulation. If the agents had given up advertising after round 11, they would have been a bit better off, as measured by the coefficient of resource utilization. The last few rounds of advertising simply wasted resources.

5.4.3 Trader accounts

We can see more about the simulation by looking at the accounts in Table 5.1. We see that every agent bid in the first round, and that trades reached a very intensive level by round 2, with 198 trades among the 100 traders. After this, trading and bidding gradually tapered off as traders exploited the possible gains from trade in their neighborhood.[13] Advertising costs gradually eroded the original endowment. The mean log of the marginal rates of substitution was originally negligibly different from zero (as the distribution method was intended to achieve), and remained there throughout the trading process. The standard deviation of the logs of the marginal rates of substitution, however, declined sharply as a result of trade, from 1.72 at the initial allocation, to .44 at the final allocation. Mean utility (which closely corresponds to the coefficient of resource utilization) rose from 39.11 to 47.33, while the standard deviation of utility declined from 10.6 to 7.52, due to the gains from exchange. Mean wealth declined (due to the costs of advertising), but the standard deviation of wealth, which was initially 0, rises to 14.93. The reason for this is that there are many exchanges at disequilibrium prices in the model. Agents who have the misfortune to have initial endowments very different from the average will make a lot of their trades at very high (or low) prices in the mechanism simulated here. As a result, these agents lose wealth to agents whose original endowment proportions were closer to the average.

---

[12] Compare this to a Walrasian system whose auctioneer consumes 3% of the endowment to achieve a first-best allocation of the remaining goods.

[13] The first phase of trading bears close resemblance to patterns produced by the third most complex type of cellular automaton. The second phase produces periodic patterns typical of the second most complex form. A cellular automaton system that is capable of producing these two patterns and terminating is known to be of the highest complexity type. See Wolfram (1986, 1.3).

(This effect may be reduced if an agent with an outlying endowment has a neighbor whose endowment is extreme in the opposite direction, because their trades with each other will be at prices close to the eventual equilibrium price.) The fall in inequality as measured by the standard deviation of utilities is in sharp contrast to the rise in inequality as measured by the standard deviation of wealth.

5.4.4 Comment

While we have no very good standard of comparison, we were somewhat surprised that this decentralized exchange mechanism performed so well. Despite the lack of a centralized market, and the necessity for goods to travel at a cost from one neighborhood to another through a chain of traders in order to equalize marginal rates of substitution, this decentralized process reallocates the original endowment effectively and fairly cheaply. Despite the crudeness of our agents' rules of behavior, they manage to figure out that they should stop advertising soon after advertising becomes futile. Of course, the distribution of original endowments did not pose the toughest test of this type of mechanism, because endowments in neighborhoods were not correlated.

5.4.5 A second illustrative example

Figure 5.3 and Table 5.2 show another run of the model in which the stopping rules did not work so well. Here the neighborhood size is 4, and the advertising cost is a relatively low .025. The system works well initially, generating a blizzard of trades in the first few rounds, and raising the coefficient of resource utilization to .965 in eight rounds. At this point trading quickly tapers off, and most of the agents give up. But four agents keep on bidding far too long. An investigation of this situation shows that these agents do not know each other's marginal rates of substitution. The cycling is caused by their assumption that large gains from trade are possible with each other, and their inability to get on the opposite side of the market because their probability models indicate a higher probability of the other trader keeping the same bid in the next period.[14]

5.5 Information cost and efficiency

We view our study as a first step toward a more detailed examination of the role of information transmission and processing costs in the micro-

---

[14]Evolutionary improvements might, of course, improve agent performance in this as in other respects.

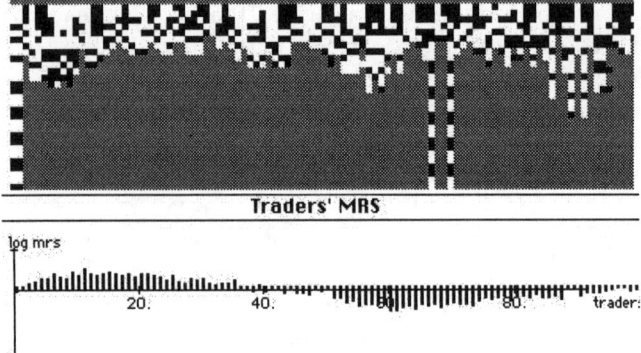

Figure 5.3: The 28th round of a simulation with neighborhood size 4 and advertising cost .025. Cycling of bids is evident.

microbehavior of market economies. The costs of information processing and transmission are multidimensional. We must consider the costs involved in the fabrication of a message, the cost of communication of the message, the cost of extraction of useful intelligence from received messages, the costs of decision in determining the actions to be followed once information has been exchanged, and the resources embodied in the infrastructure necessary to support the system of communication. We have encountered each of these facets of the information problem in setting up our model. An additional group of simulation experiments illustrates some of the important cost interactions.

5.5.1 Interactions of advertising cost and neighborhood size

Figures 5.4 to 5.8 summarize the behavior of the coefficient of resource utilization over simulations run for fixed levels of advertising cost in eight steps from .01 to .75, with neighborhood sizes ranging from 1 to 5. Similarly Figs. 5.9 to 5.16 summarize the behavior of the coefficient of resource utilization over simulations run separately for fixed neighborhood radii of sizes 1 to 5, with advertising costs ranging from .01 (the lowest level examined), to .75 (advertising cost of 1.0 was included in the simulations, but was so high as to discourage trading almost completely).

These results immediately indicate that exchange is more effective in this model when advertising costs are low for a given neighborhood size, and when neighborhood size is large for a given advertising cost, although very large neighborhood size shows some tendency to lower the final coefficient of resource utilization.

5.5. INFORMATION COST AND EFFICIENCY

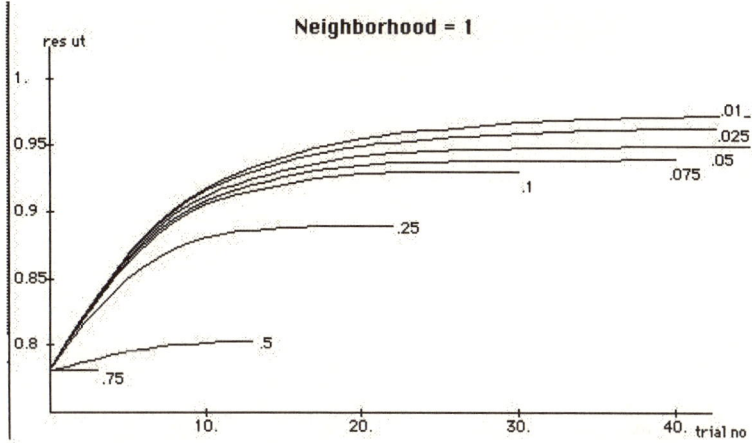

Figure 5.4: Neighborhood size = 1; advertising cost varies.

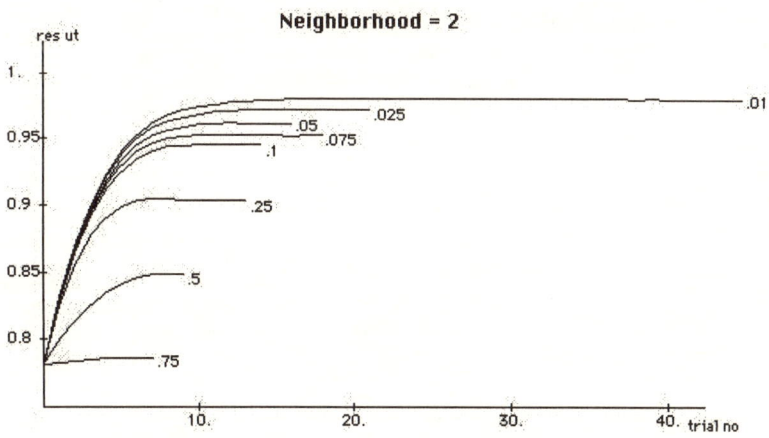

Figure 5.5: Neighborhood size = 2; advertising cost varies.

5.5.2 Interpretations

In these simulations we have fixed the capacity to extract intelligence from messages and calculate strategic decisions by assuming that all actors follow the procedures described in Section 5.3 and that there is no effective difference in intelligence and decision-making costs for neighborhoods of radii from 1 to 5.[15] Each step in neighborhood size can be interpreted

---

[15] Concern with data complexity and resource-bounded player intelligence is an emerging theme in game theory (Rubinstein, 1986; Binmore and Das Gupta, 1986, 11–13).

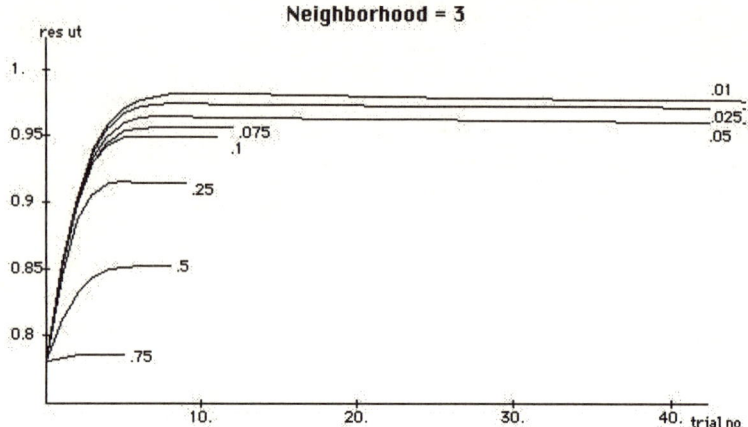

Figure 5.6: Neighborhood size = 3; advertising cost varies.

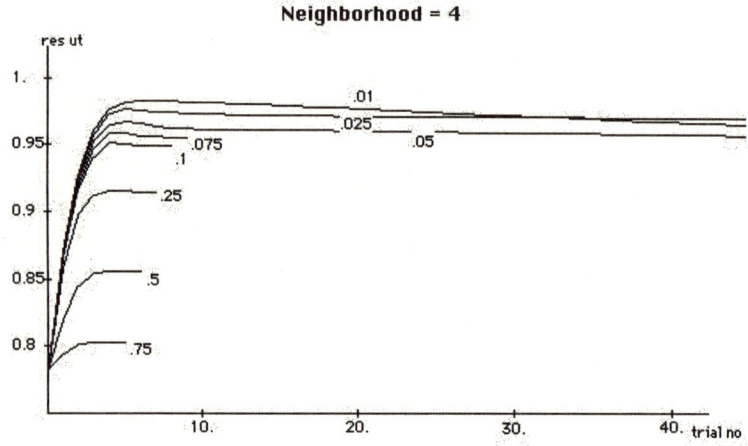

Figure 5.7: Neighborhood size = 4; advertising cost varies.

Each of our agents operates with the abstract equivalent of a programmable hand calculator. In effect, the required calculating resources for an agent following our protocol within a neighborhood of radius r is a finite device containing r fixed-size sectors of memory to store current local data. In contrast, a comprehensive, full-rationality system in which each agent seeks to model the states of all N agents in the economy (including the information possessed by these agents) requires a data store which grows with N and the number of recorded iterations. The cost of calculations entailed by this construction—in principle, an unrestricted Turing machine for each player's agent—may grow exponentially with N. This type of knowledge system may entail intractable computations for economies of realistic size. We suggest that, if calculating costs are

5.5. INFORMATION COST AND EFFICIENCY

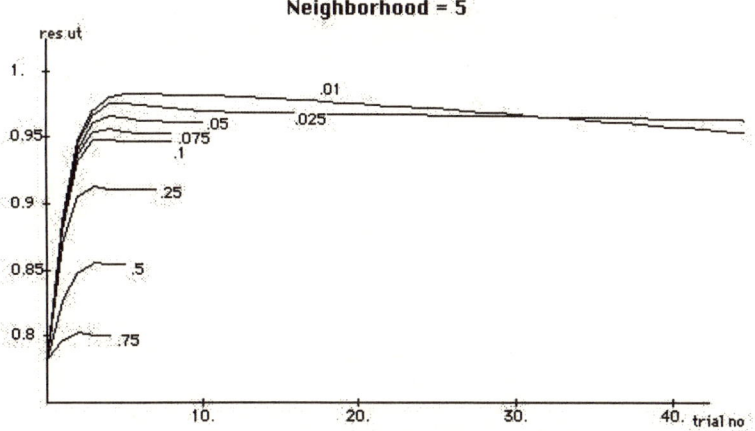

Figure 5.8: Neighborhood size = 5; advertising cost varies.

as reflecting a particular technology and cost structure for the communications function. For the sake of argument, say that "local calls" are extremely cheap and "long distance calls" are prohibitively expensive. The neighborhood radius defines the "local calling area". The simulations thus determine the efficiency outcome for a particular message fabrication cost within a local market of a particular area. In taking this cost into account, two effects play a role: the unit cost per potential recipient, and the distribution of trading opportunities offered by the particular market area. The results indicate that expansion of the local market area has diminishing marginal effectiveness in improving efficiency. The fact that the coefficient of resource utilization reaches its asymptote in our simulations for $rN = .05$ suggests that enlarging r to approximate N would not be cost-effective. We conjecture that the efficiency outcomes attained in these simulations represent a practical upper limit to the coefficient of resource limitation unless one specifies full rationality (with the ensuing problems of computational intractability) or the full Walrasian *tâtonnement* apparatus.

---

taken into account, the rational player will accept the bounds on intelligence inherent in the former construct. We note again that the data properties and dynamics of the overlapping-neighborhood configuration have been extensively studied in cellular automata representations of physical systems (Wolfram, 1986, 1.1,3) and of interfirm signaling (Albin, 1987, 1989). These approaches use the qualitative complexity classifications of Noam Chomsky (1963), which associate virtual hardware requirements with data trajectories—and implicitly with the rationality required to analyze them. In later research we plan to investigate the efficiency payoffs to investment in data handling and computation and to study the properties of systems with a distribution of resources devoted to the intelligence function.

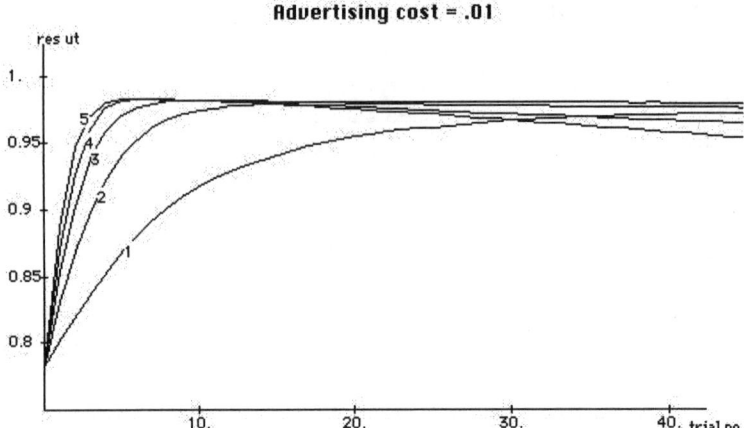

Figure 5.9: Advertising cost = .01; neighborhood size varies.

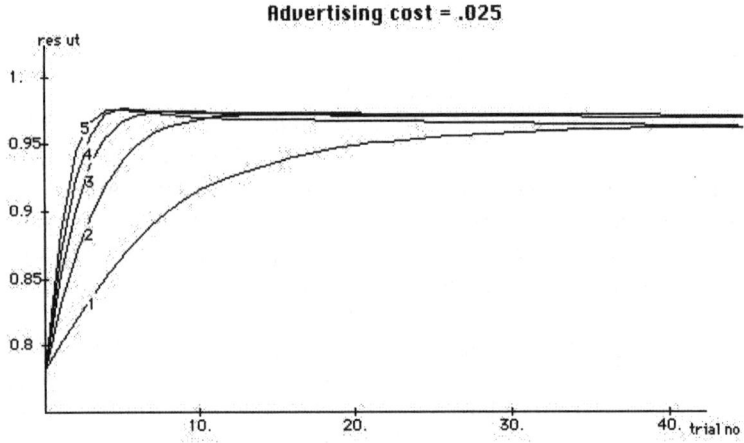

Figure 5.10: Advertising cost = .025; neighborhood size varies.

5.6 Concluding comments

Our study engages issues raised in several important literatures, although out model does not derive directly from existing formulations. We associate our work most closely with the study of nonWalrasian search technology in the spirit of Peter Diamond (1984). In Diamond's generalization, search to accomplish transactions by seller-buyer pairs is viewed as an operational alternative to the "fiction" of the Walrasian auctioneer, who "performs two functions: the matching of buyers and sellers and the calculation and

5.6. CONCLUDING COMMENTS

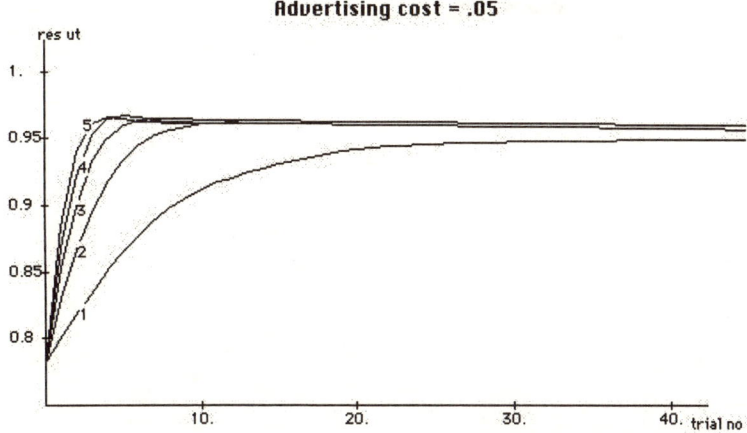

Figure 5.11: Advertising cost = .05; neighborhood size varies.

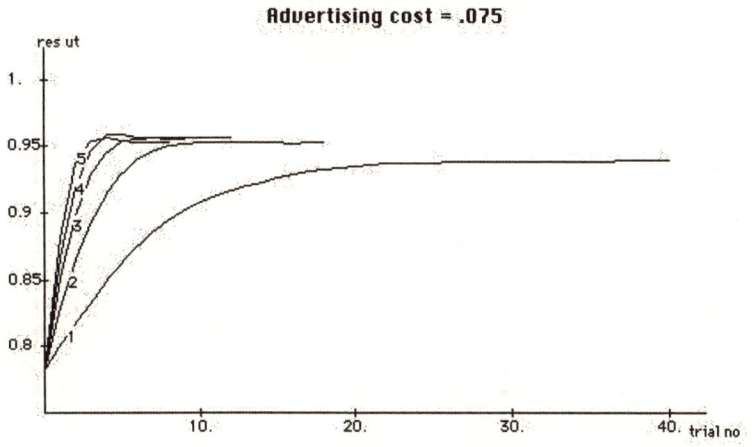

Figure 5.12: Advertising cost = .075; neighborhood size varies.

announcement of equilibrium prices." In Diamond's words: "A search technology [replaces] the frictionless matching of the Walrasian auctioneer. [But preserved is] . . . the second role of the Walrasian auctioneer [with the assumption of] correct forecasts of future prices and rates of trading opportunities" (1984, 1–3). Our analysis extends "technology specification" into this last domain. Compared to classic general-equilibrium formulations, treating a market process as a technology forces specificity and realistic costs into the model.

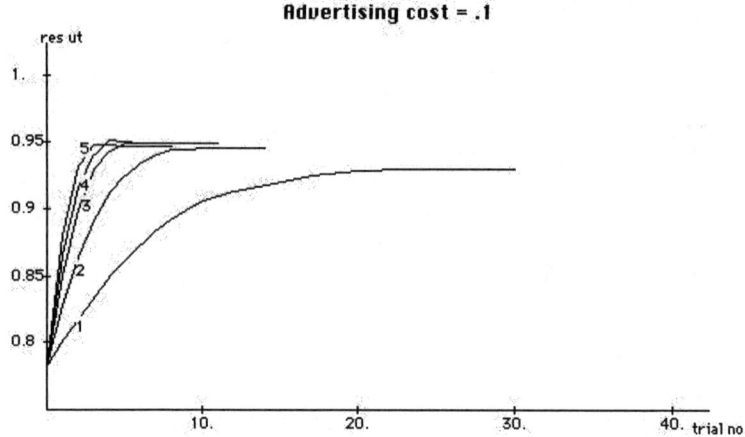

Figure 5.13: Advertising cost = .1; neighborhood size varies.

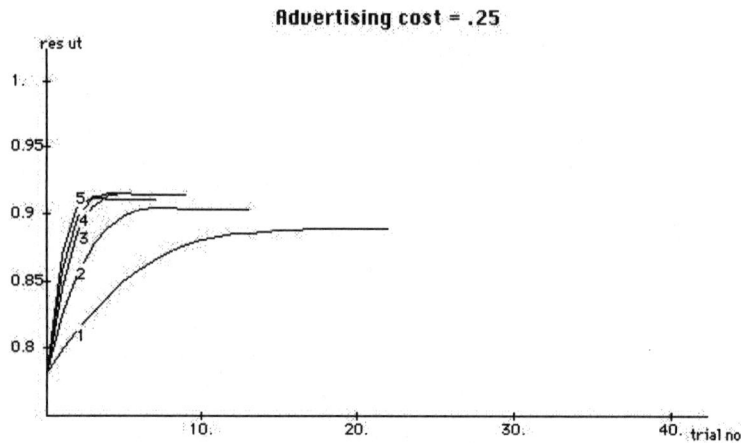

Figure 5.14: Advertising cost = .25; neighborhood size varies.

Walrasian prices do not enter the calculations of agents in our model. They appear only as references used by an external observer to evaluate the distributional impact of exchange. Trading takes place at nonequilibrium prices in a fashion analogous to that in Frank Hahn and T. Negishi's early study (1962). Although costs of coordination are strictly controlled by our assumption of local calculation, the system attains high levels of efficiency. The non-*tâtonnement* effects are exhibited in the unequal final distribution of utility and wealth.

Of particular importance in our system are costs of preparing and com-

5.6. CONCLUDING COMMENTS

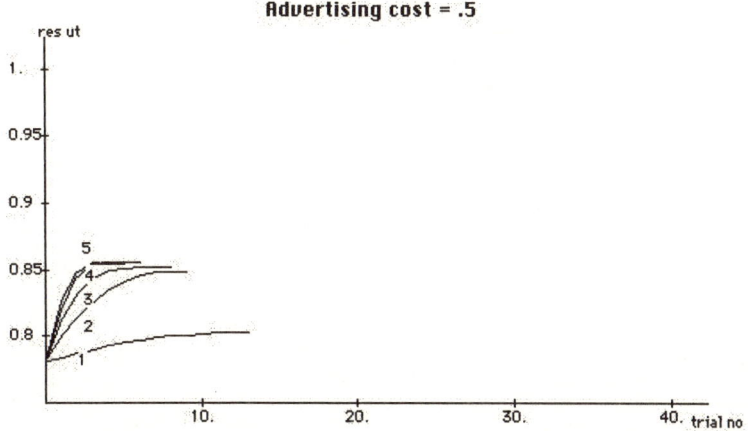

Figure 5.15: Advertising cost = .5; neighborhood size varies.

municating signals. Our work can be extended quite naturally in this direction into studies of how and to what extent access to communication nets should be publicly supported. Costs of intelligence and decision making are treated here as structural parameters that determine the computational resources carried into the process. It is interesting to conjecture that, with the local formulation we use, the unit cost of coordination does not rise with the size of the economy. In other words, for an economy of N agents sensitive to the costs of computation and organized in neighborhoods of radius r, the efficiency outcome is essentially ruled by the radius parameter and is independent of N.

It would also be possible to imagine much more sophisticated strategic behavior of agents in this model. Individual agents might attempt to maintain a model of the state of the N-agent economy conditioned on the information they have gained from past encounters with other agents, and might use this to try to predict the strategic responses of their neighbors (which will depend on information neighbors have about agents outside the particular agent's neighborhood). Such fully rational strategies would be very demanding in terms of computer storage, central processing time, and programming. The myopic rationality of our agents represents a crude attempt to economize on these costly resources. It is interesting to contemplate what technological advances would be required to make such comprehensive coordination economically feasible given the excellent efficiency performance of the simpler process.

Future research should attempt to make these various costs of information explicit and endogenous. For example, we treat neighborhood size as a parameter in our simulations, but it might be viewed as an endoge-

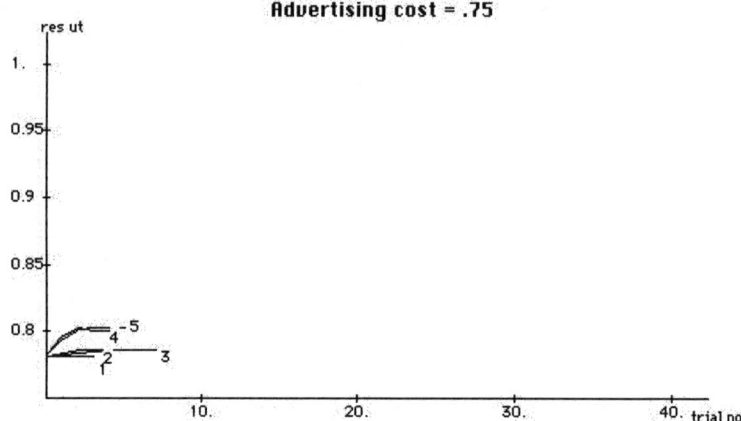

Figure 5.16: Advertising cost = .75; neighborhood size varies.

nous variable, if agents were permitted to decide how far they wanted to broadcast their advertising messages. Of course, making neighborhood size endogenous imposes higher decision-making costs on the agents as well.

Acknowledgments

We would like to thank Cecilia Conrad, the New York University Microeconomics Seminar, and anonymous referees for helpful comments.

Table 5.1   Initial Distribution: TRADER TEST 1A   Parameters: neighborhood: 2 adv.cost: 0.1

	inc ut	no bid	no trd	CRU	% good1	ln mrs mean	ln mrs sd	utility mean	utility sd	wealth mean	wealth sd
0	0	0	0	0.7812	1.0000	-0.0001	1.7200	39.1180	10.6600	100.0000	0.0000
1	89	100	195	0.8281	0.9960	-0.0048	1.4600	41.4737	9.7700	99.5956	2.3700
2	91	100	198	0.8638	0.9920	-0.0051	1.2600	43.2551	9.2900	99.1957	4.5700
3	87	99	196	0.8903	0.9879	-0.0025	1.0900	44.5808	8.8900	98.8000	6.5700
4	87	95	189	0.9110	0.9840	0.0008	0.9200	45.6098	8.3800	98.4195	8.5900
5	82	90	168	0.9257	0.9801	0.0010	0.7700	46.3543	7.9900	98.0591	10.4800
6	63	75	130	0.9353	0.9769	-0.0009	0.6600	46.8356	7.8100	97.7589	11.7000
7	50	62	97	0.9411	0.9744	0.0034	0.5800	47.1183	7.6700	97.5112	12.9100
8	45	51	76	0.9442	0.9724	0.0012	0.5100	47.2802	7.5700	97.3066	13.9700
9	17	38	30	0.9444	0.9712	0.0021	0.4900	47.2916	7.5600	97.1546	14.2900
10	21	31	30	0.9454	0.9700	0.0005	0.4600	47.3347	7.5200	97.0304	14.6700
11	9	18	17	0.9454	0.9693	0.0012	0.4500	47.3376	7.5400	96.9585	14.8500
12	3	6	4	0.9455	0.9692	0.0004	0.4500	47.3387	7.5200	96.9345	14.8600
13	0	4	2	0.9454	0.9692	-0.0005	0.4400	47.3349	7.5200	96.9185	14.9300
14	0	0	0	0.9454	0.9692	-0.0005	0.4400	47.3349	7.5200	96.9185	14.9300

Table 5.2   Initial Distribution: TRADER TEST 1A   Parameters: neighborhood: 4 adv.cost: 0.025

	inc ut	no bid	no trd	CRU	% good1	ln mrs mean	ln mrs sd	utility mean	utility sd	wealth mean	wealth sd
0	0	0	0	0.7812	1.0000	-0.0001	1.7200	39.1180	10.6000	100.0000	0.0000
1	97	100	373	0.8690	0.9980	0.0029	1.2300	43.5197	8.8700	99.7950	3.8700
2	100	100	378	0.9246	0.9958	0.0108	0.8700	46.2970	7.6700	99.5948	7.1200
3	95	100	347	0.9568	0.9938	0.0064	0.6000	47.9106	6.9100	99.3955	9.6400
4	93	100	327	0.9727	0.9917	0.0065	0.4000	48.6992	6.4500	99.1953	11.8700
5	64	100	245	0.9763	0.9898	0.0022	0.3100	48.8850	6.3600	98.9950	12.7500
6	24	97	146	0.9759	0.9879	-0.0002	0.2900	48.8586	6.3500	98.8013	12.7900
7	5	84	64	0.9749	0.9862	0.0004	0.2800	48.8075	6.3600	98.6334	12.8100
8	7	64	67	0.9742	0.9849	0.0004	0.2700	48.7757	6.3700	98.5053	12.7600
9	3	44	45	0.9736	0.9838	0.0001	0.2700	48.7477	6.3800	98.4170	12.7800
10	0	38	26	0.9731	0.9830	-0.0005	0.2600	48.7190	6.3800	98.3413	12.8400
11	1	27	18	0.9727	0.9824	0.0021	0.2600	48.6992	6.3900	98.2872	12.9000
12	2	19	8	0.9725	0.9820	0.0006	0.2600	48.6846	6.3900	98.2492	12.8900
13	0	14	1	0.9722	0.9816	0.0005	0.2600	48.6720	6.4000	98.2212	12.9300
14	0	12	2	0.9720	0.9813	0.0010	0.2600	48.6612	6.4000	98.1972	12.9400
15	0	7	0	0.9719	0.9811	0.0009	0.2600	48.6549	6.4000	98.1832	12.9400
16	0	6	0	0.9717	0.9810	0.0012	0.2600	48.6493	6.4000	98.1712	12.9400
17	0	6	0	0.9716	0.9808	0.0011	0.2600	48.6436	6.4000	98.1592	12.9300
18	0	6	1	0.9715	0.9806	0.0011	0.2600	48.6378	6.4000	98.1472	12.9300
19	0	4	0	0.9714	0.9806	0.0012	0.2600	48.6342	6.4000	98.1392	12.9300
20	0	4	0	0.9714	0.9805	0.0011	0.2600	48.6305	6.4000	98.1312	12.9300
21	0	4	0	0.9713	0.9804	0.0011	0.2600	48.6270	6.4000	98.1232	12.9400
22	0	4	0	0.9712	0.9803	0.0011	0.2600	48.6232	6.4000	98.1152	12.9400
23	0	4	0	0.9711	0.9802	0.0011	0.2600	48.6196	6.4000	98.1072	12.9400
24	0	4	0	0.9711	0.9802	0.0011	0.2600	48.6159	6.4000	98.0992	12.9400
25	0	4	0	0.9710	0.9801	0.0011	0.2500	48.6123	6.4000	98.0912	12.9400
26	0	4	0	0.9709	0.9800	0.0011	0.2500	48.6087	6.4000	98.0832	12.9400
27	0	4	0	0.9708	0.9799	0.0011	0.2500	48.6050	6.4000	98.0752	12.9500
28	0	4	0	0.9708	0.9798	0.0012	0.2500	48.6013	6.4000	98.0672	12.9500
29	0	4	0	0.9707	0.9798	0.0011	0.2500	48.5975	6.4000	98.0592	12.9500

Chapter 6

Approximations of Cooperative Equilibria in Multiperson Prisoners' Dilemma Played by Cellular Automata

6.1 Introduction

In this chapter a two-dimensional cellular automaton is used to model Schelling's (1978) multiperson prisoners' dilemma (MPD) as a repeated N-person game. In the version of MPD considered here, player payoffs are determined in a neighborhood, a field for a local subgame engaging n players, where n is substantially smaller than N. Neighborhoods, which are also local information sets, overlap to form the full N-person system or "society." Attention is directed to a model where the neighborhood is restricted to eight players but the total number of players dynamically involved through neighborhood overlaps can be quite large—in principle, equal to the number of persons in an actual society. In the simulation version of this model, upward of 65,000 players are specified. Within this framework, we examine the problem faced by full-rationality players who seek to improve expected gains above those that associate with universal defection in games with prisoners' dilemma payoff structure. Each *player* is represented by a bounded-rationality (finite automaton) *agent* with access only to the local n-person information set. The player may, however, project the implications of a local rule in the full N-player game. Players use game-theoretic reasoning to assess payoff prospects and to select optimal instructions for agents.

Not much is known or has been published about games in this size range, although the importance of the setting has been strongly maintained by Schelling and elsewhere acknowledged (Binmore and Dasgupta, 1986; Elster, 1989b; Shubik, 1984). The "commons," environmental decay, overcrowding, and many other phenomena of collectively perverse mass behavior form obvious contexts. It is, of course, obvious why the many-player game has been neglected despite its institutional and policy significance. The number of potential strategies that must be considered can seem intractably large. For example, suppose a player must choose one of two actions (i.e. "cooperate" or "defect") in a local subgame with eight neighbors. Suppose further that information sets are restricted to just the immediate past plays of the neighboring participants. Despite these restrictions there are still 2^{2^9} distinguishable mappings from information sets to the set of actions. Each of these mappings constitutes a distinguishable rule for a one-period action or an element in a strategy for repeated play. Can this daunting strategic richness be resolved?

The key result of the chapter is an exclusion theorem which shows that N-person games formed from n-agent neighborhoods and bounded-rationality rules can be partitioned into four distinct classes. All rules in a class are strategically equivalent with respect to MPD. Rules in three of the classes cannot support an equilibrium other than uniform defection. Rules in the fourth class may support such equilibria and also turn out to be relatively rare. This fact narrows the search for candidate rules. Through simulation one such rule is shown to form an equilibrium in the spirit of Nash. Players who use this rule in some (but not all) games with MPD structure can approximate the negotiated-game outcome.

The model with its description of agent rules and player strategies is presented in Section 6.2. Section 6.3 explains the partition of rules into classes of strategic equivalence. The classification method derives from a system of classifying cellular automata according to formal complexity properties (Packard and Wolfram, 1985; Wolfram, 1986). This classification system is treated at an intuitive level within the text and an accompanying appendix. Section 6.5 gives the theorem and some of its implications. Section 6.6 gives simulation results that demonstrate equilibrium properties of the candidate rule and the effectiveness of the rule in disciplining players who depart from it.

6.2 The model

The conventions given in Section 6.2.1 specialize MPD as a cellular automaton system. Players' rational strategic choices on criteria outlined in Section 6.2.2 control the system.

6.2.1 Subgame and sub-subgame structure of MPD

6.2.1.1 Play within a cellular space

Each player is represented by a finite-automaton agent who occupies a cell formed by the lattice division of a plane or a plane segment. For example, in the "video-game" topology used for the simulation version considered in Section 6.6, the lattice consists of a 256×256 array of cells. Opposite edges of the array are wrapped around and joined to form a cylinder and the ends of the cylinder are joined to form a torus. This construction is shown in Fig. 6.1a.

6.2.1.2 Local organization into homogeneous overlapping neighborhoods

A subgame domain of local play, called the cell neighborhood, is a parameter of the game. In the simulation version shown in Fig. 6.1b, n_i, the neighborhood of the ith cell, is a set consisting of the eight orthogonally and diagonally adjacent cells—that is, those to the N, NE, E, SE, S, SW, W, NW of it. This neighborhood plan, called the "Moore neighborhood" in the cellular automata literature, is specified for all $N = 256 \times 256$ cells in the lattice. Consequently, all cells are connected indirectly through neighborhood overlaps (and bidirectionally because of the toroidal topology). Given the potential propagation of locally initiated actions through the entire cellular space, the repeated game becomes an N-person game.

6.2.1.3 Timing of actions

Prior to time t each agent separately and without negotiation with other agents draws information from n_i and then selects the single-period action or cell state a_i, an element of the set $a = \{$Cooperate or Defect$\}$. The specification of the game dictates that this single choice a_i holds for period t in each of player i's eight (sub-sub)games with neighbors in n_i.

6.2.1.4 Information sets and rules

The information set of the ith agent is $A_{iL} = \{a_{k[t-T]} | k \in n_i\}$ for a sequence of $T = 1, ..., L$ stored lagged values. A rule is a mapping from A

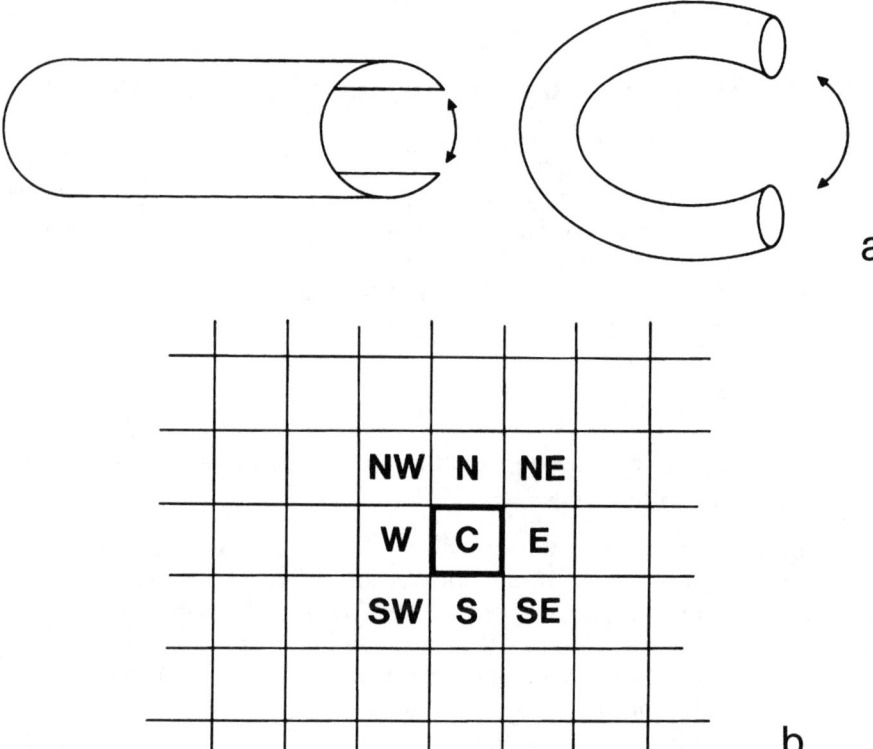

Figure 6.1: (a) Model topology. (b) Neighborhood structure. *Notes:* A lattice sheet is rolled into a tube and the north and south edges are joined. The tube is then formed into a torus with the original east and west edges joined. The Moore neighborhood shown in Fig. 6.1b is identical for all cells and is calculated on the toroidal topology for the 256 × 256 sheet in CAM-6, the experimental parallel computer used for the simulations presented in this chapter. Thus, cells in column 256 have (NW, W, SW) neighbors from column 255; (N, S) neighbors from column 256; and (NE, E, SE) neighbors from column 1. Corresponding reindexing is applied to the boundary rows.

6.2. THE MODEL

into a given by an algorithm. Myopic rules, where $L = 1$, suffice to generate the main results of this paper. Figure 6.2 depicts the logic of a finite automaton capable of reproducing such rules.

6.2.1.5 Rule format

We develop the analysis for a subset of myopic rules whose argument is S_i the sum of neighbors choosing C in the preceding period. These rules are impersonal in the sense that they do not distinguish which neighbor took which action. The rules are written in the form $a_i = S_i <s>$, where the $<>$ notation has the meaning, "pick the S_jth element from s, a string of C or D actions." Thus, the "Goodguy" rule $S_i < CCCCCCCC >$ is the pure strategy that returns C for all neighbor actions. To notate rules that are sensitive to the agent's preceding action, it is convenient to write (a) for $a_{i(t-1)}$ and (n) to denote the negation or complementary action to $a_{i(t-1)}$. Important sensitive rules are "majority" $S_j < CCCC(a)DDDD >$ and LIFE $S_j < CCCCCD(a)CC >$. In LIFE, a previous defector continues to defect if surrounded by two or three other defectors; a previous cooperator with exactly three defecting neighbors switches to D; in all other cases C is played. A "transient trigger rule" (cf. Radner, 1980; Friedman, 1986) corresponds to a rule with a C in the final position of the string (corresponding to no defecting neighbors) and at least one D in a previous position. LIFE is such a rule. A "wiseguy" rule contains a D in the final position signifying the act of defecting against uniform cooperation. These and several other rules considered in the chapter are grouped in Table 6.1.

6.2.1.6 Strategies

The strategic choice P_i of the ith player consists of the selection of a rule for the ith agent prior to repeated play. The information set and economic rationality of a player are assumed to be unrestricted. Thus, the player can take into account payoffs and the expected global interaction of a rule with the same rule or others selectable by the $N - 1$ counterpart players. The choice will also reflect the player's assumption of a particular arbitrary initial position or random seed according to which some number of agents play D. Thereafter, the interaction of agent rules proceeds deterministically. Because of the stipulated bounds on agents, trajectories of actions are recursively computable from any initial configuration. As we will see, the calculations can also be streamlined considerably using results from the complexity theory of cellular automata to obtain a full characterization of agent-rule interaction potentialities.[1] The theorem of this paper identifies

---

[1] An early survey of cellular automata research appears in Aladyev (1974); Wolfram (1986) provides an extensive annotated bibliography as well as a compilation of impor-

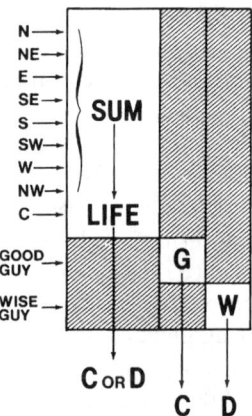

Figure 6.2: Agent rules and transition functions. *Notes*: Each agent receives data along the communication lines (top of the figure) from its Moore neighbors including self (the data line on the left labeled "C"), on actions taken in the previous period. Data received on auxiliary lines determine the agent's state, that is, which of several rules the agent will next follow. In the case illustrated the default rule is LIFE. The sum of Moore-neighbor C plays is calculated and C or D is played according to rule. If an auxiliary signal is received the agent switches to the designated rule, for example, Wiseguy or Goodguy. The hardware allows the auxiliary signals to be set adaptively or, as here, set under experimental control.

6.2. THE MODEL

Table 6.1
A selection of cellular automata rules

Rule (type)	Number of cooperators (defectors)								
	$S=0$ (8)	1 (7)	2 (6)	3 (5)	4 (4)	5 (3)	6 (2)	7 (1)	8 (0)
Pure cooperation (1)	C	C	C	C	C	C	C	C	C
Pure defection (1)	D	D	D	D	D	D	D	D	D
LIFE (4)	C	C	C	C	C	D	(a)	C	C
LlFEvar1 (4)	D	C	C	C	D	C	(a)	C	C
LlFEvar2 (4)	(a)	C	C	C	C	D	(a)	C	C
LlFEvar3 (4)	(n)	C	C	C	C	D	(a)	C	C
Majority (2)	D	D	D	D	(a)	C	C	C	C
Anneal (2)	D	D	D	(a)	(n)	(a)	C	C	C
Noise (3)	(a)	(n)	(a)	(n)	D	D	D	D	D

Notes: (a)=return own value in previous period; (n)=return complement of own value in previous period.

the rational player's optimal strategic decision when faced with the payoff implications of these potentialities.

6.2.1.7 One-period player payoffs

Payoffs to player i in each individual (sub-sub)game within n_j are given by the 2 x 2 prisoners' dilemma (PD) matrix in the left-hand portion of Table 6.2(a). The player's total payoff in the neighborhood subgame is the sum of sub-subgame payoffs in n_j on the assumption of transferable utilities. The rows in the right-hand portion of the table give total payoffs to player i at time t for the actions C and D, where S_j, the sum of neighbors in n_j selecting C, ranges from 0 to 8 (columns). Thus, the entry $C, 8$ corresponds to the uniform cooperation outcome and $D, 0$ to uniform defection. Table 6.2(b) gives corresponding figures for PDb, an alternative sub-subgame with PD ordinal structure but different cardinal payoffs.

6.2.1.8 Payoffs in the iterated game

The player receives the (undiscounted) sum over time of subgame payoffs. If the player is risk-neutral, it is appropriate to calculate this prospect as an expectation. For a simple equilibrium, such as play of D by the Nth

---

tant recent studies including his own seminal papers and the study of two-dimensional cellular automata by Packard and Wolfram. Foundation works relating to von Neumann's original conception appear in Burks (1970) and also see Smith (1971). My 1975 book formalizes economic applications of the von Neumann and "life" automata. For an overview and compilation of results on Conway's "life," see Berlekamp, Conway, and Guy (1984). The CAM-6 machine which realizes cellular automata neighborhoods as hardware is described by Toffoli and Margolus (1987).

Table 6.2
Payoffs in prisoners' dilemma sub-subgames and multiperson subgames

Sub-subgame		subgame								
		Number of cooperators (defectors)								
C	D	S = 0	1	2	3	4	5	6	7	8
		(8)	(7)	(6)	(5)	(4)	(3)	(2)	(1)	(0)
Table 6.2(a)						MPDa				
Data for: PDa										
C [3,3]	[1,4]	8	10	12	14	16	18	20	22	24
D [4,1]	[2,2]	16	18	20	22	24	26	28	30	32
Table 6.2(b)						MPDb				
Data for: PDb										
C [9,9]	[1,10]	8	16	24	32	40	48	56	64	72
D [10,1]	[2,2]	16	24	32	40	48	56	64	72	80

player against uniform defection played by the remaining $N - 1$ players, the expected outcome can be simply projected from the table. Where complicated trajectories of strategic interaction occur, expectations and distributions of payoffs must be calculated from simulated histories of the game. In most of the cases considered here trajectories of C and D actions reach stable or predictable final configurations. Payoff expectations are calculated for distributions of C and D actions in these configurations.

6.2.2 Threshold conditions for equilibria in repeated play

Inspection of the right-hand portions of Tables 6.2(a) and 6.2(b) shows that the action D dominates action C for $S_i = 0, ..., 8$ and that the game possesses MPD structure in the sense of Schelling (1978, ch. 7). Thus, in single play the uniform outcome $D, 0$ with value D' is a Nash equilibrium on the usual reasoning. (Henceforth, expected payoffs to a strategy will be designated by a prime.) In a repeated game with no discounting, player i would also select D unless there were the option of a strategy P^* that would support an equilibrium superior to universal defection. If such a strategy exists it will perforce satisfy the following necessary conditions:

Condition 1: Global payoff incentive. The payoff $P^{*\prime}$ to P^* must exceed D' the payoff to the uniform defection equilibrium.

Condition 2: Local defection disincentive. $(D_k|P_j = P^*$, if $i \neq k)'$ is the expected payoff to the kth player whose agent defects repeatedly against $N - 1$ players whose agents adhere to P^*. Analogously $((P_j)^*|D_k)'$ is the expected payoff to player i who plays P^*, conditional on all other players k defecting, $k \neq i$. For P^* to be sustainable as an equilibrium it is necessary that:

6.2. THE MODEL

2a: $(D_k|P^*)' < ((P_k)^*|P^*)'$, and that

2b: $(P^*|D_k)' > D'$

Comment. Conditions 1 and 2 form a screening test for potential equilibrium strategies that is very much in the spirit of Nash. Condition 1 is a first sorting for eligible strategies with payoff potential above that of uniform defection. Is a strategy P^* the best-reply strategy for a rational individual player confronting $N-1$ players playing P^*? At a minimum, the expected payoff $P^{*\prime}$ must equal or exceed the payoff to repeated defection against the remaining $N-1$ players adhering to P^*. This is expressed by 2a. Yet the reactions of the P^* adherents in disciplining defectors cannot result in expected returns below that of the default strategy, else an equilibrium based on P^* will be unsustainable. This requirement, which turns on interactions within the neighborhood of a "wiseguy defector" is formalized by 2b.

Conditions 2a and 2b, however, only screen out continued defection as the best reply for the individual player against P^* played by the remaining players. Might there be some "saboteur" strategy P^{**} which is a better reply than P^* for the individual player but which undermines an equilibrium? Might there be some "superior" strategy P^{***} which is a better reply than P^* for the individual player and also sustains a superior equilibrium when recognized by all N players? As we will see in Section 6.5, systems which contain a strategy P^* that satisfies Conditions 1 and 2 are also inherently "rich" in the metamathematical sense of Gödel.[2] This fact forces weakening of the usual Nash tests which rely on identification of the "best" reply strategy. Such a strategy may be identifiable for a specific set of bounds on agent rationality and specific parameters n and N. In this sense, a strategy to be proposed in Section 6.6 is a Nash equilibrium for the N and agent rule restrictions chosen for the simulation model. However, a theorem seeking to extend this finding to games of arbitrary size (or for systematic relaxation of the agent rationality bounds) is formally equivalent to propositions known to be Gödel undecidable. One can still make

---

[2] Games such as multiperson "coordination" played over the Moore neighborhood have unambiguous Nash equilibria that are unaffected when rationality bounds are relaxed. This is not so for MPD, hence I suggest the expression "Nash-like equilibria." Players have the standard motivation (described in Binmore and Dasgupta's, (1986), survey introduction) and equilibria can be demonstrated for given tightly specified calculating resources. However, as suggested in the conclusion, there is pressure to escape the bounds; but propositions on what might happen thereafter are, in principle, undecidable. Further work is required before one can properly refine the appropriate equilibrium concept.

considerable progress in resolving MPD without the strong Nash test, but a full strategic analysis requires examination of intrinsic complexity properties. As the following sections will show, the complexity of MPD is such that undecidability cannot be excluded.

6.3 Strategic equivalence and the complexity of cellular automaton rules

The problem of the iterated multiperson game is, of course, the immense number of possible strategies even where the game is restricted to bounded-rationality agents operating with restricted information sets. One seeks means to narrow the search for eligible strategies. For MPD a key is found in a body of results bearing on the computational complexity and dynamic properties of two-dimensional cellular automata. The correspondence between cellular automata and the neighborhood-agent-rule specification of Sections 6.2.1 – 6.2.1 is exact, as can be ascertained by consulting definitions in any of the sources given by note 1. A verbal definition should suffice for present purposes.

> Cellular automata are mathematical models for systems in which many simple components act together to produce complicated patterns of behavior.... A cellular automaton consists of a regular lattice of sites. Each site takes on (a finite number of) possible values, and is up-dated in discrete time steps according to a rule that depends on the value of sites in some neighborhood around it. (Wolfram, 1986, 1.4, 126).

With abstract cellular automata serving as the model for agent-rule interaction, we digress to consider: first the background to classification of cellular automata dynamics according to computational properties; and, second, the generality of cellular automata corresponding to the bounded-rationality model. These preliminary discussions prepare the way for translation of cellular automaton complexity classes into classes of rules that are strategically equivalent in MPD.

6.3.1 Digression: Study of cellular automaton complexity properties

The study of the evolution of cellular-automaton trajectories over time and across space (the lattice structure of the N-person game) has been described by Wolfram (1986, 1.5) as an "empirical" research program based

6.3. STRATEGIC EQUIVALENCE

on experimentation. Data are drawn from computer simulations of cellular-automaton rules and then tested via statistics and experimental mathematics. Observed "empirical regularities" become the subject of investigations using conventional theoretical methods and constructive demonstration. The program of trajectory classification for one-dimensional cellular automata is now virtually complete. That for two-dimensional cellular automata in the size range of the model for MPD is sufficiently well advanced for its use here as a method for determining the strategic equivalence of rules. In brief, rules are differentiated according to whether trajectories triggered by a one-time shock (e.g., a random string of C and D actions) evolve to: (1) "homogeneous state"; (2) "simple separated periodic structures"; (3) "chaotic aperiodic patterns"; or (4) "complex pattern[s] of localized structures" (Wolfram, 1986, 1.5, 172). The analogs to the first three of these behaviors in continuous dynamic systems are: limit point, limit cycle, and strange attractors, respectively. The analogy for the first two types is obvious. That between chaotic continuous systems and type 3 cellular automata is supported by many similarities in their corresponding descriptive statistics (e.g., entropies, Lyapunov exponents, fractal dimensions). However, there is no known analog in continuous dynamic systems to type 4 cellular automata (the type relevant for MPD) so an additional basis for classification turns out to be required.

A cellular automaton can also be viewed as an information processing system that produces a configuration of states (e.g., CD strings) at time $t = T$ when triggered by an arbitrary configuration of states at $t = 0$. From this perspective the string-generating capacity of cellular automata equates to computing capacity. There is an exact correspondence between the string-generating behavior of a type 1 cellular automaton and the capacities of a computing device without memory; between that of a type 2 cellular automaton and that of a device with a memory of fixed size; and between that of a type 3 cellular automaton and a finite device with a memory that grows with t. The last construct is frequently described as a Turing machine with a restricted program.

Within the class of type 4 cellular automata—and only there—one can find systems with string-producing capacities that correspond to those of unrestricted ("universal") Turing machines. Proof that a system possesses this ultimate level of computing capability is by direct demonstration. One shows first, that certain local configurations of cells can function within the larger system as components of an actual general-purpose computer; and then, that these configurations can be formed through the operation of the cellular automaton rules. The first such demonstration (von Neumann, 1966) employed a cellular automaton with a large number (29) of active states. It has since been shown (recounted in Berlekamp, Conway, and Guy, 1984) that the LIFE rule of Section 6.2 can generate configurations corresponding to a clock, transmissible data, and all memory devices and logic gates required for general computation. Most of these forms are observable in the course of a routine computer simulation. Thus, although we as outside experimenters may be interpreting a trajectory of C or D actions as an outcome of local strategic choices that determine player payoffs, the agents may unknowingly(!) and haphazardly have wired themselves together so that they collectively perform a calculation of significant depth. This calculation may effect a type of decentralized coordination that allows the great majority of agents to obtain the cooperative return, mobilize themselves in specific locales to discipline or deter isolated defectors and yet contain the spread of retaliatory defection.

For reasons that should now be becoming clear, the four levels in this classification system are commonly described as "qualitative levels of computational complexity" where it is understood that a system of a higher type has significant string-producing capabilities which are unmatched by a system of a lower type and that the four classes embrace all known computational capacities. Economists unfamiliar with the notion of qualitative system complexity can get a feel for the distinctiveness of the four cellular automata behavior classes from snapshots of the evolution of one-dimensional cellular automata. These figures allow one to view the complete history over time of a trajectory across space. A selection of such snapshots is given in the appendix along with additional commentary on technical properties and on other economic applications.

6.4 The complexity of bounded-rationality forms

The complexity types are defined for generic cellular automata. Are we losing anything of substance by working within the specific bounded-rationality setup of this chapter? Another important result in the experimental classification program for cellular automata is the finding that trajectories of all four qualitative complexity types can be generated in systems the size of the MPD model by a relatively small set of "legal" rules. Legal rules satisfy two criteria. First, they are representable in the "impersonal" $< S_i >$ form (this rule restriction is frequently labeled "totalistic" in the cellular automata literature). Second, they are of the transient trigger type: if an agent and all its neighbors play C in $t = T$, the agent will play C in $t = T + 1$. Since the four complexity types are known to exhaust all computational possibilities and represent all potential qualitative dynamics for trajectories of agent actions, there is no loss of qualitative content in confining attention to the bounded-rationality forms corresponding to legal systems. Accordingly, we turn to examination of their strategic properties.

6.4. COMPLEXITY AND BOUNDED RATIONALITY

6.4.1 Classes of strategic equivalence in multiperson games

Whether the complexity types codify critical strategic properties in all games is a conjecture beyond the scope of this chapter. They do identify properties of significance in MPD and several other multiperson games described by Schelling (1978). The text now describes for rules of each class the expected distributions of C and D actions that follow an initial perturbation consisting of a seeding of the cellular space with some D actions. Game-theoretic implications follow.

Complexity types 1 and 2. Rules of the first type result, after a brief transition, in all cells assuming a uniform state. For example, the "hair-trigger" rule $< DDDDDDDDC >$, "select D if you or any of your neighbors previously selected D," will result in uniform play of D if any agent ever plays D. Rules of the second type partition the cellular space into zones of like uniform or periodic behavior. The type 2 rule $< DDDD(a)CCCC >$, "play the way the majority of your neighbors play—include your own play in the summation," generates a gerrymandered sorting of defectors and cooperators when the lattice is seeded with a random initial distribution of defectors. Such rules are effective in generating provably Nash equilibria in "sorting" games and games of coordination. (See Figs. 6.3a and 6.3b and the accompanying notes which describe a counter-intuitive improvement to the majority rule.)

Complexity type 3. Rules of the third type propagate from both small seeds of localized defection and from broad random sowing to cover the entire cellular space with chaotic aperiodic patterns—some noiselike, some with fractal regularities. (Type 3 cellular automata are actually used as random-number generators.) Although the system is deterministic following the initial seeding and has stable statistical properties, it is impossible as a practical matter to predict the pattern within a neighborhood at time t without knowledge of cell states outside the neighborhood—even if the agent possessed the entire history of patterns in the neighborhood to $t - 1$. This property, "sensitivity to exterior contexts," contrasts to rules of types 1 and 2 and marks a watershed with respect to agent rationality. If $N - 1$ players employ a type 1 or type 2 rule, the Nth player gains no advantage from additional agent computing power or an expanded agent information set. This is not so for the Nth player facing a context-sensitive system—knowledge from an expanded information set increases near-term predictability of nearest-neighbor actions. Nonetheless, for given bounds on agent rationality, some neighbor actions will appear as indistinguishable from random data. Inferentially, the only nontrivial equilibria that type 3 rules can support are in games with mixed-strategy solutions.

Complexity type 4. Trajectories of cell states produced by a particular

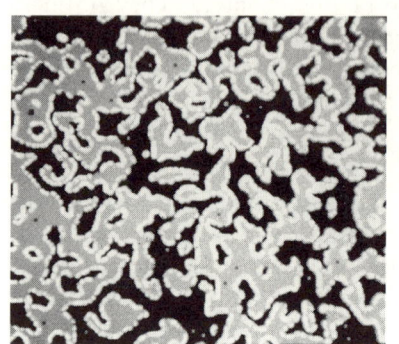
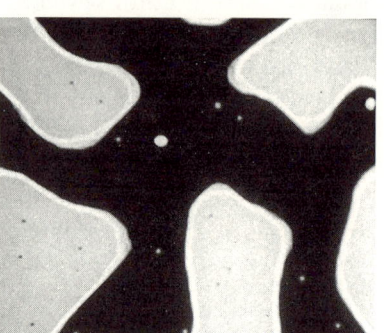
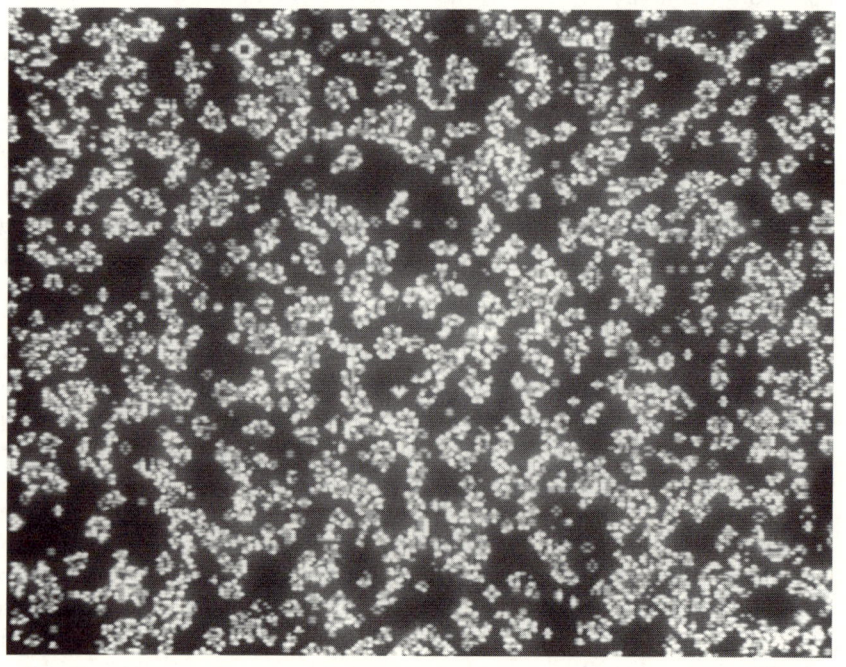

6.4. COMPLEXITY AND BOUNDED RATIONALITY

type 4 rule from different initial seeds will usually present different—and unstable—descriptive statistics. Instead, type 4 rules give rise to stable local configurations, periodic local configurations, and some special propagating structures. Since these structures can, in principle, act as components of a general computing device they can potentially reproduce any interaction within a local zone of the game space during the transient phase of a trajectory. This phase corresponds to active calculation. More to the point, if a type 4 system reaches a steady state in a local domain or within a finite cellular space such as the game space of the MPD model, the configurations that remain are unpredictable in their distribution but predictable in local structure. The steady state corresponds to a calculation that "halts." For example, in LIFE played on a finite plane segment the only steady-state forms are "still LIFEs" in which a defector has two or three defecting neighbors along with a few simple oscillating structures. Such local predictability, in effect, permits a player to calculate best-case and worst-case bounds on payoffs in the steady state. These facts when taken in conjunction with experimental data on the distribution of structures provide the rational player with sufficient information to assess the payoff potential of candidate equilibrium strategies. This establishes the setting of the theorem and simulations to follow.

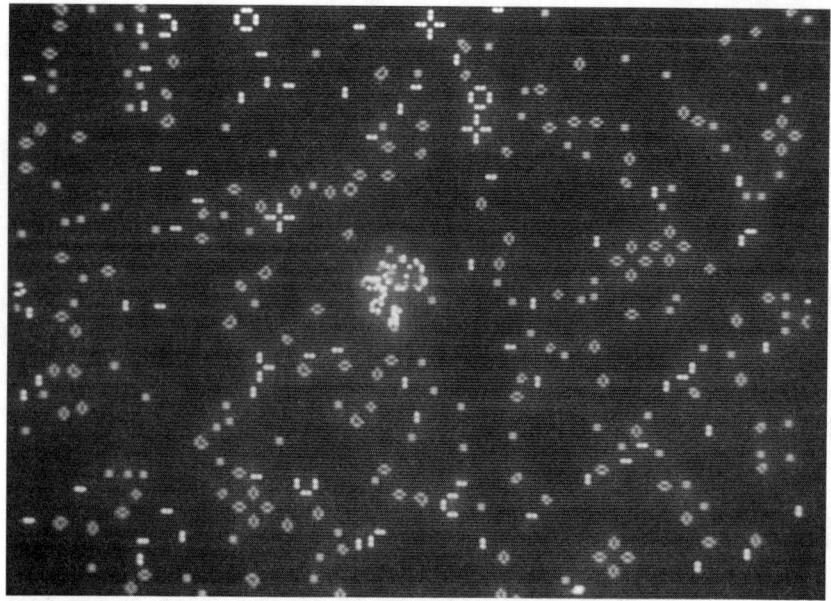

Figure 6.3: Configurations and trajectories in multiple-player games. *Notes:* The figure is reproduced from photographs of a CAM-6 monitor screen. In all cases trajectories were generated from an initial perturbation of 50% defections distributed randomly. Light pixels represent defectors; dark, cooperators. Panel (a) is a screen image of a stable configuration reached after 40 iterations of the "follow the majority in your neighborhood" rule. The string notation for this type 2 rule is $S_i < DDDD(a)CCCC >$. The same simulation somewhat later after substituting the Vishniac (1986) "anneal" rule $\{S_i + (a)\} < CCCCDCDDDD >$ is shown in Panel (b). This rule, also of type 2, seems less intuitive than the "majority" rule but is effective in "ungerrymandering" the field of play. Both rules are equilibria for coordination games: but "anneal" is superior since it reduces the number of players in boundary positions. As shown by the theorem, these type 2 configurations would not be sustainable as strategies in MPD. (c) – (e) show stages in a simulation of LIFE. (c) is a stop-action screen image shortly after the initial perturbation. Local configurations of defection take many different complicated forms. Figure 6.3d is a time exposure covering 30-odd steps of the trajectory. The bright clouds are zones of active defection. The bright diamondlike forms are locally fixed oscillating defectors; the less bright fixed forms are various stable configurations. Finally, the two faint lines running upward from left to right are trails left by "gliders." The interactions of gliders with gliders and with other stable forms (including some which perpetually release gliders) have been shown to reproduce all logical functions required for universal computation. Figure 6.3e is a stop-action image of the same simulation just before reaching steady state with all remaining configurations in stable or locally oscillating states.

6.5 A theorem on "Nash-like" equilibria in MPD

A Nash equilibrium in a many-person iterated game corresponds to a rule or equivalent procedure for instructing agents which, if selected by $N-1$ full-rationality players, will be selected by the Nth as a best-reply strategy. In addition, the equilibrium must hold for a class of institutionally permissible initial perturbations. For generality, this class is taken to contain the null perturbation, arbitrary configurations of defection, and random seedings of defection. For MPD we seek an equilibrium strategy that raises the expected payoff to all players above that corresponding to $D, 0$. Does such an equilibrium strategy exist? If so, then it must be true that there exists at least one strategy P^* which is superior to D as a reply to P^*. That is, P^* satisfies Conditions 1, 2a, and 2b of Section 6.2.2. Call such a strategy a "Nash-like equilibrium strategy." A Nash-like strategy P^*, however, may not be provably the best reply to P^*. Thus the existence of a strategy P^* is not sufficient to guarantee the existence of a Nash equilibrium P^+. Among the possibilities are: the identity of P^+ and P^*; the existence of P^+ with $(P_k^+|P^*)' > (P_k^*|P^*)'$; the existence of a saboteur strategy P^{**}; and P^* provably a best-reply strategy for only a restricted set of candidate rules. The following theorem applies to this weaker equilibrium concept.

Theorem 6.1 *(1) A Nash-like equilibrium strategy for MPD with expected value above that of uniform defection cannot be formed from rules in the first three complexity classes. (2) If such a strategy exists it must be formed within a system at the fourth complexity level.*

Proof. Part (1) of the theorem follows from the remarks of Section 6.5 regarding the first three complexity/strategy types.

Complexity type 1. Suppose $N-1$ players choose an agent rule that forms a system of the first complexity type. The game space must quickly reach a state corresponding to either uniform defection or cooperation. In the first instance, the Nth player must elect an agent rule corresponding to pure defection. In the second instance, the player, following the usual prisoners' dilemma reasoning, would have an incentive to defect. Since all players are in a symmetric position, this potentiality would have been universally recognized and the postulated strategic decisions would not have occurred.

Complexity type 2. The proof for systems of the second complexity type is essentially the same as that for type 1. Player N visualizes four possibilities: being in a region of predominant defection, in a region of predominant cooperation, on a boundary between regions, or in a zone of periodicity. Each could be identified by a finite agent but that is unimportant since defection is the optimum action in each case. Since these are the only possibilities, a strategy forming a type 2 system is also strategically unsustainable in MPD.

Complexity type 3. Trajectories in type 3 systems present themselves as pseudorandom fluctuations that are unforecastable within agent neighborhoods because of context sensitivity. Such fluctuations would be indistinguishable from a mixed strategy, against which a pure strategy of uniform defection is optimal.

In summary, none of these cases is sustainable, hence none would be chosen by a rational player over the equivalent of a pure strategy of defection. Are there any solving strategies of type 4? An analytical proof of part (2) of the theorem would require judgments as to the calculating properties of a finite approximation of a system known to be capable of universal computation if unbounded. Declarations as to the generality of a method for deriving an equilibrium strategy in this metamathematical setting are undecidable on Gödelian reasoning and on the reasoning of the "busy-beaver" version of the halting problem (cf. Albin, 1982, for references and economic interpretations; also see Albin, 1975, appendix 7A: Proof of the pundit theorem). Thus, cases satisfying the theorem can only be demonstrated for specific scale parameters N and local information restrictions. With this caveat in mind, a solution that satisfies the theorem will be given in Section 6.6.

Remark. The effects of the theorem are threefold potent. First, part (1) of the theorem excludes from candidacy all MPD societies which are known (i.e., through cellular automaton study) to be incapable of supporting type 4 dynamics. This exclusion bans all myopic 2-action MPDs with local neighborhoods smaller than the Moore form. For nonmyopic smaller-neighborhood systems it determines minimum memory or state-complexity requirements. At the limit of the one-neighbor game (i.e., two-person PD), the requirement implies the confrontation of two Turing machines! This is an intriguing reduction to the setting examined by Rubinstein (1986). Second, part (2) of the theorem provides an effective guide for search: the number of candidate type 4 systems is conveniently small. Finally, the setup provides a convenient framework for extending the analysis to cover the "robustness" of P^* in the face of a limited number of wiseguy defectors with greater computing power and or larger information sets.

6.6 A "Nash-like" solution to MPD

One extremely well-known type 4 system for the Moore neighborhood and myopic legal rules is the LIFE rule $S_i < CCCCCD(a)CC >$. The

6.6. "NASH-LIKE" SOLUTION

Table 6.3
Values of LIFE in MPDa and MPDb

Strategic action	Number of defectors in neighborhood									Sums
	0	1	2	3	4	5	6	7	8	
All-C	57538	2626	2925	288	104	198	3	0	0	63682
LIFE-D	0	284	932	632	6	0	0	0	0	1854
Wise-D	0	0	0	0	0	0	0	0	0	0
All-D	0	284	932	632	6	0	0	0	0	1854
Cells	57538	2910	3857	920	110	198	3	0	0	65536
										Values
C-PDa	24	22	20	18	16	14	12	10	8	
D-PDa	32	30	28	26	24	22	20	18	16	
vLIFE										22.99
C-PDb	72	64	56	48	40	32	24	16	8	
D-PDb	80	72	64	56	48	40	32	24	16	
vLIFE										70.41

Notes: The entries in the upper portion of the table give the number of agents classed according to chosen action who have 1, ... ,8 defecting neighbors in the final configuration of a game in which there were 65,536 LIFE players. The middle portion of the table gives payoffs in the static neighborhood subgame PDa. The values in the final column are expectations for the LIFE strategy calculated from the static payoffs and the distribution by outcome in the upper portion of the table. The lowest portion of the table gives like data for PDb.

only other type 4 rules for these information conditions are close variants such as $S_i < DCCCD(a)CC >$; $S_i < (a)CCCCD(a)CC >$; and $S_i < (n)CCCCD(a)CC >$. The qualitative behavior of variant LIFE is close to that of LIFE itself; so the chapter reports only on LIFE simulations.

Since LIFE is a transient trigger rule, it yields uniform cooperation when started with the null perturbation of uniform cooperation. A test of Condition 1 involves calculating payoff expectations after perturbing a system of LIFE players (that described in Section 6.2 and simulated on a CAM-6 parallel computer) with initial shocks of randomly distributed defections (probability $(D) = 0.2$ to 0.9). After approximately 50 rounds of sub-subgames the number of defectors remaining begins to approach a limiting value for that initial shock. An order-of-magnitude drop in the number of defectors is typical for the transition following a massive shock during this early period. Until the system reaches a final configuration of stable groups of defectors—this may take thousands of rounds—agents may at any time play D or C. In all cases observed (corresponding to hundreds of billions of sub-subgames in hundreds of separate trials) every agent played D at one time or another during the transition. In the final configuration, a "soup" of stable forms and simple oscillators, the number of remaining defector clusters is always quite small—usually well below 1 percent of N with approximately 3 percent of the agents playing the

Table 6.4
Values to different strategies when LIFE is played in MPDb (number of players)

Players	LIFE	Goodguy	Wiseguy	Steps (defectors)
L	70.41			4000
	(65536)			(1854)
L, W	69.55		64.94	3783
	(65519)		(17)	(2878)
L, G	70.32	64.22		4023
	(65518)	(18)		(1936)
L, G, W	69.40	70.66	66.76	9026 interim
	(65492)	(18)	(26)	(3010)
L, G, W	70.34	69.77	70.15	13916 final
	(65492)	(18)	(26)	(1910)

Notes: The entries give estimates of the expected value of a strategy in MPDb as calculated from simulated trajectories for 65,536 players. The columns give values for LIFE, Goodguy (always cooperate), and Wiseguy (always defect). The row labels give the strategies played in a particular run. The entries in parentheses give the number of agents programmed to play each strategy. The final column gives the number of steps that were required to reach a final stable configuration and the number of defecting agents—either LIFE players or Wiseguys—in the final configuration. For reference, the final four rows give values for the nth player playing the lower-case strategy versus $n-1$ neighbors playing the upper-case strategy in the static game.

defector role. Figures 6.3c – 6.3e illustrate stages in such a representative trajectory.

Payoff expectations calculated for representative final configuration of LIFE are given in Tables 6.3, 6.4, and 6.5. Table 6.3 reports on such a final game configuration. The rows in the upper part designate player strategies (i.e., Wiseguy and LIFE) and agent actions taken according to the strategies. There is a record on the numbers of player-agents of each strategic type surviving into the final configuration, classified (by column) according to the number of defectors in their neighborhoods. The columns of the middle section of the table give the payoffs to these outcomes for PDa (taken from Table 6.2 but printed in reverse order) and the columns of the lower section give the corresponding payoffs for PDb. The summary values in the final column are the average payoffs to players whose agents play C or D according to the LIFE rule (see notes to the table). These average payoffs exceed the D' value of 16 in both PDa and PDb. Thus a player who takes these averages as an expectation would see Condition 1 satisfied. However, the risk-averse player might note that there are 198 instances in which an agent playing C has 5 defecting neighbors and three instances of an agent with 6 defecting neighbors. The individual player unlucky enough to have an agent in this position would receive a payoff below D' in PDa. In PDb the payoff even in this adverse individual outcome exceeds that for D'.

Table 6.5
LIFE versus Goodguy and Wiseguy

Strategic action	Number of defectors in neighborhood									Sums
	0	1	2	3	4	5	6	7	8	
Good	15	1	2	0	0	0	0	0	0	18
All-C	57218	2838	2929	290	87	237	9	0	0	63608
LIFE-D	0	290	982	612	0	0	0	0	0	1884
Wise-D	16	0	2	4	4	0	0	0	0	26
All-D	16	290	984	616	4	0	0	0	0	1910
Cells	57249	3129	3915	906	91	237	9	0	0	65536
										Values
C-PDa	24	22	20	18	16	14	12	10	8	
D-PDa	32	30	28	26	24	22	20	18	16	
v LIFE										22.96
v Wise										29.53
C-PDb	72	64	56	48	40	32	24	16	8	
D-PDb	80	72	64	56	48	40	32	24	16	
v LIFE										70.34
v Wise										70.15
v Good										69.77

Notes: The format of this table is similar to that of Table 6.3. The entries in the upper portion of the table give the number of agents classed according to chosen action who have 1,...,8 defecting neighbors in the final configuration of a game in which there were 18 Goodguys, 26 Wiseguys, and 65,492 LIFE players. The tabulation distinguishes LIFE cooperators from Goodguy cooperators and LIFE defectors from Wiseguy defectors. The middle portion of the table gives payoffs in the static neighborhood subgame PDa. The values in the final column are expectations for the strategy calculated from the static payoffs and the distribution by outcome in the upper portion of the table. The lowest portion of the table gives like data for PDb. It is seen that the outcome for LIFE exceeds that for Wiseguy and for Goodguy and approximates the outcome for pure cooperation.

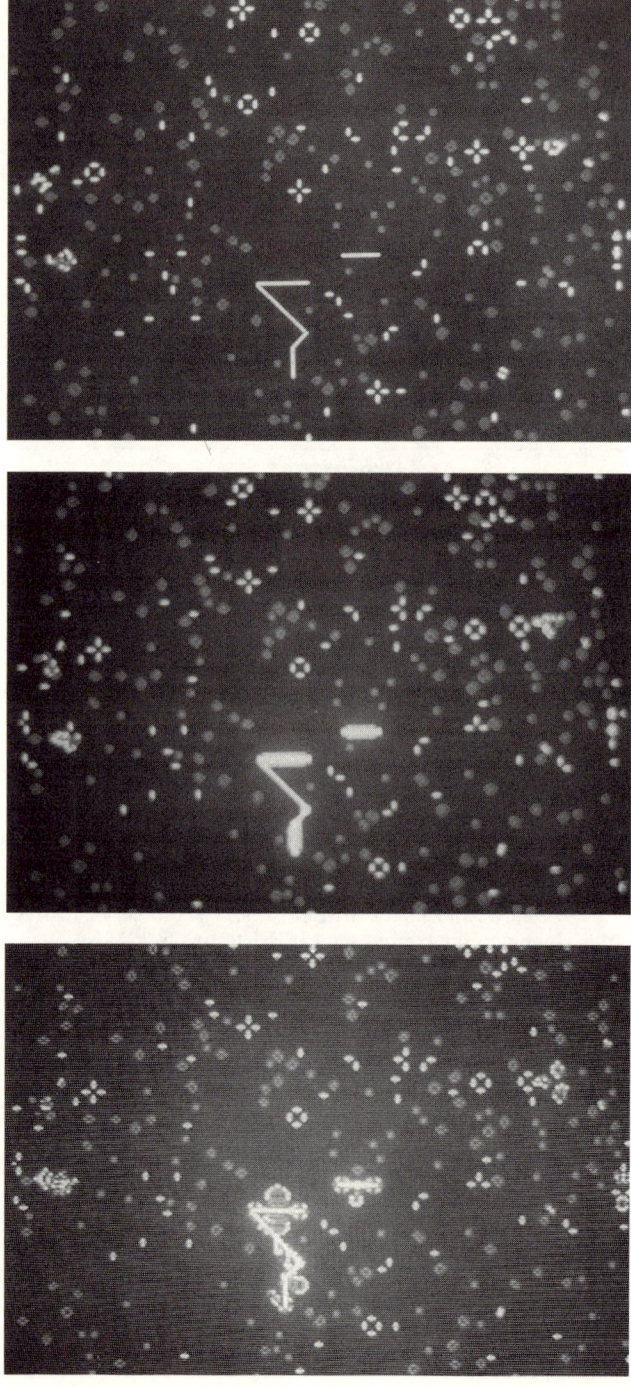

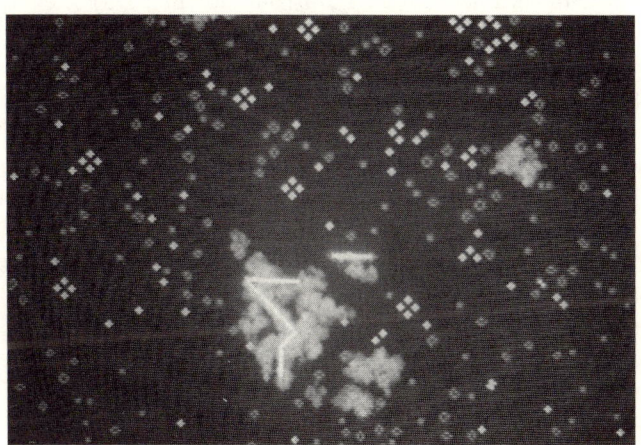

Figure 6.4: LIFE punishes Wiseguy defectors. *Notes:* Fig. 6.4 is reproduced from photographs of a CAM-6 monitor screen. (a) Wiseguy defectors occupy zones of previous uniform cooperation at the location of the zigzag configuration and the horizontal line above and to the left of it. These positions would have been judged safest for invasion by players with information-set radius wider than that of the Moore payoff neighborhood. Immediately, these defectors are surrounded by LIFE players switching to the defection action. (b) A few steps later the retaliation intensifies. (c) Still later, as shown in a time exposure. (d) Defection remains intense around the Wiseguys but has also unsettled a new area above and to the left through glider transmission. The original Wiseguys would have taken a heavy cumulative loss in MPDb. Even when the Wiseguys revert back to LIFE, the residual activity in their neighborhood penalizes them.

To test Conditions 2a and 2b a small number (20) of agents were randomly selected as "Wiseguys" who played D throughout the simulation against the remaining LIFE players. Additional trial simulations introduced a small number of "Goodguy" agents who always played C, or a mixture of Goodguys and Wiseguys. The results of these simulations are summarized in Table 6.4 as expectations in PDb for the LIFE, Wiseguy, and Goodguy strategies. Table 6.5 gives detailed results in a format similar to that of Table 6.3 for a simulation mixing Goodguys and Wiseguys. The simulations demonstrate that in PDb (but not in PDa) the expected return to LIFE exceeds that to the Wiseguy strategy in a setting representing Conditions 2a and 2b under a variety of control conditions. It is perhaps gratifying to observe that the free-riding Goodguy strategy fares poorly as well.

In a final experiment, robustness was tested by simulating agents with larger information sets than n. If the agents could identify themselves as being in a zone of uniform cooperation they would shift to D for some time. When several agents had this capacity and located in the same zone they ended up triggering D actions by LIFE players and getting swamped in a storm of defections—see Fig. 6.4 and the accompanying explanation. Even one-shot Wiseguy defectors could trigger defection storms in their immediate neighborhoods that canceled out the gains from their one-period exploitations.

6.7 Conclusions

This chapter introduces a method of escaping the apparent intractability of many-person games. The approach taken here is subtly different from that of Schelling. Schelling extrapolates the global implications of locally rational micromotivations operating within a local domain. Here, agent rules do operate identically to Schelling's micromotivated procedures. However, a rational player is allowed to consider systemic as well as local consequences and selects local rules strategically. No intractabilities are confronted in this choice so long as the players' agents are subject to neighborhood restrictions on their information sets.

The setup requires an equilibrium concept weaker than that of Nash but, nonetheless, operational. We can reason only that if rational players sustain an equilibrium in the system under the given information bounds and restrictions on rules, the equilibrium will be LIFE or one of its near variants. We cannot demonstrate that an equilibrium based on LIFE will be sustained if invaded by players with superior informational resources although LIFE demonstrates some robustness in this regard. The whole question of evolutionary rule development in models of this type remains open, as does the matter of establishing a rigorous basis for the apparent correspondence between formal complexity level and strategic equivalence. The policy applicability of LIFE-like self-enforcement of cooperative behavior in real-world settings is a challenge for future research.

Developing further the implications of my distinction between the bounded-rationality agent and the fully rational player would seem on the basis of this analysis to have an extremely rich applicability in many other decision settings. I believe it represents a constructive relaxation of the usual defined informational constraints in game theory.

Appendix: The four complexity types in one-dimensional cellular automata

The cellular space of a one-dimensional cellular automaton is formed by the lattice division of a line—or, in finite cases, by the lattice division of a line segment or circle. Each cell of the space is occupied by a finite automaton. The automaton may assume one of k states according to a rule whose argument is the state of cells in a predefined neighborhood during one or more previous periods. A conventional neighborhood plan selects the r cells to the left and r cells to the right of the reference cell. Rules may take many forms; we restrict attention to a form analogous to that in the text. Associate with each state $1, ..., k$ a cardinal value v_k and construct the set $V = \{v_k\}$. Then, $v_{it} \in V$ the value of the reference cell at time t is given by $v_{it} = S_i < s >$, where s is a string of values $v \in V$ and S_i is the sum from $J = -r$ to $J = r$ of terms $v_{(i+J)(t-1)}$. The $< \cdot >$ notation again denotes selection of the S_ith element from the string s.

The trajectories of one-dimensional cellular automata are conveniently displayed by the "data bank snapshots" forming the panels of Figs. 6.5 and 6.6. In these cases $r = 2$, $k = 3$ and the v_k are $(-1, 0, +1)$—depicted by the colors gray, white, and black, respectively. The cellular space is a horizontal line segment containing 100 cells. The ends of the segment are bordered by cells with $v_k = 0$. The offset topmost line of each panel is a random perturbation at $t = 0$. The next line denotes cell values at $t = 1$ determined by the rule and so on successively to the last line generated at $t = T$. The snapshots thus give the T-period history of a system. The conventional graphs to the right of some of the panels give the algebraic sum of values for each iteration. The reference line indicates the point at which the aggregate has value zero. These figures were produced for earlier chapters (Albin, 1987, 1989, Chapters 3 and 4 in this volume) which demonstrated the chaotic potential in bounded-rationality search procedures where the signals were the past investment actions of economic neighbors. In some applications, neighborhoods correspond to industries; in others, lines of a supplier-customer relationship. Information sets were restricted to neighborhoods on the assumption of high information costs or delays for data generated beyond the immediate locale. The data were thought of as leading indicators used to form expectations regarding possible (unfavorable, normal, favorable) investment climates. It should be noted that the same "overlapping-neighborhood" setup can also depict a strip market of local monopolistic competition. The pricing behavior of gasoline retailers sited at highway interchanges and serving partly overlapping market areas fits this case. In still another application (Albin and Foley, 1992, Chapter 5 in this volume) the overlapping-neighborhood setup was used to model signaling in decentralized non-Walrasian exchange—albeit with more intricate rules.

On these several interpretations the local patterns in the snapshots identify domains of relative investor optimism (or zones of discounting in the strip-market case) based on only local rule-based reactions to signals. Supplementary economic calculations of standard type are required to determine the payoffs to a rule and possible systemic implications of the aggregates—including adaptive learning. For the present, the point to note is that a naive signaling structure can give rise to the full range of system complexities. These translate variously into systemic tendencies toward uniform, periodic, or aperiodic behavior. In the latter cases plausible local rules can lead to "sectoral bubbles." In type 4 systems local irregularities are particularly dramatic.

Thus, in scanning the snapshots it may help to think of them as representations of a segment of a data bank giving the qualitative levels (low, normal, high) of an observed economic variable for firms in adjacent activities (i.e., as recorded by SIC codes). Type 1 and type 2 snapshots are easily identified and their correspondence to simple attractors is apparent. Some of the different chaotic aspects of particular type 3 systems can be picked out by visual inspection. The "noisier" versions reproduce each possible string pattern of a particular length with approximately equal frequency in both vertical and horizontal directions. These systems register relatively high calculated entropies compared with the systems in which the triangular block patterns appear (Wolfram, 1986, 1.3, 116). These latter, however, strongly suggest standard fractal forms such as the "Sierpinski arrowhead" (Mandelbrot, 1983, 142; and see the addendum on cellular automata, 463). Dimension calculations—Richardson's geometric "coastline" approximation can even be directly used on the snapshots—establish the fractal character of type 3 cellular automata and their association with chaotic dynamic systems.

Only a hint of the richness of type 4 systems is conveyed by Figs. 6.5 and 6.6. Fig. 6.7 gives a trajectory of a $K = 4$, $r = 2$, type 4 system in

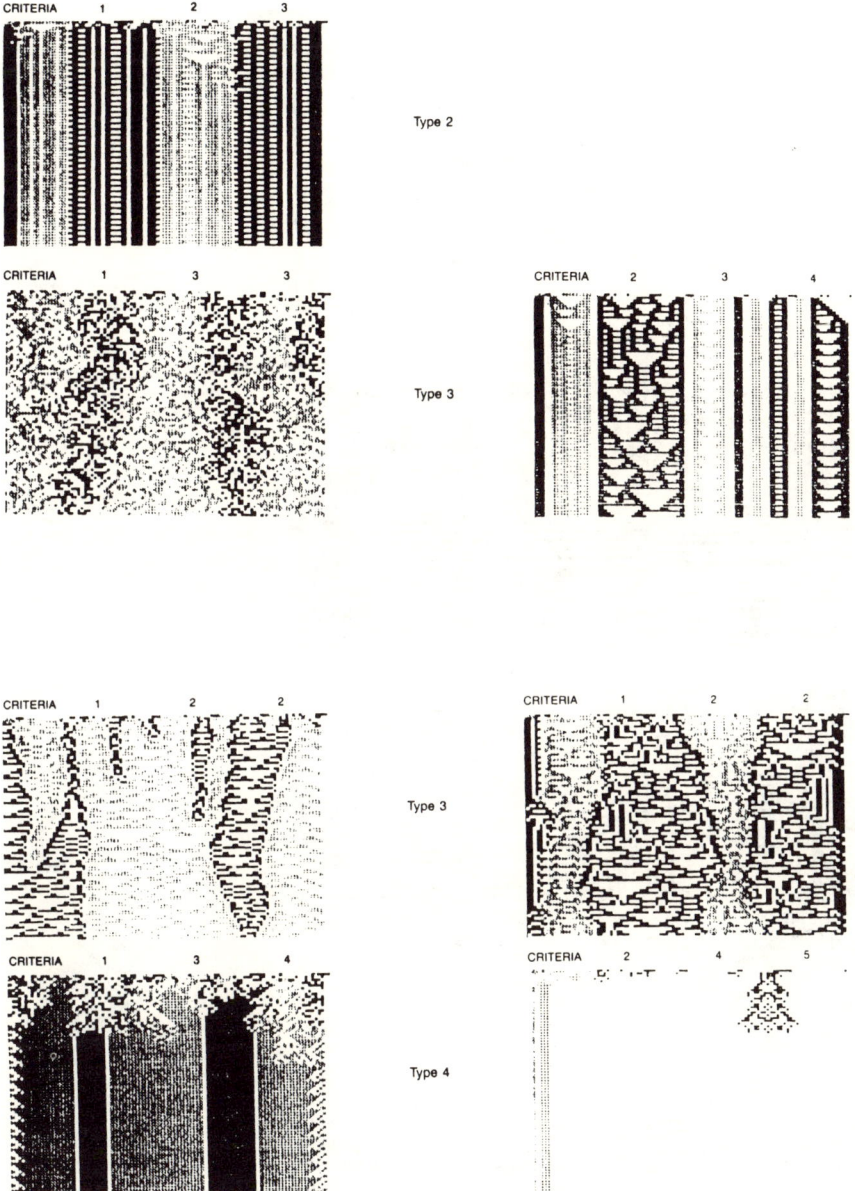

Figure 6.5: Qualitative behavior of one-dimensional cellular automata (three-state models). *Notes:* Type 1 cases (all black, white, or gray) are not shown. The case in row 1 is type 2. The case on the right in row 2 is transitional. The other type 3 cases display "pseudosectors" of like activity. The case to the left in row 4 is transitional in the line-segment topology; it displays long transients with type 4 properties.

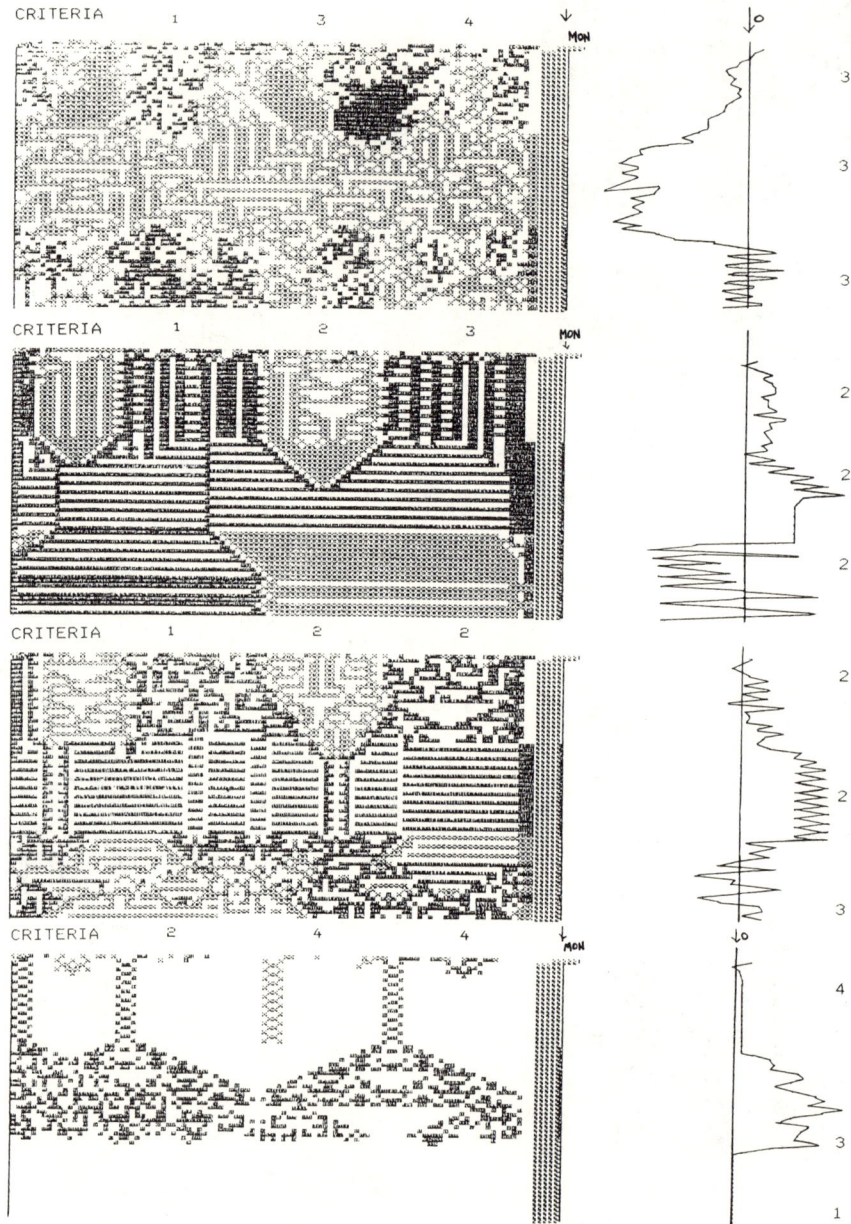

Figure 6.6: Complexity types.

APPENDIX   209

Figure 6.7: Trajectory of a type 4 one-dimensional cellular automaton (four-state model).

which the suggestions of "data transmission," "memory," and "calculation" are particularly dramatic. This system is conjectured to have underlying computational power approximating that of LIFE. Note, finally, that cross sections of trajectories of two-dimensional cellular automata will closely resemble the full-trajectory snapshots of one-dimensional cellular automata of corresponding complexity type.

Acknowledgments

The author gratefully acknowledges suggestions and comments from Eileen Applebaum, Christopher Bliss, Steve Brams, Alain Lewis, Roy Radner, Ariel Rubenstein, Andrew Schotter, Avner Shaked, Chuck Wilson, and Ted Yanow. Financial support was received from the Jerome Levy Economics Institute and the P.S.C./CUNY Faculty Research Program. The research was accomplished while the author was on sabbatical leave to Nuffield College, Oxford University.

Chapter 7

The Complexity of Social Groups and Social Systems Described by Graph Structures

7.1 Introduction

Recently a broad literature has developed in which specific types of group interactions are described as equivalent to specific directed graphs. These descriptions have great value as they lead toward defining a relatively small number of characteristic graph patterns which typify classical interactions and group behaviors. The limitations of the approach have been described by Todd La Porte[1] who has also been one of the strongest advocates of directed graph methodology and an insightful practitioner.

Three criticisms seem most telling: first, that directed graph representations do not give adequate quantitative information about the complexity of relationships; second, that the methodology is awkward if not completely impractical where the number of subjects is large; and third, that causal or substantive aspects of the behavior of individual subjects are imperfectly modeled.

This is not to say that the qualitative analysis is in any sense misdirected. For example in Mitchell's work[2] there is the categorization of *morphological attributes* ("anchorage," "density," "reachability," and "range")

---
[1] See the introductory article and references in La Porte (1975).
[2] See the survey introduction in Mitchell (1969).

7.1. INTRODUCTION

and *interactional criteria* ("content", "directedness", "durability," "intensity," and "frequency").[3] The *attributes* correspond to formal structural properties of the graph which possess behavioral relevance. Thus, as a formal property "density" pertains to the comparative degree of a node, the average number of interaction paths which connect to a subject relative to the maximum number for that graph or graph region—in other words, the ratio of node degree to the order of the graph. In various behavioral interpretations "density" relates to local isolation, degree of integration, or completeness of the social framework. The morphological description only tells part of the story; it clearly matters how the "content" of the interaction might be judged or how frequent or intense the interactions might be. In many instances, characterization of graphs according to morphological and interactional attributes may give a full description of the significant behaviors under examination. However, in other instances—particularly in comparative studies—there may be ambiguities: as, for example, where "content" is high relative to "density" in one setting and low in another. A common measure over these dimensions is lacking.

It should be noted, however, that although each of the attributes and criteria is associated with a distinguishable phenomenon, each can be characterized as pertaining to a general variable which can be labeled "complexity" and may be perceived as such by social actors.[4] Thus, increases in the density, range, and reachability of potential interaction along with increases in the information content of the typical interaction and increases in interaction frequency, duration, and intensity are reasonably described as increases in the complexity of the social setting or interaction system. This aspect is tacitly recognized in the literature—the phrases "more com-

---

[3] "Anchorage" refers to the designation of a specific node as the focus for analysis; "density" (discussed in text) pertains to graph completeness; "reachability" to path properties; and "range" to degree and fan out (in part). "Content" pertains to the informational transactional meaning assigned to the relationship represented by a graph link. "directedness" to the logic or control of relationships represented by a link. "Durability", "intensity", and "frequency" can be thought of as informational properties of messages or transactions across a link.

[4] Note the following questions pertaining to perception:
(1) Is there a direct relationship between subjective "perceived complexity" and "measured complexity" as calculated by an observer?
(2) Are there perceptual thresholds above which (or below which) alterations in complexity are not distinguished?
(3) Are perceived alterations in complexity (general or of specific types) evaluated favorably or unfavorably?
(4) Do individuals perceive overall system complexity or do they approach a high-complexity system through heuristics?
(5) Do the answers to (1) – (4) depend in a systematic way on situational variables pertaining to social position or personality?
These are not answered in the text. The analysis presents a method for calculating "measured complexities" which can be presented as situational or structural variables in perceptual experiments or hypothesis tests.

plex" or "less complex" appear with considerable frequency—but there is lacking a comprehensive methodology, or integrating analysis in terms of overall system complexity.

The present chapter seeks a corrective. We show that the same data which are used to develop a directed graph description can be used to construct a composite description consisting of an undirected graph and one or more descriptions of the communications logic needed to generate the directed graph. The elements of the composite can be separately analyzed to give: first, a description of and complexity measure for the undirected graph as a separate form; second, descriptions and measures for the undirected graph treated as a reduction from a complete graph; third, a description of the communications logic needed to realize the observed interactions along with measures of the complexity of the required communications/control system needed to generate the directed graph; and fourth, a measure (or measures) of the complexity of the overall system.

It should be made clear at this point that "complexity measures" mean either cardinal numbers or indices which will preserve rankings under linear transformations. In most instances such measures will expedite comparisons between different interaction systems or permit comparisons over time. In many instances trade-off calculations are possible. For example we show that the complexity of one type of arrangement (e.g., nonhierarchic) could be approximated by another pattern (e.g., hierarchic) only where there are at least K times as many participants, K being a derived parameter falling within definite limits. Finally, we note that in a number of cases, there will be more than one way to describe the control logic and, accordingly, several ways to calculate associated complexity measures. This apparent ambiguity is not a defect of the methodology but rather represents the methodology, in effect, prompting the behavioral scientist to ask the right questions to complete the analysis. For example, a directed graph shows an arrow leading from individual A to individual B but not from B to A. Question: Does B inhibit communication? Question: Does A reject communications? Question: Is there actually a channel between them? Question: Is there something in the particular replication of the experiment which causes there not to be communication from B to A, although in some other replication the flow could take place?

It is clear that skilled observers bring information on just these points into the commentaries that accompany and give meaning to their graphical descriptions. The methodology we are proposing will permit handling such material in a formal and rigorous way. Available information will either permit the analysis to be completed leaving no residual uncertainty; or, if there is in fact a lack of knowledge (say, as to who is inhibiting a communication or interaction), the uncertainty of the situation will itself be expressed as a measurable attribute of the system.

Two additional introductory comments are called for. First, it should be emphasized that the methodology proposed here does not simply duplicate the theoretical content of existing directed graph methodology. A number of theorems and results flow from the proposed forms. These theorems, which correspond to classic themes in *Weberian sociology*, cannot be derived within existing models. Second, there are alien aspects to the methodology in that the constructions inject abstract machines or automata into the positions occupied by human beings within social groups; so that in effect, we will be examining the complexity of societies of machines. It turns out that complexity is well-defined in that specific context and there are reasonable measures for the complexity of a device that stands where a person does and engages in identical signal processing. There are also reasonable measures for the complexity of ensembles of machines that perform as groups. The numbers that are thereby generated can be called indicators of social complexity. They appear to be highly plausible, but whether they correspond to system attributes as perceived by human actors is, of course, the real question—a question left unanswered here.

7.2 Directed graphs and their representation by "logic and nondirected graph" methodology: An overview

We begin with a brief description of directed graph methodology. More complete descriptions are given by La Porte (1975), Mitchell (1969), and Harary (1965), whose works contain extensive bibliographic references.

Figure 7.1a gives a constructed example of a directed graph such as one which might arise in the context of a sociological study. The arrows represent binary relationships between the elements A, B, C, D, E (persons, groups, or organizations, according to context). Suppose the relationships were "uses the familiar (e.g., *tu, du*) form of address." Figure 7.1a would then be read "A and B *tutoyent* each other; B and A use the familiar form in addressing E but without reciprocation; C does not use the familiar form in conversation with D (if any); . . . ." This description might arise in the analysis of interactions among colleagues of differing ages and distinctions in a small French Sociology department. Alternatively the relationship might be "initiates inter-departmental information flow" (e.g., "sends memos"), in which case an interpretation could be: "A and B circulate memos to each other; D receives memos but only through E's transmission; C can only contact D through E, but C cannot contact A or B; . . . ." Such a description might arise in an analysis of actual interoffice behaviors in a bureaucracy; it could also arise in a simulation of a projected table of organization. In the latter instance, the analysis could serve some useful purpose such as uncovering potential impediments to communications within the organization.

Figure 7.1b gives the undirected graph corresponding to the directed graph in Fig. 7.1a.[5] The interpretation of Fig. 7.1b is more general: for example, "there is some unspecified direct relationship between A and C or A and D; . . .; etc." The directed graph clearly carries more specific information as to the relationships among and between the participants A, B, C, D, E, than does the undirected graph. One can also say that Fig. 7.1a represents a single example of an element drawn from the set of directed graphs associated with the undirected graph given by Fig. 7.1b.

The undirected graph of Fig. 7.1b can also be thought of as a single example drawn from the set of partial connected graphs (subgraphs) derived from the complete graph of order 5 (Fig. 7.1c). The complete graph can be interpreted as a representation of all possible interactions among and between N objects ($N = 5$ in this case). The number of subgraphs increases dramatically with order, and subgraphs of a particular order vary dramatically in apparent complexity (Fig. 7.1d gives some representative cases for order 5). We contend that a significant component of the complexity in the actual social situation modeled by the directed graph is intrinsic to the general social setting as given by the appropriate undirected graph (which can also be described as a subgraph of the designated order). Our first task is, therefore, isolation of the complexity of the undirected graph itself.

To resolve these various components of complexity we propose the "logic and nondirected graph" (LANG) convention in modeling. Figure 7.1e gives a general model of the LANG system. We imagine the edges of the graph connect at each node to a "socket" or switchboard. The jth participant in the system is modeled as the composition of a logical device $L(j)$ which plugs in at the socket and controls communication into and out of the node, and a general structure $S(j)$ which can be unspecified but which could characterize the persona of the jth participant in some way. Figure 7.1f pictures the logical system for individual A. His communication system is that which enables him to transmit data to E and B and receive data from B. For the moment we will also assume that he plays no other role in communications control. His persona is represented by the structure $S(A)$ which is otherwise left uncharacterized.[6] We also note that his *persona* is plugged into certain other social groups in which he interacts separately.[7]

---

[5] See Berge (1962) for full discussion of the basic properties of undirected graphs.

[6] We are not concerned with the richness of this personality, itself; the subject for analysis is the social matrix and the adjustments made by the individual to link to the matrix.

[7] We assume each of these exterior groups to be separable for the purposes of analysis. In other words, we are saying something like the following: the personality of individual

7.2. METHODOLOGY

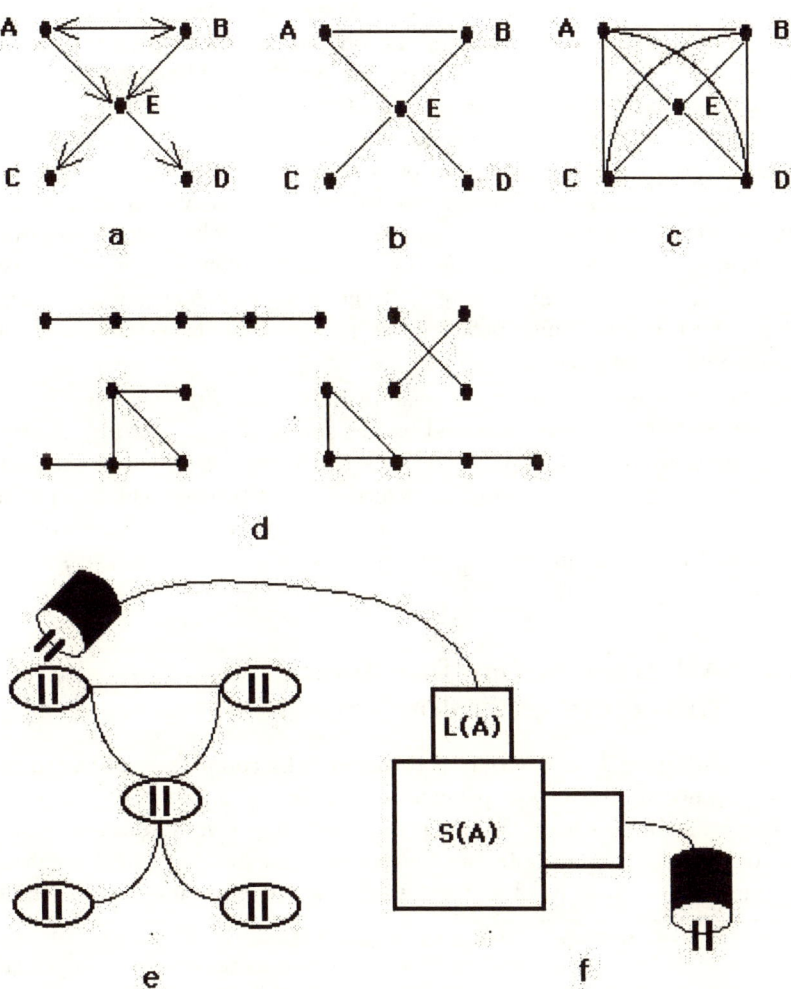

Figure 7.1: Reference graph types: (a) directed graphs; (b) undirected graphs; (c) complete graph of order 5; (d) some partial graphs of order 5; (e) the LANG system; (f) A's logical system.

This description has not yet considered the richness of communication or behavior within the system. This attribute, which embraces the linguistic content of the system, is determined in part by the personae and in part by the resources of the system. Suppose the nodes of the graph are occupied by Mozart, Kant, Goethe, Marx, and Freud, but the communications hardware only permits one bit per month to pass through a channel. Or suppose there to be a system which would satisfy the communications needs of Mozart, Kant, Goethe, Marx, and Freud; but the nodes are occupied by trivial mechanical devices that emit only one bit per month. In practice it turns out to be a relatively simple task to specify the complexity of logical elements needed to permit Kant to expand his communication rate from one bit per month to a twelve-page memorandum per day. We elide the problem of analyzing the complexity of the text of that memorandum—only noting that the analysis can surely determine whether there is dissonance between the potential of the system and the requirements of the personae.

In short, we have resolved the system into a *nondirected graph* which is the setting for processes governed by the specific *logic*, *controls*, *requirements*, and *restrictions* needed to generate the behaviors observed and codified as the directed graph; and the *richness* of the process which depends proximately upon the symbol, behavioral, or informational richness of the transmitted messages and ultimately on the symbolic richness invested in the situation by the personae.

7.2.1 Arbitrary system functions: "Structure generators"

A particular convention is required to resolve the complexity of the undirected graph component and provide a basis for all subsequent analyses. The first stage involves specifying a type of action or communication which could be accepted by an outside observer as a meaningful social transaction. The second stage involves specifying a general machine design which

---

A is not a subject for analysis. A is a participant in Group G_1 (his office staff); the complexity of his interactions in G_1 and his contribution to the complexity of G_1 are matters for analysis. Similarly A participates in G_2 (the volunteer fireman's association in his town); his interactions in G_2 etc. are matters for analysis. He also participates in $G_3, ..., G_n$ which are also potential subjects for analysis. Experiences in one group role may carry over to influence the character of A's participation in some other group or A may conceivably take on a role in which he acts to change intrinsic characteristics of a group. These matters essentially lie in the portion of A's persona which is outside the proper scope of our analysis. To be sure, it is reasonable to examine hypotheses such as: "A takes on a structure-changing role with respect to groups in which he participates if the complexity measures attaching to his present roles are (high/ low)." But such hypotheses use complexity measures for group participation only as data and do not engage far deeper problems of personality itself.

7.2. METHODOLOGY

can accomplish this transaction. In the third stage, a variant of the basic machine is constructed for each node in the undirected graph so that the machines when started up simulate the arbitrary social behavior. It is understood that each machine (automaton) has sufficient internal complexity to perform the arbitrary function for its locus in the graph but no excess capacity. The final stage calls for computing the complexity of the set of automata.

We will see in later sections that the constructions and computations just outlined are feasible, practical, and even reasonable. Their effect is to translate the undirected graph from a "structural framework" into a "structure", where "structure" is interpreted in the sense of Piaget (1972, ch. 1 and 2), that is, as a complete algebraic group-type process.[8] Given a benchmark structure generator we would be able to describe any undirected graph as a structure with measurable complexity. And with suitable choice of a generator, complexity measures turn out to vary with number of nodes, degree of interconnectedness, and so on, in an intuitively clear way. Thus we would know that any system framed say by Fig. 7.1b has a base level of complexity intrinsic to that particular undirected graph. And the implications of this measurement would be understood.

Going further, we see that the directed graph based on observation is also a structure, but one composed of the base structure plus incremental functions. The base complexity of the system given (Fig. 7.1a) is thus, the complexity of a composite machine consisting of the base structure which takes into account the number of nodes and the pattern of their connections plus the structure generators which delimit paths and control transmissions. This structure is the basic design for a family of structures—the members of which differ according to the richness of the symbol strings they process and speed of processing. We should note that the base structure and the augmented directed graph structure are specified for a particular level of symbol richness and/or a particular rate of social transactions. The augmented directed graph structure can be further augmented by structure generators to achieve more computational power and speed. These incremental structure generators add systematically measurable complexity to the model and complete the representations of an observed system.

---

[8] "Structure" in this sense means association of the system (action plus framework) with a finite semigroup, or, equivalently, with a composition of finite automata. The algebra of automata is described in a large literature. See Minsky (1967), Ginzberg (1968), and Hopcroft and Ullman (1969) which are standard references. An accessible introduction to the complexity- measurement methodology of Krohn and Rhodes (1965) which closely relates to the methodology here can be found in Gottinger (1978b). The most general form for complexity measurement is the cellular automaton, an automaton modeled with a structural framework for interactions with like automata. Complexity measurement for social and technical systems modeled with cellular automata is described in Albin (1975).

Working backward, we would be able to distinguish that component of complexity which associates with the fact that the system must handle information units consisting of twelve-page memos as against single bits. By taking account of the complexity associated solely with the level of symbol richness we would be able to reduce the system and isolate the complexity associated only with the augmented directed graph. Reducing further, we would be able to compute the complexity needed to reduce the augmented graph to the base undirected graph structure. Let us examine these processes in some detail.

7.2.2 Analysis of the undirected graph

There are many functions which could give information about the social properties of a graph. The function "Rumor transmission with recorded path" is presented later in this section as an example on which an interesting and potentially rich system can be developed. We begin, however, with a description of the salient graph parameters.

7.2.3 Parameters of the undirected graph

We are given G, the undirected graph of the system under analysis. G is a connected graph with N nodes (thus G is described as being of order N). If a system consists of a series of U disconnected graphs we merely replicate the analysis for $G_u, u = 1, 2, ..., U$. We possess two pieces of knowledge: first we know d_j for $j = 1, 2, ..., N$ nodes; where d_j is the degree of the jth node, that is, the number of edges which connect to that node. This set of facts is easily determined by inspection, by simple enumeration, or by a "census" of the graph carried out by a computer. Second, we know the longest path $P(G)$ through G where no edge is retraced. This parameter is established by graph theory (see Berge, 1962) to be a computable attribute of any connected graph. But we can even relax our knowledge requirements and permit $P(G)$ to be known only to some degree of approximation. It turns out that in graphs with large N where calculation of $P(G)$ is somewhat more laborious, the sensitivity of derived complexity measures to errors in $P(G)$ is relatively small. The examples given in Fig. 7.2 should clarify these notations.

7.2.4 The function "rumor transmission with recorded path"

The function "rumor transmission with recorded path" abbreviated RTRP or RTRP(G) is described as follows: A "tidbit" of information is given from

7.2. METHODOLOGY

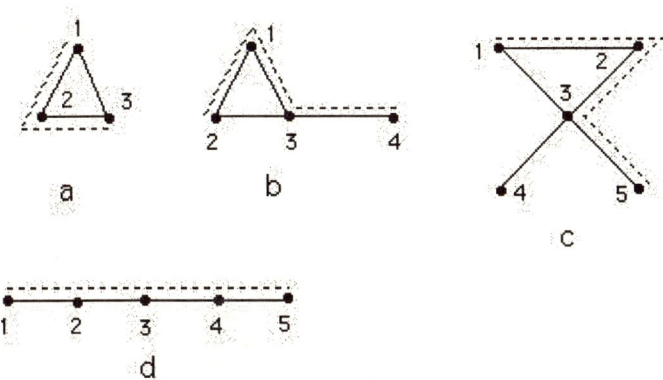

Figure 7.2:
Parameters of representative graphs. A "longest path," $P(G)$, is indicated by a broken line.
(a) $N = 3; d(1) = d(2) = d(3) = 2; P(G) = 2$.
(b) $N = 4; d(1) = d(2) = 2, d(3) = 3, d(4) = 1; P(G) = 3$.
(c) $N = 5; d(1) = d(2) = 2, d(3) = 4, d(4) = d(5) = 1; P(G) = 3$.
(d) $N = 5; d(1) = d(5) = 1, d(2) = d(3) = d(4) = 2; P(G) = 4$.

outside the system to the ith individual (e.g., to the ith node). The individual transmits this information to all of its neighbors during the period from one tick of an external clock to the next tick. In each succeeding clock interval, each individual who has just received the information transmits to those neighbors who have not already received the tidbit.

Information is also passed on as to the path the tidbit has taken to this point. Taking graph (d) in Fig. 7.2, supposing the tidbit entered at 1, individual (1) would say to (2) ("'Tidbit,' I heard it from a burning bush"). Individual (2) would say to (3) ("'Tidbit,' I heard it from (1) who heard it from a burning bush"). (3) would say to (4) ("'Tidbit,' I heard it from (2) who heard it from (1) who heard it from a burning bush"), and so forth. We require that the automaton at each node be able to handle the largest possible rumor which the system can generate. This rumor will take the form $R = (B; P(G) \cdot L)$ where B is the tidbit: for all intents and purposes we can take B to be a binary bit, the minimum unit of information. B is then followed by a data field divided into $P(G)$ separate words of length L. $L = \log_2 N$ bits[9] will permit a unique identifier for each of the N participants. In other words the rumor message grows larger according to the need to have larger words to identify each participant in the chain and according to the length of the longest possible chain.[10]

---
[9] Rounding up to integer value.
[10] We can now see why it is not all that critical to know $P(G)$ exactly. Suppose $P(G)$

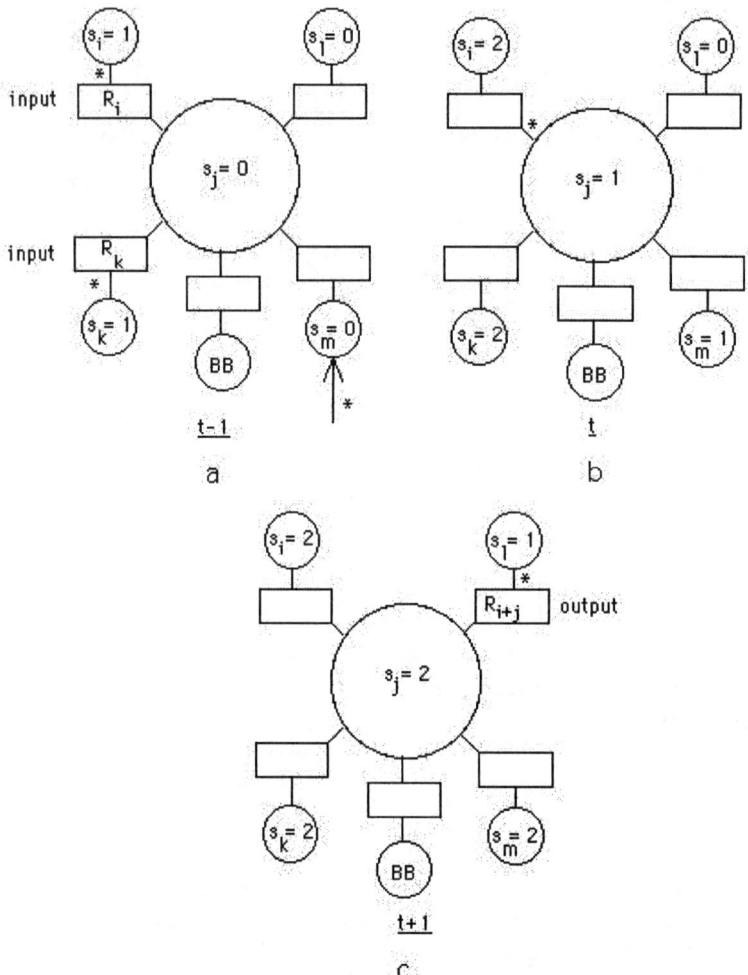

Figure 7.3: Operation of rumor machine j. At $t-1$, the machine is in the quiescent state: it receives R from both machine i and machine k. These data with the appropriate identifiers are stored in input buffers. At time t the machine senses that it has data in its buffers; it instantly switches to state 1 and according to some arbitrary ranking of its buffers, it draws the data from the buffer connecting with neighbor i and adds its identifier to R which now reads " 'BIT,' I heard it from j who heard it from i who heard it from . . . a burning bush." The data are now shifted to data lines 3 and 4 and passes down these lines to the buffers of the corresponding neighboring automata. If these automata are in state 0, they will accept the data in their buffers; if not, the data are disposed of in a rumor mill. Having completed its propagation to l and attempted propagation to m or R the machine moves into state 2 and, in effect, closes down its data links.

7.2. METHODOLOGY

We now ask what types of automata can perform the communication of the rumor R. We focus on the logic needed to communicate a single bit of data and then generate machines for a rumor of the required length. We describe a device A_j ($j = 1, 2, \ldots, N$) which can be in one of three possible states $S_j = 0, 1, 2$. The 0 state is described as the quiescent state with regard to the rumor R. All automata in the system are in the 0 state prior to intervention by the burning bush. The 1 state is defined as the state of active communication: suppose that during the interval $(t-1, t)$ the jth automaton received the rumor from automaton k. For the interval $(t, t+1)$ automaton A_j moves to the calculating and communicating state, for example, shifts from $S_j = 0$ to $S_j = 1$. During the interval the device adds the phrase equivalent of "I heard it from k" to R and transmits the now-incremented R to those of its neighbors which are still in the 0 state. Having done its duty to society, the automaton ponders the rumor in the private corners of its mind and passes on to state 2. The process ends when all automata are in the 2 state.

There are a number of machines which could realize these functions. As a matter of taste we choose the machine design $\bar{A}$ of which the four-neighbor version is pictured in Fig. 7.3 for node j.

At $t-1$, the machine is in the quiescent state; it receives R from both machine i and machine k. These data with the appropriate identifiers are stored in input buffers. At time t the machine senses that it has data in its buffers; it instantly switches to state 1 and according to some arbitrary ranking of its buffers, it draws the data from the buffer connecting with neighbor i and adds its identifier to R which now reads ("'Tidbit,' I heard it from j who heard it from i who heard it from . . . a burning bush.") The data is now shifted to data lines 3 and 4 and passes down these lines to the buffers of the corresponding neighboring automata. If these automata are in state 0, they will accept the data in their buffers; if not, the data are disposed of in a rumor mill. Having completed its propagation to l and attempted propagation to m of R the machine moves into state 2 and, in effect, closes down its data lines.[11]

---

is in fact 250 and we approximate with the number $P(G) = 100$. That is, we truncate the message after 100, "I heard it from i who heard it from j who heard it from k . . ." steps. In many instances a complete rumor will be transmitted, e.g., ("'Tidbit,' I heard it from 174 who heard it from a burning bush.") In some instances the rumor message will take the form ("'Tidbit,' I heard it from 231, who heard it from 225, . . . who heard it from 211, but I don't know who 211 heard it from.") Since the RTRP(G) function is itself arbitrary the function RTRP(G)$_{100}$ which restricts the length of the message is by no means an improper particularization.

[11]The reader will note that the system could actually run as a $(0,1)$ state machine. Instead of lapsing into the quiet contemplation of state 2 the machine once activated would stay in state 1. Each period it would ask its neighbors "Have you heard . . .," and each period it would get the answer "Yes, I told you I heard it yesterday and the day before and the day before . . . ."

Without going into all the intricacies of the circuit logic (and the greater intricacies of a functioning electronic circuit), it is seen that the behavior of the automaton is essentially given by a table like Table 7.1, which describes the behavior of the machine when in the 1 state and for a given priority assignment. (Note that it says "I heard it from 1" when both 1 and 2 fill its buffers; "I heard it from 3" when 1, 2, and 3 feed its buffers; and "I heard it from 2" when 2, 3, and 4 feed its buffers. This arbitrariness is no more than what one would expect from such a machine.)

7.2.5 Complexity of the rumor propagating machine

The device, $\bar{A}_j$, requires the switching of 2^{d_j} input channels into d_j output channels. We can now describe the complexity of this particular automaton. It is a device which handles a word of length $W = 1 + L \cdot P(G)$ bits. It has input complexity of $2^{d_j} \cdot W$ and output complexity of $d_j \cdot W$. Its input-output capacity is therefore:[12]

$$C_j = d_j \cdot 2^{d_j} \cdot W^2 \quad \text{bits} \tag{7.1}$$

$$C_j = (d_j \cdot 2^{d_j})(1 + L \cdot P(G))^2 \quad \text{bits} \tag{7.2}$$

Despite the forbidding notation a simple social meaning remains: "If this minimum social transaction is to be performed, its logical demands are that all of the potential senders and receivers of the message be linked (the first term in braces) and that the full message be received and sent (the second term in braces)."

This is not the full picture, however; recall that the machine has the ability to add its identifier to R; we designate the complexity of this function as $\bar{c}W$ including within $\bar{c}$ the complexity of various housekeeping and timing tasks performed by the device. The precise form of $\bar{c}W$ need not concern us at this time. Note simply that the addition function is literally an "add on" accessory and the device complexity alters by the amount plus $\bar{c}W$.

Now let us put things together. We have at node j a machine with complexity equal to that given by equation (7.1) along with the additional factor, $\bar{c}W$.

---

[12]Equations (7.1) and (7.2) represent an arbitrary machine design which contains significant redundancy. The composing of input and output complexities to yield a W^d term involves, in effect, inefficient use of memory. An alternative construction would give $C_j = d_j 2^{d_j} W$ bits. The construction principle used in the text gives greater weight to $P(G)$—and, inferentially, N—than does the alternative form which gives weight in the index to degree of the node. The ultimate tests of which construction principle to use depend upon empirical context.

Table 7.1
Input-output behavior of a rumor machine. Note that there are 2^4 input combinations plus the external BIT. Combinations 1–15 result in a change of state as does the BIT input. Combination 16 leaves the automaton in state 0.

Input combinations from predecessor machines				Outputs to successor machines			
1	2	3	4	(1)	(2)	(3)	(4)
*					$R+1+j$	$R+1+j$	$R+1+j$
	*			$R+2+j$		$R+2+j$	$R+2+j$
		*		$R+3+j$	$R+3+j$		$R+3+j$
			*	$R+4+j$	$R+4+j$	$R+4+j$	arbitrary
*	*					$R+1(\text{or }2)+j$	$R+1(\text{or }2)+j$
*		*			$R+1(\text{or }3)+j$		$R+1(\text{or }3)+j$
*			*		$R+1(\text{or }4)+j$	$R+1(\text{or }4)+j$	
	*	*		$R+2(\text{or }3)+j$			$R+2(\text{or }3)+j$
	*		*	$R+2(\text{or }4)+j$		$R+2(\text{or }4)+j$	
		*	*	$R+3(\text{or }4)+j$	$R+3(\text{or }4)+j$		
*	*	*					$R+1(\text{or }2\text{ or }3)+j$
*	*		*			$R+1(\text{or }2\text{ or }4)+j$	
*		*	*		$R+1(\text{or }3\text{ or }4)+j$		
	*	*	*	$R+2(\text{or }3\text{ or }4)+j$			
*	*	*	*				
BIT				$R+j$	$R+j$	$R+j$	$R+j$

$$C_j = d_j 2^{d_j} W^2 + \bar{c}W \qquad (7.3)$$

Summing over the entire graph we have:

$$C_G = \sum_{j=1}^{N} C_j = \sum_{j=1}^{N} d_j 2^{d_j} W^2 + \sum_{j=1}^{N} \bar{c}W \qquad (7.4)$$

$$= W^2 \sum_{j=1}^{N} d_j 2^{d_j} + N\bar{c}W \qquad (7.5)$$

and with substitutions from (7.2):

$$C_G = ((1 + L \cdot P(G))^2)(\sum_{j=1}^{N} d_j 2^{d_j}) + (1 + L \cdot P(G))\bar{c}N \qquad (7.6)$$

Equation (7.5) gives the complexity of a graph which has been translated into a structure that performs the RTRP function with a word of length W.[13] Equation (7.6) is identical but resolves the word into its components. It should be noted that in the (7.6) form the complexity expression consists entirely of standard graph parameters and as such stands as a pure measure, a cardinal number dimensioned in bits. Thus, in the equation (7.6) form the complexity measure is a result in pure graph theory aside from its sociological implications. We will examine some implications of these expressions in the next three sections, which are labeled "digressions" implying that they could be read at any point in the text. They give some practice in complexity calculations, first, in examining the trade-off and, second, in a solution to an ideal type of committee problem. The third digression should give the reader some reassurances about the measurement properties of the complexity indices derived here.

Digression 1. The trade-off between number of participants and degree. We should take it as a given that an objective in observation of groups is to develop sufficient information to specify the directed graph of interactions. With this in mind, analysis of the undirected graph can be useful only in an advisory way, say, to give some idea as to how connectedness trades off against number of participants or to sketch characteristics of ideal types.

Let us begin by examining large system properties of equation (7.6). The third expression in parentheses can be simplified into an expression

---

[13] Note that if each node has the same logical structure (e.g., is of the same degree, as in a cycle), the summation condenses for a graph with node degree d' to $C_G = N(W^2 + d'2^{d'} + \bar{c}W)$.

7.2. METHODOLOGY

that depends primarily on N. We note that $P(G)$, the longest path in a connected graph, can be no longer than $N - 1$ for that graph; and we therefore approximate $P(G)$ by N. Thus, the third term in the parentheses can grow no faster than N^2 and we replace the expression by $\bar{c}LN^2 + \bar{c}N$. In a rough approximation we can ignore L and $\bar{c}$, which remain fixed for varying N, giving the expression $(N^2 + N)$.

On the identical argument, $(P(G))^2$ becomes the dominating term in the first expression in parentheses; $(P(G))^2$ can grow no more rapidly than N^2 and we replace the first expression in braces by $(N^2 + 2N + 1)$.

The term in the second set of braces then becomes critical. Of course d_j cannot exceed $(N-1)$, but even moderate d_j (relative to N) can be the dominating factor. We adopt the following conventions: Select $\bar{d}$ as an "average," "representative," or "typical" value of d_j.[14] The expression in the second set of parentheses then is approximated by $\sum \bar{d} 2^{\bar{d}}$. We now have as an approximating equation:

$$C_G = (N^2 + 2N + 1)(N\bar{d}2^{\bar{d}}) + (N^2 + N) \tag{7.7}$$

On undoing the parentheses this expression becomes the polynomial in N:

$$C_G = N^3 \bar{d} 2^{\bar{d}} + N^2(2\bar{d}2^{\bar{d}} + 1) + N(\bar{d}2^{\bar{d}} + 1) \tag{7.8}$$

For large systems, then, the complexity will be dominated by the order of the graph so long as the interconnection parameter $\bar{d}$ for the representative individual is relatively small. Once $\bar{d}$ rises appreciably, it becomes the dominating fact.

If complexity is a relevant consideration, this relationship should give rise to testable hypotheses. For example, in a context where complexity can be presumed to be a dissatisfier or a burden, we would expect to see one or more of the following:

(a) evidence of dissatisfaction, disorder, or pathology where complexity is relatively high;

(b) evidence of adaptation to offset complexity—for example, if resources or technology can be used to reduce effective or experienced complexity,[15] one would expect to see the application of such technology biased toward eliminating initially high complexity;

---

[14]This approximation is satisfactory only where the range of d_j is narrow.

[15]I am still attempting to avoid the important issue of distinguishing between the *subjective* complexity felt by the social actor and the *objective* complexity discovered by the observer. It is quite human to ignore imposing complexities or to make them the occasion for a game.

(c) evidence of structural optimization—for example, if it is possible to choose between two organizations of a group, there will be a tendency to choose that organization which reduces overall system complexity;

(d) evidence of group dysfunction or breakup where expedients (b) or (c) are not followed.

Like hypotheses could be developed for settings in which complexity is a satisfier or for the more interesting cases in which the first increments of complexity are valued but where, beyond a threshold, complexity becomes a burden. However, this goes beyond the scope of the chapter. Instead in digression 2 which follows we will examine a possible structural adaptation along the line of hypothesis (c).

Digression 2. Effective committee/subcommittee structures. A group of 24 persons is to be formed into one committee of 24 members (1×24), or two subcommittees of 12 persons (2×12), or three subcommittees of 8 persons (3×8), or four subcommittees of 6 persons (4×6), or six subcommittees of 4 persons (6×4), or eight subcommittees of 3 persons (8×3), or twelve subcommittees of 2 persons (12×2), or 24 subcommittees of 1 person (24×1), or any of the vast number of unbalanced committees. The first order of business is to explore the complexity of the subcommittee structures.

Figure 7.4a shows one node in a committee of the whole (1 committee of 24 members) in which all participants can be in communication and contact. In this case, the complete graph becomes the model of reference. Figure 7.4b shows one possible subcommittee structure for the 6×4 case, clearly there are many other ways to assemble the participants.

In Fig. 7.4a complexity will be dominated by the $2^{\bar{d}}$ term (all nodes are of degree 23 with node complexity of 2^{23}) while in Fig. 7.4b node complexity is relatively small (12 nodes are 3rd degree and 12 nodes are 4th degree). In both figures the longest paths are 23 steps (shown in Fig. 7.4b by the curly line), so the approximation of $P(G)$ by N is reasonable and equation (7.8) is usable. We repeat it here:

$$C_G = N^3 \bar{d} 2^{\bar{d}} + N^2(2\bar{d}2^{\bar{d}} + 1) + N(\bar{d}2^{\bar{d}} + 1) \qquad (7.9)$$

For the purpose of this approximate comparison only the first term need be considered, that is, $N^3 \bar{d} 2^{\bar{d}}$. For the complete graph, the degree is nearly equal to N ($\bar{d} = 23$), so an order of magnitude approximation gives a first term of $24^3 \times 23 \times 2^{23}$ which is close enough for our purpose to $24^4 \times 2^{23}$. For the subcommittee structure we approximate with $\bar{d} = 4$, but even with this overstatement of actual complexity we have a first term of only $24^3 \times 4 \times 2^4 = 24^3 \times 2^6$. The ratio of the committee to subcommittee complexities (again using only the first term) is of the order of magnitude of $(24^4 \times 2^{23})/(24^3 \times 2^6) = 24 \times 2^{17} = 3 \times 2^{20}$.

7.2. METHODOLOGY

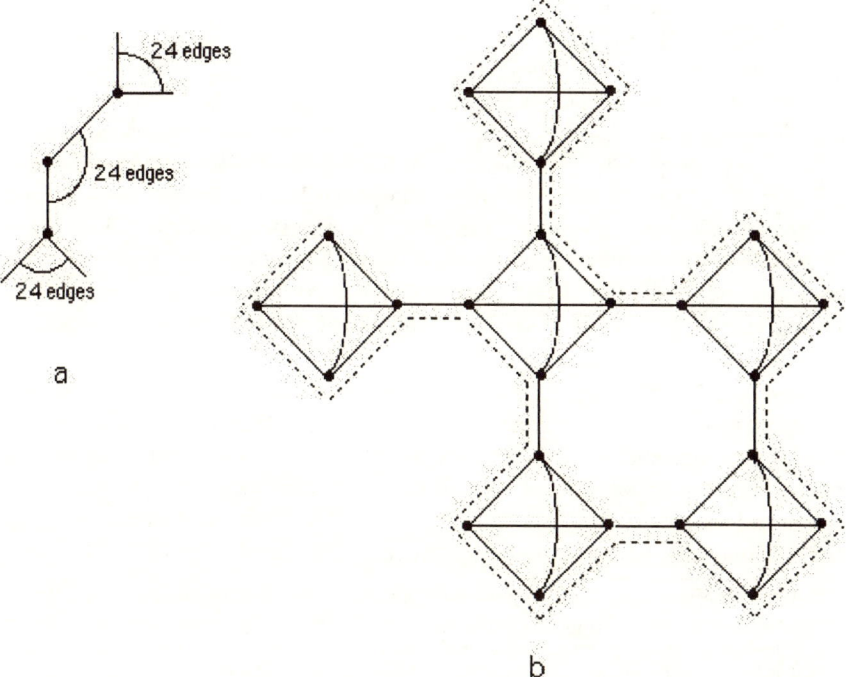

Figure 7.4: The committee problem: (a) a sector of the committee of the whole; (b) b subcommittee problem.

228   CHAPTER 7. SOCIAL COMPLEXITY

The weight of complexity in the full committee associates primarily with the high level of interaction which is implicit in representation by the complete graph. Actual assemblies or committees-of-the-whole develop mechanisms such as rules-of-order, speakers lists, scheduled entertainment or infrequent meetings to keep the potential interaction-complexity in check. These adaptations, which may be costly in resources (to purchase entertainment) or members' time, are examples of complexity offsets as suggested by hypothesis (b). The subcommittee arrangement is an example of a structural adaptation as suggested by hypothesis (c). The example is, of course, extremely restricted since no procedures have been specified, nor authority relationships, nor any information as to the objectives of the committee. All we have supplied to the case is the RTRP function and a suggestion that the benefits of having many participants can be lost where the interaction burden is too high. The subcommittee structure results in reduced complexity parameters. Whether this reduction means that complexity has been reduced to a manageable level (or what is perceived to be a manageable level) is a question for empirical analysis. The question of "what subcommittee structure?" may be approached in like fashion with like strengths and disadvantages. For example, consider the organization shown in Fig. 7.5 for a committee of sixteen and three possible subcommittee-of-four arrangements.

Figure 7.5b is similar to Fig. 7.4b: the graph features small interaction groupings and a long maximum path for information flow ($P(G) = 15$). Could this committee structure be effective? Perhaps, yes, in a context in which there is no significant loss in this inhibition of communication between individuals in separate subcommittees.[16] Figure 7.5c shows a structural framework in which the four inner participants labeled 1, 5, 9, and

---

[16] Again, the reminder that we have been looking at committees and subcommittees as abstract structures without explicit regard to objectives and functions. Why might it not be useful to have more people in the overall pool linked by the structure? Why might it be useful to reduce the complexity of interactions in the specific subcommittee? Suppose the function of the committee were to develop policy responses to a problem, say "urban fiscal crisis." By increasing the size of the pool (on some reasonable sampling or representational principle) one increases the likelihood of soliciting a relatively complete list of options including independent or novel solutions. The smaller "subcommittee" or discussion group in principle permits there to be full discussion and criticism of even the more *outré* types of construction or plan.

The value of the large N/small committee scheme might be described by a scenario in which a novel idea but one which is difficult to explicate is aired with apologies in one of the many small committees; it survives criticism there and is communicated to adjoining subcommittees where it gains polish and is strengthened in its details and particulars. Eventually it gains consensus support; and, to make a long story short, a city is saved. The alternative scenario, of course, is one in which the idea is exposed under serious time constraints within the committee only to be tabled. The idea is rediscovered eons later by an archaeologist digging the ruins.

I have treated the explanation lightly since the basic truths of committee structure are well-known to political organizers. It is interesting, I think, to have a means of for-

7.2. METHODOLOGY

13 form what is, in effect, a subcommittee of "key men." In addition the short circuit through the key-man subcommittee results in a shorter longest path. The overall system calculations rank 7.5b as more complex but of the same order of magnitude—compare with the disconnected graphs (Fig. 7.5d) and the complete graphs (Fig. 7.5a). However, the detailed calculations point out the relatively high complexity associated with the key-man position.

This result seems slightly counterintuitive in that the path factor rates as the major determinant of Fig. 7.5b's complexity. For example, the recalculation in the lower section of 7.5b indicates that a truncated graph significantly reduces the complexity of 7.5b. Is it playing fair to make such an adjustment after the fact? I believe such adjustment can be legitimate in certain situations: for example, if in the empirical referent there was no indication that communication was forced into the longest path and in fact the interior path (designated by a broken double line) was followed, it would make sense to use the truncated path. If, however, the referent was one in which exquisite bureaucratic delay was an operative characteristic, the greater complexity in the original calculation would be appropriate. This example shows the use of the complexity measure as what is essentially a heuristic device.

Digression 3. Complexity parameters as measures. Although the operations given in equations (7.7)–(7.8) calculate numbers it may not be clear that the numbers are measures in some appropriate sense. This digression examines some properties of the parameters derived here. The expressions given calculate complexity C_G as an arithmetical expression in *cardinal numbers* (N and $\bar{d}$) applying to the graph and *measures of information* (bit, wordlength). A hidden dimension includes *data pertaining to a process device* (e.g., a two-state switch or a binary adder). The dimension of the complexity measure is then in the form $K(N, \bar{d}) \cdot$ bit $\cdot$ processes; where $K(N, \bar{d})$ is a cardinal number, a bit is a well-defined measure of information, while "process" seems somewhat vague. Actually, process measurement poses no substantive problems or conceptual problems beyond those involved in using dimensioned numbers such as foot-pounds, horsepower, calories, watts, or other measures related to physical work.

In computer science. the complexity of intricate devices, such as a powerful computer, is commonly measured in terms of the number of "primitive units" which would be required to simulate the performance of the subject machine (see Albin, 1978b). In such calculations a "primitive unit" is some

---

malizing their practical knowledge. It is clear, for example, that on various information-theoretic assumptions and for particular values placed on members' time and the need to closely approximate a "solution," one can in principle "optimize" structure. Action groups, task forces, and think tanks take this sort of matter very seriously. Whether, in principle, one should optimize structure is another question entirely.

device whose input output behavior is well understood Thus, we can analyze the complexity of a finite computing device (a sequential machine) in terms of a measure of simpler "grouplike" machines needed to realize the larger machine; or the measure of the complexity of a program can be expressed as a composition of sequential machines; or the complexity of a system of rich and varied interactive relationships as a composition of many automata, each with a fixed interaction neighborhood and each with the internal complexity of a sequential machine. In these cases a more complex process unit can be analyzed "downward" as a composition of more primitive devices or "upward" as an element in the decomposition of a larger system. It is a matter of convenience as to which level is chosen. We add only the following comments:

(1) Where the complexity of a device at one level is to be inferred by analysis of simulations carried out by devices at another level, the measure usually is expressed as a trade-off (e.g., the device D calculates an input-output chain in T time units). D is simulated by K devices of type d but the production of identical output from identical input requires T' units.

(2) In many important instances there are significant "thresholds" of complexity: for example, certain calculations require a large-scale computer with a potentially infinite memory (the "tape" of a Turing machine). The simulation of such calculations by a finite system of finite-state machines is an act of folly. Clearly, there is no such thing as an infinite tape, but the Turing machine model is such that a measure of "undecidability" accompanies its operation on major problems. The point of this comment is that, although the graph structure outlined here is capable of computation, it is essentially a low-complexity device relative to Turing machines and human beings. Although Mozart and da Ponte might be members of a social group modeled by the graph G, the graph structure as modeled will not produce *Don Giovanni* (nor will a Turing machine).[17] The graph structure only pertains to stereotyped communication (e.g., the momentary symbol exchange); it does not pertain to the creation of thought which comes from members' brains which are effectively outside of the system as was the source of the tidbit in the rumor process.

(3) As there are higher thresholds of complexity than present in the graph model, there are lower levels as well. The model we are using contains components which will produce a complete Boolean algebra: that is, by suitable construction of functions in the model all natural logical operations can be realized (this was the point of inserting the adder function). This

---

[17]The reader should be aware that these statements anticipate a more general theory of structural forms which embrace linguistic components and cognitive structures. Although the topic is beyond the scope of this chapter, I note that the algebraic approach extends in this direction and that a theory of complexity applies in this rich domain as well.

7.3. THE DIRECTED GRAPH 231

turns out to be the appropriate level for modeling control over the directed graph, although we could have spread simpler rumors with more primitive logic.

In summary, the graph model which will operate the RTRP function over any connected graph constitutes a composition of individual machines, each of which contains a complete Boolean algebra. A description of the set of machines (specified according to the graph parameters N, the number of nodes, M, the number of neighbors at each node, and P, the longest path through the graph) is sufficient to generate a measure of complexity in terms of symbol processing units.[18]

7.3 The directed graph

We have seen how the complexity of a nondirected graph (NDG) may be calculated where the NDG is transformed from a structural framework into a structure by a generating function. We turn now to an analysis of the complexity of the reference directed graph (DG). Several points emerge immediately. One observation is that if the reference communication is at least as complicated as that in the generating function to the NDG and if the DG is "total," (i.e., all arrows are two-way), then the complexity of the DG is no less than that of the NDG. Otherwise we need to deal with the special case of the total graph and (for a directed graph that is less than total) the distinct cases where the complexity of the actual communications function is at the same level or at a higher level or at a lower level than the generating function.

The number of cases could proliferate, particularly when one recalls the enormous variety of graph types. To deal with this embarrassment of riches we will propose some intuitive lines of analysis and describe strategies for attacking characteristic and significant problems.

7.3.1 The graph that is less than total

Consider the DG's pictured in Fig. 7.6a. The nontotal version to the left, the total version to the right. The total version which we have studied before could be transformed into the nontotal version according to four distinct strategies (and many other combined strategies) each of which corresponds to a different sociological understanding.

---

[18] Note that in the present model we have modeled processes at the level of larger-scale "byte" processing (as opposed to bit processing) within a sequential machine. This is convenient as the logical devices needed to realize a directed graph are expressible at this level as well.

Strategy 1. General inhibition. Following this strategy we will apply an inhibiting device to each node where there is observed to be a reduction of communications channels below the potential number given by the NDG structure. Thus, taking each node in turn, we will apply inhibitors (not i) to inhibition of transmission and (not i)' to reception. Figure 7.6b illustrates.

Strategy 2. Social specific inhibition. According to this strategy, the observer brings a priori information to bear on the problem of just who is inhibiting communication. For example, suppose we know that E was manipulating information channels against the wishes of the other participants who wished total communications; the logical structure would then be as shown in Fig. 7.6c.

Even without the a priori information that would allow the observer to draw Figs. 7.6b and 7.6c directly, we would suspect that framing the model as in Fig. 7.6a is sufficiently unsatisfying so that there is enough inducement to commence a search for the data which will delineate the specific inhibitions. Is this a contrived case?

Consider the directed graph of the example with certain alterations in the edge labeling (e.g., that shown below).

Regardless of the plausibility of these structures the issues implied by the strategy of disclosing specific inhibitions are clear. What then is the measurement effect of adding inhibitions? As we are modeling the system, the inhibitions actually seem to be increasing complexity in that we have added distinct inhibiting units to the system. The complexity of the inhibiting units can be calculated in a manner that compares with the calculations of the preceding section. The calculations will give individual measures C_i^I, for $i \in H$, the set of inhibiting participants and a composite measure

$$C^I = \sum_{i \in H} C_i^I$$

The full directed graph system has complexity $C + C^I$. This might be thought a counterintuitive result. One can surely argue that the inhibited system is less rich than the uninhibited system, since the uninhibited system can effect transformations which can not be reached in the inhibited system (e.g., if data enter the system at D they cannot be communicated to the other nodes.)

The issue raised in the preceding paragraph has no simple resolution. According to the setting or social context, an inhibiting restriction may increase complexity, for example, as where a caste restriction makes ordinary social transactions "more complicated." Or it may "simplify" things by reducing the complexity of the core transactions (analogous to reducing

7.3. THE DIRECTED GRAPH

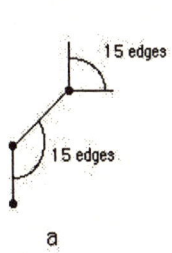

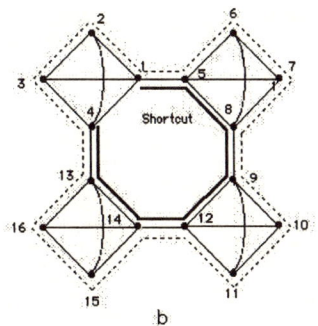

Complexity analysis for (7.5b)

Eight exterior members
$j = (2, 3, 6, 7, 10, 11, 15, 16)$ for whom
$d = 3$ and
$c_j = (3 \times 2^3) \times (1 + 4 \times 15)^2 = 84304$
$\Sigma c_j = 714432$

Eight interior members
$j = (1, 4, 5, 8, 9, 12, 13, 14)$ for whom $d = 4$
and $c_j = (4 \times 2^4) \times (1 + 4 \times 15)^2 = 138144$
$\Sigma c_j = 1905152$

total complexity = 2 619 584 bits
complexity analysis on "shortcut" path in (7.5b), $P = 7$
complexity of 8 interior members = 430 592
of 8 exterior members = 161472
total complexity = 592 064 bits

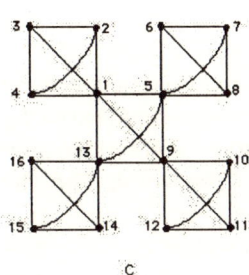

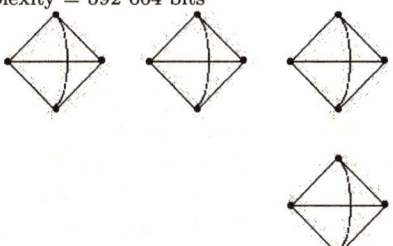

Complexity analysis for (7.5c)

Twelve "ordinary" members
$j = (2, 3, 4, 6, 7, 8, 10, 11, 12, 14, 15, 16)$ for
whom $d = 3$ and
$c_j = (3 \times 2^3) \times (1 + 4 \times 9)^2 = 32856$
$\Sigma c_j = 394272$

Four "key" members
$j = (1, 5, 9, 13)$ for whom $d = 6$ and
$c_j = (6 \times 2^6) \times (1 + 4 \times 9)^2 = 525696$
$\Sigma c_j = 2162784$

total complexity = 2 497 056 bits

Figure 7.5: Alternate subcommittee structures: (a) a segment of the committee of the whole : $N = 16$, $P = 15, d(j) = 15, c_j = (15 \times 2^{15}) \times (1 + 4 \times 15)^2 = 1828940000$, $\Sigma c_j = 29263000000$ bits; (b) linked subcommittees; (c) "key member" subcommittees structure, $N = 16$, $P = 9$; (d) discrete subcommittees, $N = 4$, $P = 3$, $d = 3$ at each node, $c_j = (3 \times 2^3) \times (1 \times 2 \times 3)^2 = 1176$, $\Sigma c_j = 18816$ bits.

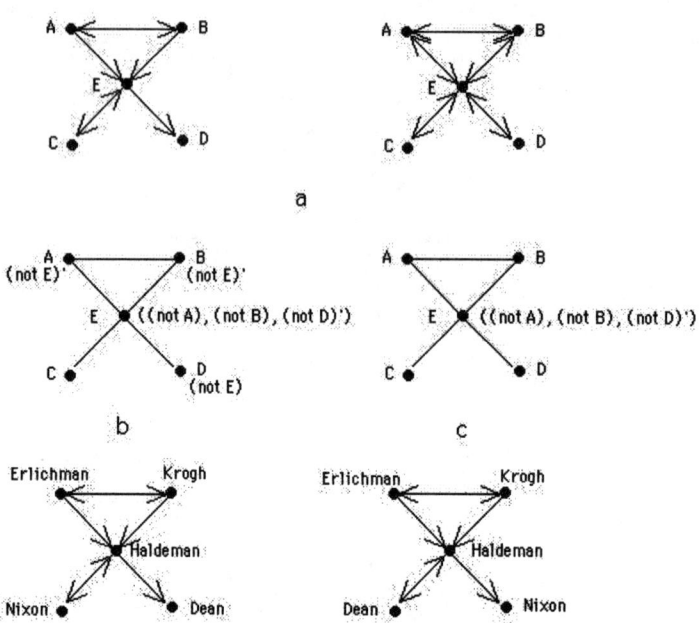

Figure 7.6: Directed graph structures.

the complexity of the generating function). One test on this is the following question: Does the individual *feel* that life is made more complicated by the restriction, that is, does he or she attempt "natural" interactions only to find them frustrated by constraints, forms, taboos, red tape, and the like? Or does the individual know that only a reduced form of interaction is possible and consequently never attempt more than will be routinely satisfied? In the first instance, complexity of inhibitions should be treated as an additive element on the logical network. In the latter instance, a restriction should be treated in a second stage of calculations in which vestigial functions are virtually amputated (Strategy 3) or through a simplification of the generating function (Strategy 4).

Strategy 3. Amputation of vestigial organs. If the context is clearly one in which there is degradation of complexity for specific participants, it is appropriate to enter a second stage of calculation in which node complexities are selectively altered. Suppose, for example, that inhibitions imposed by node (j) result in a situation in which node (k) never transmits to node (l) and node (p) never receives from node (q). In calculations according to equation (7.1) it is reasonable to reduce the input-output complexity of node (k) to $(d_k - 1)2^{d_k}$ and that of node (p) to $d_p 2^{(d_p-1)}$. The recalculated system complexity would include the augmented complexity of inhibitions

7.3. THE DIRECTED GRAPH

at the critical nodes and the decremented complexity at the passive nodes. Again, these operations are reasonable if there is clear evidence of the vestigial nature of inhibited functions.

Strategy 4. Reprogramming of the generating function. Where the interaction potential of the system is apparently much reduced, a reasonable representation of the situation might be reached through use of a simpler structure generating function. Detailed discussion of Strategy 4 is essentially beyond the scope of this chapter. We again remind the reader that the RTRP function is an arbitrary device and other structure- generating functions can be used as circumstances merit. The only restriction to keep in mind is that comparisons between graph structure complexity measures are only valid where there is a common generating function.

7.3.2 Complexity measurement for the directed graph

The imposition of an inhibition on communications is equivalent to placing a logical gate on an input or output channel that will either switch the channel open or closed. The RTRP function requires a channel width equal to the word length so the logical gate structure need be no more than $2W$: the gate simply adds on to the existing system so the increment to complexity at an inhibiting node need be no larger than the term $X \cdot 2W$ where X is the number of specific inhibitions. However in certain calculations node (j) might be observed to have power to exert any or all of the possible inhibitions open to it. Since there are 2^{d_j} possible input combinations and 2^{d_j} output combinations the full table of inhibiting combinations would contain 2^{2d_j} elements. One possible representation of the power to control (not the most efficient representation from the standpoint of programming) would be to include a memory of this size in the device along with a full complement of logical gates. The addition to the complexity of the inhibiting node could be as high as:

$$2^{2d_j} + (2d_j \cdot 2W) = 2^{2d_j} + 4d_j W$$

The first term is the memory size; the second term gives the number of input and output channels times the channel width.

Following strategy (1) or strategy (2), inhibiting elements on the constructions would be added as appropriate. Supplementary calculations according to strategy (3) would be made according to the procedures given in the previous section. The reader is again reminded that the complexity parameters derived for a graph structure are intrinsically tied to the observation process. The numbers produced can do no more than formalize an observer's reading of a social context. Their usefulness or lack of usefulness

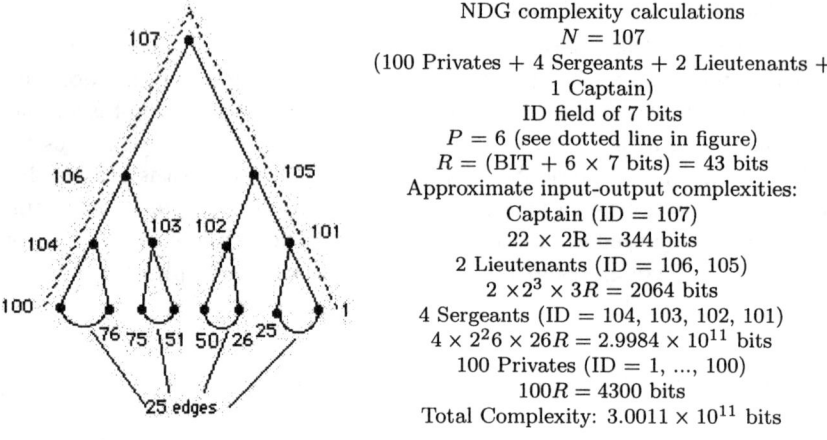

Figure 7.7: Complexity of a hierarchical organization in NDG form.

will be exhibited as they are used to generate subsequent stages of analysis. Does satisfaction or frustration derive from an individual's exposure to a particular level of complexity? Do resources flow to offset or enhance implied complexity buildups? Does the viability of organizations or groups depend upon the presence of particular complexity patterns? Hypotheses of this type can be investigated using the measures, and the investigative processes will be the testing ground for the methodology.[19] An illustration is in order and this section concludes with the elaboration of such hypotheses in the context of organizational structure.

7.3.3 Case example: Complexity of organizational structures

Figure 7.7 illustrates the familiar "tree" framework for an organizational "chain of command." Complexity calculations for the RTRP function are

---

[19]The author and his colleagues are using procedures similar to those described here to investigate the complexities of job designs and the complexities of social interactions within work groups. The empirical setting is a factory floor and detailed data are available pertaining to technical specifications of work tasks, the scope of decisions, and actual social interactions. Calculated complexity measures are included in higher-level statistical models as variables that presumably influence job satisfaction and other behavioral variables pertaining to work.

7.3. THE DIRECTED GRAPH

attached.

Figures 7.8 and 7.9 give analyses for this framework as an "in tree" and as an "out tree" respectively. The "in tree" structure can be thought of as an information-collecting mechanism; the "out tree" structure as a device for propagating information directives, orders, and the like. The calculations are performed according to Strategy 2 with the higher tree levels imposing inhibitions.

As shown in Fig. 7.7, the complexity of the NDG structure for the RTRP function is dominated by node complexity in the level at which the graph "fans out." Noncommissioned officers are undoubtedly nodding their heads at this accurate portrayal of reality while senior officers are protesting that their personae are involved in other structures in which weighty and complex determinations are made.[20]

In Figs. 7.8 and 7.9 "ingraph" and "outgraph" structures are produced according to Strategy 2 by placing inhibitions on downward communication and upward communication respectively. The complexity is the same in both instances. The graph structures produce interesting contrasts, however, when we move to recalculation stages under Strategy 3.

(a) The ingraph. Looking at the ingraph from the bottom up we make the following modifications to produce a simple information gathering system. At the lowest level, since there is no internal path of communication the rumor message becomes: $R_0 =$ "'Bit.' My name is XXX and I heard it from a burning bush" and the lowest-level device becomes an automaton that switches R_0 or (not R_0) onto a single line. The complexity of this device is no greater than $2R_0$.

At the Sergeant's level we produce a modified rumor: $R_1 =$ "'Bit.' I am Sergeant YY, XXX told it to me, and he heard it from a burning bush; by the way, $m'(= 1, 2, ..., 24)$ other people reported the bit." The Sergeant can generate 2^{25} different messages of this type but transmits them on only one line. There is at least an order of magnitude reduction in his inherent complexity and he can be further simplified.[21] The Lieutenant stays at approximately the same complexity level. His rumor R_3 has the structure of (a 1-bit data field for the Bit (and burning bush); a field for his ID; a 2-bit field for the Sergeant's ID; a 5-bit field for the Private; and a 7-bit field for the poll of Privates). He receives on two channels and sends on

---

[20]The analysis is, of course, inappropriate to most hierarchical organizations since the interactive processes implied in the RTRP function are not supported as norms and restricted DG structures are more representative. Nevertheless, echoes of the latent complexity potentiality of the NDG will be heard.

[21]The Sergeant's complexity is actually overstated. Although there are 2^{25} different input configurations of the rumor, efficient programming of his functions might result in a machine that operates $1 + 25 \times 24$ distinct messages: a null message + (1 of 25 identified participants) × (the count of additional messages received).

CHAPTER 7. SOCIAL COMPLEXITY

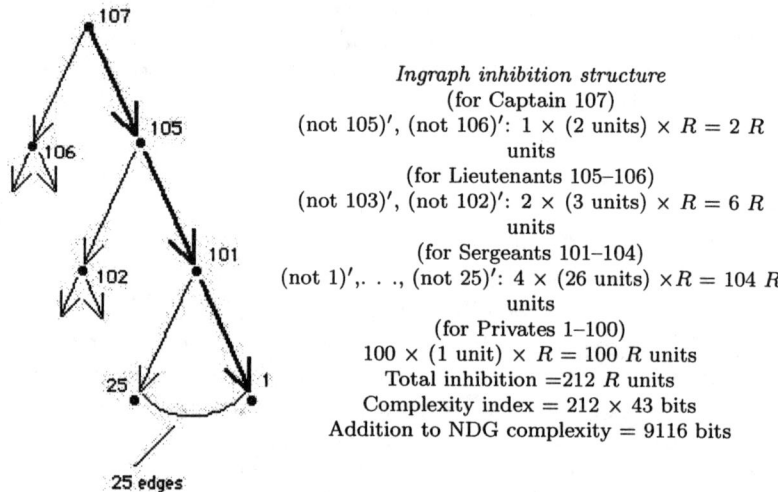

Ingraph inhibition structure
(for Captain 107)
(not 105)′, (not 106)′: $1 \times (2 \text{ units}) \times R = 2\,R$ units
(for Lieutenants 105–106)
(not 103)′, (not 102)′: $2 \times (3 \text{ units}) \times R = 6\,R$ units
(for Sergeants 101–104)
(not 1)′,..., (not 25)′: $4 \times (26 \text{ units}) \times R = 104\,R$ units
(for Privates 1–100)
$100 \times (1 \text{ unit}) \times R = 100\,R$ units
Total inhibition $= 212\,R$ units
Complexity index $= 212 \times 43$ bits
Addition to NDG complexity $= 9116$ bits

	Reprogramming of ingraph	
Private's rumor =	(BIT xxxxx) = 6 bits.	
Complexity =	2 × 6 bits × 100 Privates =	1200 bits
Sergeant's rumor =	(BIT xx xxxxx xxxxx) = 13 bits	
Complexity =	$2^{25} \times 13$ bits × 4 Sergeants =	1.74483×10^9 bits
Lieutenant's rumor =	Sergeant's rumor + 5 bits = 18 bits	
Complexity =	4 × 18 bits × 2 Lieutenants =	144 bits
Captain's rumor =	2 × Lieutenant's rumor =	36 bits
Complexity =	2 × 36 bits × 1 Captain =	72 bits
Total complexity =		1.74483×10^9 bits

Figure 7.8: Ingraph analysis.

7.3. THE DIRECTED GRAPH

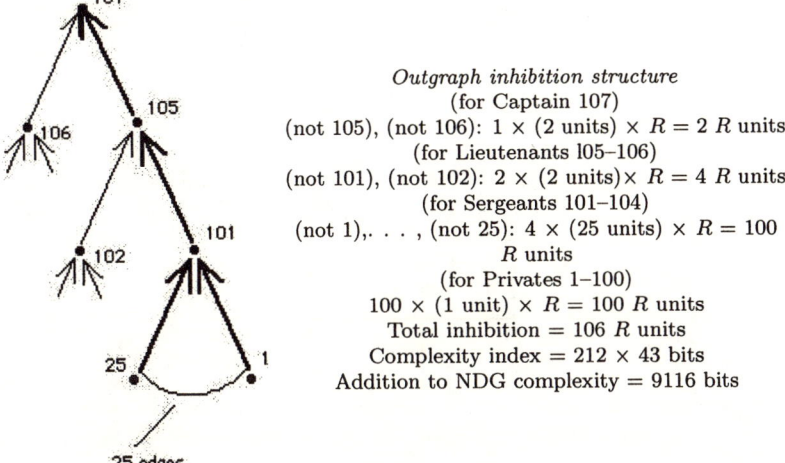

Figure 7.9: Outgraph analysis.

one. The Captain receives the augmented message from Lieutenants on two channels. It is not at all clear what he does with this information.

(b) *The outgraph.* It is plausible to reconstitute participant complexities so that there is a quite dramatic reduction of system complexity. The Captain transmits a single command-rumor to his Lieutenants who pass it to the Sergeant. In Fig. 7.9 the path through the chain of command is added to the rumor. At these levels complexity is much reduced compared to that in the ingraph. At the Sergeant's level, however, we reprogram significantly on the convention that an order is to be propagated to all Privates uniformly and without distinctions and individual identification. In effect, the rich fan-out structure of Fig. 7.9 is replaced by the simple structure in Fig. 7.10 where the term TR is understood to be a transistorized bullhorn or highly developed vocal chords. In order to make this structure effective the Privates must be severely reprogrammed to accept the order without question. Basic training is therefore an adaptation that enables

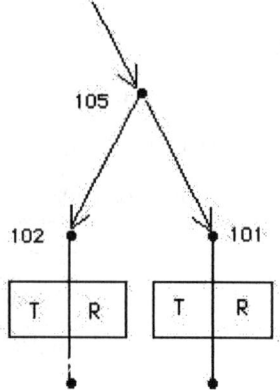

Sergeant's rumor = $R_2 = 5$ bits
    Complexity =   5 bits × 4 Sergeants =   20 bits
     Private   as in Fig. 7.9

Figure 7.10: The stentorian Sergeant.

the less complex structure. There may be a degree of oversimplification in this representation, but its logic appears to be instructive. The NDG as a generalized structure is extremely rich even as a tree form. The associated DG representing an in-tree is less rich, but may still require a degree of complexity in its participants. The highly transformed DG representing an authority or command structure requires an abridgment in participant complexity in order to be effective.

There should again appear to be an ad hoc quality to the calculations and again it was my intention to foster this impression. Complexity measures are instruments that can assist the course of an analysis. For example, it would be entirely appropriate to reexamine the forms of this section and test the complexity implications of highly interactive subsquads inserted below the Sergeant's level, or test how interaction and information exchange above the noncom level would affect structural complexity.

It should also be recalled that complexity at a particular level or node of a structure may require significant resources in order to be realized.[22] For example, if a classical outgraph chain of command is to be transformed

---

[22] The actual expedients which a real-life organization will follow to realize its functions include buffering and queuing routines to offset a need for high internal complexity. These also can be modeled as abstract machines with computable complexity. As a matter of convenience the text imposed the convention of an external clock which determines the time span for a stage of communication and calculation. Real-time systems may effect a trade-off of a larger decision time span for less internal complexity.

7.4. CONCLUSION

into an ingraph or interactive structure, complexity requirements jump enormously and this should trigger enormous resource demands for a supporting bureaucracy. It should also be noted that the representations given here have not allowed for control or oversight functions. If there is a high level of complexity at, say, the Sergeant's level, a monitor at higher levels must embody the complexity to a substantial degree. The question of whether a system is or can be controlled is a related question but one beyond the scope of the chapter (see Gottinger, 1978c).

7.4 Conclusion

The objective of this chapter was to present a method whereby (1) numerical measures of complexity could be attached to graph representations of social contexts, (2) large-scale systems could be analyzed, and (3) behavioral attributes could be modeled to the fullest extent. I believe the text has realized the objective, while at the same time presenting a rigorous theory of structural forms. A few points of interpretation and emphasis remain.

The text has, perhaps, overemphasized heuristics and the modeling flexibility inherent in the methodology. This may, perhaps, give rise to the impression that complexity measurement is a free-form exercise that can represent any behavior or phenomenon to give any result after the fact. This would be a mistaken impression, however. It should be recalled that for a uniform specification of the representative participant, the structure generating function will give a complete ranking of all graphs of all orders. This is a very powerful result and its implications as to the conduct of research are clear. The observer has freedom to embody attributes and functions within a modeled participant. However, once these attributes are fixed, the complexity measure for the system that encompasses these participants is fixed and subject to direct comparison with complexity measures for other configurations. Similarly, there is flexibility as to the choice of generating function, but once the choice is made, the resultant model becomes a subject for rigorous comparison.

The text could not cover applications in any real detail. The treatments of the committee/subcommittee structures and tree structures were only meant to be prefaces to full analyses. The chapter dodges the question of possible discrepancies between complexity as perceived by the participants and complexity as calculated by an outside observer for a machine representation of the social context. The chapter also elides the issue of determining what types and levels of complexity may trigger satisfactions or dissatisfactions. The text has also avoided normative questions such as those concerned with optimal committee or bureaucratic structure. It should be clear, however, that complexity-measurement methodology provides instruments for incisive analysis in these areas. Finally, the text does not give great enough emphasis to cross-disciplinary and metatheoretical aspects of the methodology. It is important to note that the chapter is not really an essay in graph theory and combinatorial analysis. However, the step of attaching a machine to the node of a graph is a nontrivial extension. The graph structure that is produced is a distinct form and one that is dimensionally compatible both with economic structures (i.e., production systems), and with linguistic forms (including grammars, patterns, and higher-level cognitive structures). Structures of these types have an underlying logic and mathematics that is quite different from the calculus-based forms frequently adapted to social science applications. Lacking a continuity requirement, the automata-based forms are well configured to represent discrete interactions.

Acknowledgments

This research is supported by The National Science Foundation. The original version of this chapter was written at the Institute for Advanced Studies in Vienna where the author was visiting professor in the spring of 1978. Many of the arguments were shaped in seminal meetings with Oskar Itzinger and later refined in discussion with Hans Gottinger.

Works Cited

Aladyev, V. 1974. Survey of research in theory of homogeneous structures and their applications. *Mathematical Biological Sciences* 22: 121–154.

Albin, P. S. 1975. *The Analysis of Complex Socioeconomic Systems.* Lexington, MA: D. C. Heath and Company, Lexington Books.

Albin, P. S. 1978a. *Progress without Poverty: The Social Dimensions of Economic Growth.* New York: Basic Books.

Albin, P. S. 1978b. Measurable complexity in economic systems. *Sozialwissenschaftliche Annalen* Band 2:93–106. Wien: Physical-Verlag.

Albin, P. S. 1980. The complexity of social groups and social systems described by graph structures. *Mathematical Social Sciences* 1: 101–129.

Albin, P. S. 1982a. The metalogic of economic predictions, calculations, and propositions. *Mathematical Social Sciences* 3: 101–129.

Albin, P. S. 1982b. Complex information exchange in multicriterion decision making. *Policy Analysis and Information Systems* 6(1): 25–36.

Albin, P. S. 1983. Structural theory and structural formations. *Mathematical Social Sciences* 6: 133–152.

Albin, P. S. 1984. Job design within changing patterns of technical development. In E. Collins and L. Dewey, eds., *American Jobs and the Changing Industrial Base*, 125-162. Cambridge, MA:Ballinger.

Albin, P. S. 1985. Job design, control technology, and technical change. *Journal of Economic Issues* 3: 703–730.

Albin, P. S. 1987. Microeconomic foundations of cyclical irregularities or "chaos." *Mathematical Social Sciences* 13: 185–214.

Albin, P. S. 1989. Qualitative effects of monetary policy in "rich" dynamic systems. In W. Semmler, ed., *Financial Dynamics and Business Cycles: New Perspectives*, 168–187. Armonk, NY: M.E. Sharpe.

Albin, P. S., and D. K. Foley. 1992. Decentralized, dispersed exchange without an auctioneer: A simulation study. *Journal of Economic Behavior and Organization* 18(1): 27–52.

Albin, P. S., and F. Hormozi. 1983. Theoretical reconciliation of equilibrium and structural approaches. *Mathematical Social Sciences* 6: 261–284.

Albin, P. S., F. Hormozi, S. L. Mourgios, and A. Weinberg. 1984. An information system approach to the analysis of job design. In Shi-Kuo Chang, ed., *Management and Office Information Systems*, 385–400. New York: Plenum.

Albin, P. S., and A. S. Weinberg. 1983. Work complexity in structured job designs. *Human Systems Management* 4(2): 69–81.

Arbib, M. 1980. *Brains, Machines and Mathematics*. New York: McGraw-Hill.

Axelrod, Robert. 1984. *The Evolution of Cooperation*. New York: Basic Books.

Baumol, W. 1967. Macroeconomics of unbalanced growth: The anatomy of urban crisis. *American Economic Review* 57(3):415–426.

Benhabib, J., and R. Day. 1981. Rational choice and erratic behavior. *Review of Economic Studies* 48: 459–471.

Beniger, J. 1986. *The Control Revolution: Technological and Economic Origins of the Information Society*. Cambridge, MA: Harvard University Press.

Berge, C. 1962. *The Theory of Graphs and Its Applications*. London: Methuen.

Berlekamp, E. F., J. H. Conway, and R. K. Guy. 1984. *Winning Ways for Your Mathematical Plays*. Vol. 2. New York: Academic Press.

Bernstein, J. 1980. *Experiencing Science*. New York: E. P. Dutton.

Best, M. H. 1990. *The New Competition: Institutions of Industrial Restructuring*. Cambridge, UK: Polity.

Bienenstock, E., F. Fogelman Soulie, and G. Weisbuch, eds. 1986. *Disordered Systems and Biological Organization*. New York: Springer.

Binmore, K., and P. Dasgupta. 1986. *Economic Organizations as Games*. Oxford: Basil Blackwell.

Binmore, K., and P. Dasgupta, eds. 1987. *The Economics of Bargaining*. New York: Basil Blackwell.

Bluestone, B., and B. Harrison. 1982. *The Deindustrialization of America: Plant Closings, Community Abandonment, and the Dismantling of Basic Industry*. New York: Basic Books.

Boldrin, M., and L. Montrucchio. 1986. On the indeterminacy of capital accumulation paths. *Journal of Economic Theory* 40(1): 26–39.

Burgstaller, A. 1994. *Property and Prices*. Cambridge: Cambridge University Press.

WORKS CITED

Burks, A. W., ed. 1970. *Essays on Cellular Automata*. Urbana: University of Illinois Press.

Chaitin, G. J. 1975. Randomness and mathematical proof. *Scientific American* 232: 47–52.

Chomsky, N. 1959. On certain formal properties of grammars. *Information and Control* 2:137–167.

Chomsky, N. 1963. Formal properties of grammars. In *Handbook of Mathematical Psychology* 2: 323–418. New York: John Wiley and Sons.

Conlisk, J. 1988. Optimization cost. *Journal of Economic Behavior and Organization* 9: 213–228.

Cyert, R. M., and J. G. March. 1963. *A Behavioral Theory of the Firm*. With contributions by G. P. E. Clarkson and others. Englewood Cliffs, NJ: Prentice-Hall.

Davis, M. 1965. *The Undecidable*. Hewlett, NY: Raven.

Day, R. H. 1979. Cautious optimizing. In J. Roumasset, J.-M. Boussard, and I. Singh, eds., *Risk Uncertainty and Agricultural Development*, 115–130. New York: Agricultural Development Council.

Day, R. H. 1982a. Irregular growth cycles. *American Economic Review* 72: 406–414.

Day, R. H. 1982b. The emergence of chaos from classical economic growth. *Quarterly Journal of Economics* 96: 201–213.

Debreu, G. 1951. The coefficient of resource utilization. *Econometrica* 19 (July): 272–292.

Dewdney, A. K. 1985. Computer recreations. *Scientific American* 252:228.

Diamond, P. A. 1984. *A Search-Equilibrium Approach to the Micro Foundations of Macroeconomics*. Cambridge, MA: MIT Press.

Dosi, G. 1981. *Technical Change and Survival: Europe's Semiconductor Industry*. Sussex European Research Centre, University of Sussex.

Eichner, A. S. 1991. *The Macrodynamics of Advanced Market Economies*. Armonk, NY: M. E. Sharpe.

Elster, J. 1989a. *Nuts and Bolts for the Social Sciences*. Cambridge: Cambridge University Press.

Elster, J. 1989b. *Cement of Society: A Study of Social Order*. Cambridge: Cambridge University Press.

Freeman, C., ed. 1986. *Design, innovation, and long cycles in economic development*. London: Pinter.

Freeman, C., J. Clark, and L. Soete. 1982. *Unemployment and Technical Innovation: A Study of Long Waves and Economic Development*. Westport, CT: Greenwood Press.

Friedman, J. 1986. *Game Theory with Applications to Economics.* New York: Oxford University Press.

Gödel, K. 1931. Über formal unentscheidbare Satze der Principia Mathematica und verwandter Systeme, 1. *Monatshefte für Mathematik und Physik* 38: 173–198.

Gödel, K. 1962. *Formally Undecidable Propositions.* New York: Basic Books.

Gottinger, H., and W. Leinfellner, eds., 1978a. *Decision Theory and Social Ethics: Issues in Social Choice.* Boston: D. Reidel.

Gottinger, H. 1978b. Complexity and social decision theory. In Gottinger (1978a), 251–270.

Gottinger, H. 1978c. Problems in large scale social economic systems. *Journal of Peace Research* 15(2):131–151.

Hahn, F., and T. Negishi. 1962. A theorem on non-tâtonnement stability. *Econometrica* 30: 463–469.

Harary, F. 1965. *Structural Models: An Introduction to the Theory of Directed Graphs.* New York: Wiley.

Heal, G. 1986. Macrodynamics and returns to scale. *Economic Journal* 96: 191–198.

Hirsch, M., and S. Smale. 1974. *Differential Equations, Dynamical Systems and Linear Algebra.* New York: Academic Press.

Hofstadter, D. R. 1979. *Gödel, Escher, Bach: An Eternal Golden Braid.* New York: Basic Books.

Hollis, M. and E. J. Nell. 1975. *Rational Economic Man: A Philosophical Critique of Neo-classical Economics.* Cambridge: Cambridge University Press.

Hopcroft, J. E., and J. D. Ullman. 1969. *Formal Languages and Their Relation to Automata.* Reading, MA: Addison-Wesley.

Hopcroft, J. E., and J. D. Ullman. 1979. *Introduction to Automata Theory, Languages and Computation.* Reading, MA: Addison-Wesley.

Hurwicz, L. 1969. On the concept and possibility of informational decentralization. *American Economic Review* 59:513–524.

Kac, M., and S. Ulam. 1969. *Mathematics and Logic.* New York: Mentor.

Kornai, J. 1971. *Anti-Equilibrium.* Amsterdam: North-Holland.

Kornai, J. 1982. *Growth, Shortage, and Efficiency: A Macrodynamic Model of the Socialist Economy.* Translated by Ilona Lukacs. Oxford: Basil Blackwell.

Krohn, K., and J. Rhodes. 1965. Algebraic theory of machines. *Transactions of the American Mathematical Society* 116: 450–464.

Kuenne, R. E. 1979. Rivalrous consonance and the power structure of OPEC. *Kyklos* 32: 695–717.

Kuenne, R. E. 1984. *Rivalrous Consonance: A Theory of General Oligopolist Equilibrium*. Manuscript. Princeton University, Princeton, NJ.

La Porte, T. 1975. *Organized Social Complexity*. Princeton, NJ: Princeton University Press.

Leijonjufvud, A. 1993. Towards a not-too-rational macroeconomics. *Southern Economic Journal* 60(1): 1–13.

Li, T., and J. A. Yorke. 1975. Period three implies chaos. *American Mathematical Monthly* 82: 985–992.

Lucas, R. E., Jr. 1967. Adjustment costs and theory of supply. *Journal of Political Economy* 75: 321–334.

Machlup, F. 1962. *The Production and Distribution of Knowledge in the United States*. Princeton, NJ: Princeton University Press.

Mandelbrot, B. B. 1982. *The Fractal Geometry of Nature*. New York: W. H. Freeman.

Martin, O., A. M. Odlyzko, and S. Wolfram. 1984. Algebraic properties of cellular automata. *Communications in Mathematical Physics* 93: 219–58. Reprinted in Wolfram (1986): 51–90.

May, R. M. 1975. Simple mathematical models with very complicated dynamics. *Nature* 261: 459-467.

Minsky, H. P. 1986. *Stabilizing an Unstable Economy*. New Haven: Yale University Press.

Minsky, M. 1967. *Computation, Finite and Infinite Machines*. Englewood Cliffs, NJ: Prentice-Hall.

Mitchell, J. 1969. *Social Networks in Urban Situations*. Manchester: Manchester University Press.

Montias, J. M. 1976. *The Structure of Economic Systems*. New Haven: Yale University Press.

Muth, R. 1961. Adaptive expectations and the theory of price movements. *Econometrica* 29. Reprinted in Lucas and Sargent (1981): 3–22.

Nagel, E., and J. R. Newman. 1958. *Gödel's Proof*. New York: New York University Press.

Nath, S. K. 1969. *A Reappraisal of Welfare Economics*. London: Routledge and Kegan Paul.

Nelson, R. R., and S. G. Winter. 1982. *An Evolutionary Theory of Economic Change*. Cambridge, MA: Belknap Press of Harvard University Press.

Newell, A., and H. Simon. 1972. *Human Problem Solving*. Englewood Cliffs, NJ: Prentice-Hall.

Packard, N. H. 1983. Complexity of growing patterns in cellular automata. In J. Demongeot, E. Golès, and M. Tchuente, eds., *Dynamical Systems and Cellular Automata*, 123–138. London: Academic Press, 1985.

Packard, N. H. 1984. *Working Paper on Properties of 2-Dimensional Cellular Automata*. Princeton, NJ: Institute for Advanced Studies. Reprinted in Wolfram (1986): 305–310.

Packard, N. H., and S. Wolfram. 1985. Two dimensional cellular automata. *Journal of Statistical Physics* 38: 901. Reprinted in Wolfram (1986): 126–171.

Phelps, E. S., ed. 1970. *The Microeconomic Foundations of Employment and Inflation*. New York: Norton.

Piaget, J. 1972. *Genetic Epistemology*. New York: Columbia University Press.

Piccoli, M. L. 1973. An application of formal language and automata theory to social choice. Paper presented to the Econometric Society, December.

Piore, M. J., and C. F. Sabel. 1984. *The Second Industrial Divide: Possibilities for Prosperity*. New York: Basic Books.

Radner, R. 1980. Collusive behavior in noncooperative epsilon-equilibria of oligopolies with long but finite lives. *Journal of Economic Theory* 22: 136–154.

Reder, M. 1982. Chicago economics: permanence and change. *Journal of Economic Literature* 20: 1–38.

Révész, G. 1983. *Introduction to Formal Languages*. New York: McGraw-Hill.

Rubinstein, A. 1986. Finite automata play the repeated prisoners' dilemma. *Journal of Economic Theory* 39: 83–96.

Salop, S. and J. Stiglitz. 1982. A theory of sales: A simple model of equilibrium price dispersion with identical agents. *American Economic Review* 72: 1121–1130.

Samuelson, P. 1947. *Foundations of Economic Analysis*. Cambridge, MA: Harvard University Press.

Schelling, T. 1978. *Micromotives and Macrobehavior*. New York: Norton.

Semmler, W. 1986. On nonlinear theories of economic cycles and the persistence of business cycles. *Mathematical Social Sciences* 12: 47–76.

Shubik, M. 1984. *A Game Theoretic Approach to Political Economy*. Game Theory in the Social Sciences Ser. vol. 2. Cambridge, MA: MIT Press.

Simon, H. 1978. Rationality as process and as product of thought. *American Economic Review* 68: 1–16.

Simon, H. 1984. On the behavioral and rational foundations of economic dynamics. *Journal of Economic Behavior and Organization* 5: 35–55.

Smale, S. 1967. Differentiable dynamical systems. *Bulletin of the American Mathematical Society* 73: 747–817.

Smith, A. R. 1971. Cellular-automata complexity tradeoffs. *Information and Control* 18: 466.

Solo, R. A. 1991. *The Philosophy of Science and Economics.* Macmillan.

Solow, R. M. 1956. A contribution to the theory of economic growth. *Quarterly Journal of Economics* 70: 65–94. Reprinted in A. Sen, ed., *Growth Economics*, 161–92. Harmondsworth: Penguin Books, 1970.

Thatcher, J. W. 1970. Self-describing Turing machines and self-reproducing cellular automata. In Burks (1970).

Toffoli, T., and N. Margolus. 1987. *Cellular Automata Machines.* Cambridge, MA: MIT Press.

Tool, M. R. 1986. *Essays in Social Value Theory: A Neoinstitutionalist Contribution.* Armonk, NY: M. E. Sharpe.

Vishniac, G. 1986. Cellular automata models of disorder and organization. In Bienenstock (1986), 1–20.

von Neumann, J. 1966. *Theory of Self-Reproducing Automata.* Edited and completed by Arthur W. Burks. Urbana: University of Illinois Press.

Wainwright, R. ed. 1973.*Lifeline.* New York: Yorktown Heights.

Wan, H. 1971. *Economic Growth.* New York: Harcourt Brace Jovanovich.

Warsh, D. 1984. *The Idea of Economic Complexity.* New York: Viking Press.

Weitzman, M. L. 1984. *The Share Economy: Conquering Stagflation.* Cambridge, MA: Harvard University Press.

Williamson, O. E. 1975. *Markets and Hierarchies, Analysis and Antitrust Implications: A Study in the Economics of Internal Organization.* New York: Free Press.

Winter, S. G. 1975. Optimization and evolution in the theory of the firm. In R. H. Day and T. Groves, eds., *Adaptive Economic Models*, 73–118. New York: Academic Press.

Wolfram, S. 1983a. Statistical mechanics of cellular automata. *Review of Modern Physics* 55: 601-644. Reprinted in Wolfram (1986): 3–69.

Wolfram, S., 1983b. Universality and complexity in cellular automata. *Physica D 10: 1–35.* Reprinted in Wolfram (1986): 115–157.

Wolfram, S. 1984a. *Computation theory of cellular automata.* Manuscript. Princeton, NJ: Institute for Advanced Study. Reprinted in Wolfram (1986): 189–231.

Wolfram, S. 1984b. *Working Paper on Computation Irreducibility.* Princeton, NJ: Institute for Advanced Study Preprint. Reprinted in Wolfram (1986): 294–297.

Wolfram, S. 1984c. Software for science and mathematics. *Scientific American* 251: 188-203.

Wolfram, S. 1985. Undecidability and intractability in theoretical physics. *Physical Review Letters* 54: 735–8.

Wolfram, S., ed.. 1986. *Theory and Applications of Cellular Automata.* Singapore: World Scientific.

Index

accumulation function, 111
acquaintances, 163
adjustment costs, 109
advertising
    excessive, 169
    expected gains from, 164
advertising cost, 160, 165
    effects on market outcome, 170
advertising strategy, 158, 162
attractor
    strange, 148
automata, xix, xx
    complexity of, 140
    finite, 129, 181, 185
    pushdown, 130
    rumor mills, 221
    theory, xiii–xv
automation, xvii

Benhabib, J., 105
bilateral bargaining, 157
bounded rationality, xxv, 110, 134–135, 161, 165, 181, 189, 190, 192

cellular automata, xxviii, 127
    as model of monetary policy, 138
    complexity hierarchy, 173, 190–192, 205–209
    model of multiperson prisoners' dilemma, 183, 190
    one-dimensional, 128
    rules
        totalistic, 134
    two-dimensional, 181
chain of command
    complexity analysis of, 236–240
chaos, 131
    in growth model, 122
    theory of, 106
chaos map, 109
Chomsky ordering, 173
Chomsky, N., xiii
clocks, 128, 219
coefficient of resource utilization, 166
committees, 226–229
commons, 182
communication costs, 157, 173, 177
competitors, 115
complexity, xiii, xx–xxiii
    and directed graphs, 210
    computational, 190, 191
        of rules in multiperson prisoners' dilemma, 198
    hierarchy, xxix, 106, 113, 131, 168, 182, 190, 192
    and rules in multiperson prisoners' dilemma, 193–195
    in chaotic growth model, 118, 123, 126
    of cellular automata, 190–192, 205–209
    of dynamical systems, 140–147, 155
    of one-dimensional cellular automata, 128–131

in chaotic growth model, 113
level of economy
    and monetary policy, 156
measured and perceived, 211
measurement
    of directed graphs, 235–241
measures of, 212, 229–231
    graph nodes, 216
    of chain of command, 236–240
    of committee structures, 226
    of directed graphs, 217, 231
    of dynamical systems, 137
    of graphs, 212
    of Nash-like strategies in multiperson prisoners' dilemma, 197
    of rumor mill, 222–224
    of social networks, 225
    reactions to, 225
    system, xx, 129
    thresholds, 230
    with inhibited communication, 232
complexity levels, xxvii
complexity threshhold, xxvii
computability
    of play in multiperson prisoners' dilemma, 185
computation costs, 133, 161, 164
computation-irreducibility hypothesis, 130, 132
computational capacity, xx
    of agents in decentralized exchange model, 162
computers, xvii
    logic and architecture, xxiii
connectedness of social networks, 224
content
    of graph interaction, 211
Cournot-Nash equilibrium, 188
    in rules in multiperson prisoners' dilemma, 197
customers, 115
cycling, 169

Day, R., 105, 108, 138
Debreu, G., 166
decentralized exchange model
    Walrasian equilibrium, 158
decidability, 189
density
    of graphs, 211
Diamond, P., 174
disequilibrium prices
    trade at, 168, 176
dynamical systems
    complexity of, 140
    nonlinear, 107

economic decision making
    limits to, xxvii
economic distance, 114, 138
economic dynamics
    qualitative
        and policy, 156
economics, xviii, xxvi–xxviii
economies, 133
    as computers, 131
economists, 147
efficiency
    of decentralized market, 157
endowments, 159, 167
entropy, 129, 133
environmental decay, 182
equilibrium strategies, 189
exchange, 157
    transitory in decentralized exchange model, 161
expectations
    rational, 134
externalities
    in neoclassical growth model, 110

follow-the-leader dynamics, 117

forecasting
    impact of monetary policy, 155
    in chaotic growth model, 122, 133, 147
    type 4 patterns, 123
formal languages, 129
    Chomsky ordering, 148
    complexity of, 140
    context-free, 129, 148
    context-sensitive, 129, 148
    regular, 129
    unrestricted, 130
fractal regularity, 122

gains from trade
    estimates of, 163
game theory
    and computation costs, 171
    of large games, 182
Goodguy, 185, 201
grammar, 129
graphs
    complete, 214
    directed, 210, 231–236
    maximal paths, 218
    methodology, 212–216
    undirected, 218

Hahn, F., 176
heuristics, 211
Hurwicz, L., 134

incentive compatibility, 162
industrial leadership, 136, 138, 149
industries, 114
industry structure, 135, 149
inequality of wealth, 157, 176
inflation
    structural, 136
information costs, 138, 158, 170
information network, 132
information technology, xvii–xix
informational dimension, xviii, xxi, 106

informational system, xxii
inhibitions of communication, 232–235
intermediate-goods industries, 115
international dependence, xviii

key men, 229
Kornai, J., xxiii
Kuenne, R., *see* rivalrous consonance

La Porte, T., 210
labor
    division of, xv
labor markets, xvii
learning-by-doing, xxviii
Life
    Game of, xiv, xxi, xxviii, xxix, 187, 195
    rule in multiperson prisoners' dilemma, 185, 191, 201
    strategy in multiperson prisoners' dilemma, 198–204
limit cycle, 129, 148
limits to growth
    behavioral, 110–111
logic and nondirected graph convention, 214

Machlup, F., xvi
Mandelbrot, B., 122
marginal rate of substitution, 159
    disclosure, 162
Markov model, 164
model, xix
monetary policy, 137
    accomodative, 156
    cellular automaton model, 150
    goals, 150
    perverse effects of, 156
    pro- and countercyclical, 151, 156
myopic agents, 158

Nash equilibrium, *see* Cournot-Nash equilibrium
Nash-like strategies
    complexity of, 197
Negishi, T., 176
neighborhood, 159
    in local-interaction multiperson prisoners' dilemma, 181
    Moore, 183
    overlaps of, 181
neighborhood effects
    in prices, 158
neighborhood interaction
    in chaotic growth model, 112
neighborhood size, 165
neoclassical growth model, 105, 107, 131, 138
neutral oscillation, 125
nonlinearity
    in neoclassical growth model, 109
    microeconomic
        in chaotic growth model, 113

order of trade, 160
overtrading, 168

payoffs, 187
Piaget, J., 217
pollution, 109
    in neoclassical growth model, 110
predictability
    of chaotic growth model, 125
    of type 4 rules in multiperson prisoners' dilemma, 195
price system
    as giant computer, 130
prisoners' dilemma, xxi
    multiperson, 181
probability weight, 165
production function, xvi
productivity inhibiting effects, 109

rational choice, 126, 134
rational expectations, xxi
rationality, 161, 185
    full, 172, 177, 181
    in advertising strategy, 158
    unrestricted, 158
recursive functions, 130
regime changes, 123
rivalrous consonance, 117, 136, 139
rules
    legal, 192
    myopic, 185
    totalistic, 192
rumor mill, 218–224

Sargeant
    stentorian, 237
Schelling, T., 117, 181
search costs, 132
self-similarity, 122
Simon, H., xxv, 105
simulation, 114, 131, 135
    of decentralized exchange model, 165
    of monetary policy, 151
simulation costs, 133
Smith, A., xv
sociological studies, 213
Solow, R., 138
stabilization policy, 149, 156
statistics, 165
strangers, 163
strategic behavior, 177
strategic equivalence
    of complexity types in multiperson prisoners' dilemma, 193–195
structural formation, xxvii
structure, xiii, 217
suppliers, 115

technological unemployment, xvii

INDEX

tit-for-tat, xxi
trade
    intensity of, 168
trade step, 160, 165
trading strategy, 158
transition probabilities, 165
trigger strategy, 192
Turing machine, 130, 172, 191, 230

unbalanced growth, xxiii
utility function
    Cobb-Douglas, 158

von Neumann, J., xiv

Walrasian auctioneer, 174
Walrasian equilibrium, 157
    agents' knowledge of price, 163
wealth
    inequality in decentralized exchange model, 169
wealth effect, 109
Wiseguy, 185, 201
Wolfram, S., xiv, 127, 131, 185, 190

ABOUT THE AUTHOR AND EDITOR

Peter S. Albin is Professor Emeritus of Economics at the City University of New York and has been a Visiting Scholar at Cambridge University, the University of California at Berkeley, the University of Paris, and Oxford University. His books include *The Analysis of Complex Socio-Economic Systems* and *Progress without Poverty: The Social Dimensions of Economic Growth.*

Duncan K. Foley is Professor of Economics at Barnard College of Columbia University. Among his books are *Understanding Capital* and *Money, Accumulation and Crisis.*